LEGAL CERTAINTY IN MULTILINGUAL EU LAW

Law, Language and Communication

Series Editors
Anne Wagner, Lille University – Nord de France, Centre for Legal Research and Perspectives of Law, René Demogue Group, France and Vijay Kumar Bhatia, City University of Hong Kong

This series encourages innovative and integrated perspectives within and across the boundaries of law, language and communication, with particular emphasis on issues of communication in specialized socio-legal and professional contexts. It seeks to bring together a range of diverse yet cumulative research traditions related to these fields in order to identify and encourage interdisciplinary research.

The series welcomes proposals – both edited collections as well as single-authored monographs – emphasizing critical approaches to law, language and communication, identifying and discussing issues, proposing solutions to problems, offering analyses in areas such as legal construction, interpretation, translation and de-codification.

Legal Certainty in Multilingual EU Law

Language, Discourse and Reasoning at the European Court of Justice

ELINA PAUNIO

Routledge
Taylor & Francis Group
LONDON AND NEW YORK

First published 2013 by Ashgate Publishing

2 Park Square, Milton Park, Abingdon, Oxfordshire OX14 4RN
52 Vanderbilt Avenue, New York, NY 10017

Routledge is an imprint of the Taylor & Francis Group, an informa business

First issued in paperback 2020

British Library Cataloguing in Publication Data
A catalogue record for this book is available from the British Library

The Library of Congress has cataloged the printed edition as follows:
Paunio, Elina.
Legal certainty in multilingual EU law : language, discourse, and reasoning at the European Court of Justice / by Elina Paunio.
pages cm.—(Law, language, and communication)
Includes bibliographical references and index.
ISBN 978-1-4094-3861-8 (hardback) 1. Legal certainty—European Union countries. 2. Law—European Union countries—Language. 3. Law—European Union countries—Interpretation and construction. 4. Court of Justice of the European Communities. I. Title.
KJE962.P38 2013
341.242'2284—dc23

2013011979

ISBN 978-1-4094-3861-8 (hbk)
ISBN 978-0-367-60121-8 (pbk)

Contents

List of figures

Acknowledgments

During the course of writing this book, I have been very fortunate to be part of two distinct, inspiring settings: the Centre of Excellence in Foundations of European Law and Polity at the University of Helsinki and the Court of Justice of the European Union in Luxembourg. A warm thank you is due to Professors Thomas Wilhelmsson, Joxerramon Bengoetxea and Juha Raitio for numerous helpful comments and suggestions. I also owe a special thank you to Professors Kaarlo Tuori, Kimmo Nuotio, Tuomas Ojanen and Pia Letto-Vanamo as well as Advocate General Niilo Jääskinen.

I want to express my warmest thank you to my parents and Arto for their unfailing support and encouragement throughout this project. This book is dedicated to them.

Elina Paunio

'I don't know what you mean by "glory," ' Alice said.

Humpty Dumpty smiled contemptuously. 'Of course you don't—till I tell you. I meant "there's a nice knock-down argument for you!" '

'But "glory" doesn't mean "a nice knock-down argument," ' Alice objected.

'When I use a word,' Humpty Dumpty said in rather a scornful tone, 'it means just what I choose it to mean—neither more nor less.'

'The question is,' said Alice, 'whether you CAN make words mean so many different things.'

'The question is,' said Humpty Dumpty, 'which is to be master—that's all.'

Lewis Carroll, *Through the Looking Glass and What Alice Found There*, 1871

Introduction

Multilingualism is a central and inevitable aspect of European integration, yet its impact on the development of pan-European legal rules has remained a largely neglected field of scholarship. This book contributes to filling that gap by examining the effect of multilingualism on legal certainty in EU law.

The official languages of EU Member States are formally equal. After successive enlargements, the number of official languages has grown exponentially from the original four to an impressive 24 in 2013. In accordance with the policy of linguistic equality, EU legislation must be translated into all official languages of the Member States. From formal equality also follows that these language versions are legally authentic in that not only is legislation drafted in these languages but they also form the basis for interpreting EU law.

Given that the EU is essentially a multilingual enterprise, the issue of multilingualism is unavoidably brought into focus when discussing EU law and, more specifically, interpreting EU law. The extraordinary number of official and at the same time legally authentic languages, together with the linguistic policy of equality, means that in legal disputes the meaning of EU legal texts is, at least in theory, construed on the basis of and after comparison with all language versions.

In case of differences, the language versions must therefore be reconciled by way of interpretation at the Court of Justice of the European Union (the Court or the ECJ). However, eliminating linguistic discrepancies by way of interpretation may be argued to run contrary to the principle of legal certainty given that one or more language versions may have to be interpreted in a manner that is not in accordance with the ordinary usage of words. Mindful of this problem and aiming at guaranteeing the official EU policy of linguistic equality, the Court has stated that it is appropriate to reach a solution that does not prefer any one of the language versions. To do so, the Court resorts to the teleological method of interpretation that takes as its starting point the *telos*; that is, the purpose and objectives of the rule in question as well as contextual and systemic considerations.

This teleological approach to interpreting EU law can collide with the principle of legal certainty. The argument goes that predictability, which is often regarded as the kernel of legal certainty, is undermined because of multilingualism, thereby inevitably causing problems of clarity. This criticism is generally expressed along the following lines: eliminating linguistic discrepancies by way of interpretation and, more specifically, by reference to systemic and, perhaps most importantly, teleological considerations, runs contrary to the key tenets of the principle of legal certainty: since multilingualism requires recourse to the teleological method of interpretation, it subordinates the wording of the rule in question to considerations of purpose and consequences, thus resulting in unpredictable judicial decision-making.

Multilingualism seems to imply that legal certainty, and in particular predictability, are irreconcilable objectives. This book contends, however, that revising the notion of legal certainty by shifting the focus from clarity and unequivocal rules to acceptability and judicial reasoning can avoid a collision between legal certainty (predictability) and multilingualism. Propositions of this kind are yet to be extensively discussed in debates about legal certainty in the context of EU law.

This book rejects the notion that legal certainty must necessarily be based on objectivity and a static notion of language. It proposes a hermeneutic, interpretative conception of legal certainty that focuses on judicial reasoning and rational acceptability of judicial decision-making within a particular legal community.

The proposed conception of legal certainty that will here be termed *discursive legal certainty* finds support not only in the philosophy of language, which challenges the idea of a natural or objective meaning of words, but also in the multilingual character of EU law. There is no objective meaning of the legal provisions that the ECJ interprets and applies. Even more importantly, no uncontested language reference can be pinpointed among the equally valid official language versions in which the law is formally expressed.

The principle of legal certainty refers to more than mere predictability. In fact, legal certainty is also said to exist when judicial decision-making is acceptable, consequently fulfilling the imperatives of rationality and moral acceptability. Indeed, it is plausible to say that legal certainty comprises both formal and substantive elements. That is, it comprises both predictability and acceptability.

Drawing from both legal and translation theory, this book formulates a hypothesis as to what legal certainty is and how it should be conceptualized in this multilingual framework. Insights drawn from translation studies are combined with knowledge of the discipline to analyze multilingual EU law. Therefore, a clear overlap necessarily exists between the two fields of research. The multilingual and translated character of EU law highlights the need to draw perspectives from other fields of study to better understand problems related to multilingualism.

The book is structured as follows. Chapter 1 clears the ground by examining the interrelationship between translation, a central feature of EU law, and the interpretive techniques employed by the Court. In this context, problems of translation and the role of language in EU law-making are discussed before exploring the basic tenets of judicial reasoning at the Court.

Due to both institutional and systemic problems in translating EU legislation, the task of constructing the concrete meaning of EU legislation falls on the Court. It does so through its judgments by using arguments that can be divided into the umbrella categories of linguistic, systemic and dynamic arguments. In this regard, the different methods of interpretation used by the Court are charted with particular focus on their justificatory force in the present multilingual context. In the light of the inherently unstable foundation on which judicial interpretation at the Court is constructed, a move beyond words is proposed, in favour of teleological reasoning in interpreting translated law.

Chapter 2 shifts the focus to different meanings attributed to the principle of legal certainty. Before turning our attention to theoretical aspects of the principle following the twofold concept of legal certainty, based on the dichotomy between formal predictability and substantive acceptability, the basic tenets of the Court's case law on the meaning of the principle of legal certainty are fleshed out.

In fact, what makes the principle of legal certainty a particularly interesting and fruitful object of study is its diffuse nature: this seems to be so, irrespective of the legal system in which it is applied. Even though both extensive ECJ case law and literature are available in the field, legal certainty remains an elusive concept and, accordingly, its contours are difficult to define.

The Court has itself employed legal certainty as a fundamental principle of EU law requiring that rules imposing obligations on individuals or other private parties should be clear and precise so that those they affect are able to ascertain unequivocally what their rights and obligations are and take steps accordingly. It is therefore not surprising that the formal component of legal certainty has attracted most attention within EU legal scholarship.

Here it is asserted that substantive legal certainty is tied to judicial reasoning. The claim is made that a connection can be found between the methods of interpretation used by the Court and substantive aspect of legal certainty. The key to legal certainty in its substantive form lies in the way judicial decisions are justified.

Chapter 3 examines the role of communication in the context of legal adjudication. In this context, Habermasian discourse theory of law offers a helpful theoretical tool for exploring the communicative character of adjudication and judicial reasoning and its implications for understanding legal certainty.

On the basis of a dynamic understanding of language, Chapter 3 discusses how multilingual EU law gains meaning in discourse, in particular through discursive practices in which the ECJ engages with national courts. In that context, this chapter also puts forward the idea of different communicative spheres to identify contexts in which the Court engages in dialogue with its audience. Reaching agreement within the EU legal community about the meaning of EU law requires judicial reasoning which exposes the underlying value basis of interpretation. Similarly, the communicative concept of legal certainty sketched here reposes on deliberative communication between relevant specialists. Acceptability of judicial decision-making is not achieved by authority but by means of transparent judicial reasoning expressing the value orientation taken in judgments.

Chapter 4 addresses the concept of discursive legal certainty more closely. In support of the claim that legal certainty can be conceptualized in terms of discourse and understood as higher-order certainty based on rational acceptability of judicial decision-making in a particular legal community, this chapter makes use of the concept of ideal particular audiences and examines the role of rhetoric in ECJ reasoning and its implications for acceptability.

Just like Humpty Dumpty and Alice in the famous quote from Lewis Carroll's book, the fundamental question here is: who is to be master? Why should the EU legal community accept the Court's decisions? The key to legal certainty lies in the interaction between members of the EU legal community through an ongoing dialogue which entails that the Court gives persuasive, convincing and acceptable reasons for its judgments. This facilitates transparency, sincerity and dialogue with the Court's pertinent audience and is a pre-condition for rational acceptability and consequently for discursive legal certainty. Searching for meaning beyond the words of the law helps the Court to configure its decisions to received expectations. Deeper-level certainty is thus closely linked to *telos* and dynamic methods of interpretation as sources for constructing meaning.

Chapter 1
Lost in translation

Role of language in EU law-making

Translation is the official language of Europe.[1] This chapter sheds light on the techniques deployed by the Court to determine the meaning of multilingual EU law. More specifically, after addressing the role of translation in drafting EU law as well as uncertainties in law and language, we turn to the typical features of the Court's reasoning. The chapter formulates a claim that while insufficient without support from other types of argument, teleological reasoning is in fact necessary to make sense of statutory texts that evolve into complicated and multifaceted procedures of drafting and translation.

The Court's judgments interpreting EU law are based on translated originals to a large extent drafted by the European Commission Translation Services. In fact, intertwined with the policy of linguistic equality is the idea that translations are not really translations at all: they are equivalent official language versions. From the viewpoint of judicial interpretation, this is of particular significance since language versions are all equally authentic when judges or other competent authorities interpret and apply EU legislation. Officially, therefore, language versions are drafted, not translated simultaneously. In this sense, language versions are 'independent' in that they are not considered as derivative of any other version.[2] Irrespective of any qualitative characteristics, all versions are automatically assumed to be equivalent, or in other words, of equal value and meaning in judicial interpretation.

From this it follows that EU legal translation possesses a high symbolic value. Arguably, the communicative function of translation may in some cases be subordinate to its symbolic function: instead of conveying a particular message, the primary function of a translation may simply be existential: it must simply exist. In this sense, it might be said that EU language policy promotes 'existential equivalence'. Indeed, rather than conveying a message or facilitating communication, translation serves as proof of linguistic equality.[3]

1 Ost 2009: 12.
2 Koskinen 2000: 84.
3 Koskinen 2000: 83.

Fiction of equivalence in translated EU law

Law forms a highly institutionalized form of communication, regulating and giving specialized meaning to social action by using natural language.[4] Problems of translation specifically related to legal texts are said to be connected with the fact that legal language is closely connected to a given legal system and legal culture: in other words, legal language is said to carry and be an expression of a particular legal system and culture.[5] Traditionally, for both institutional and systemic reasons, legal texts have been regarded as particularly difficult to translate.[6] For some, the intimate linkage between law, system and culture forms a problem for uniformization of laws that cannot fully be resolved in translation.[7] For others, the very existence of multilingual EU law based on translation suggests that although language admittedly forms a barrier to intercultural communication, it is a barrier that can be overcome.[8] In addition to law-specific translation issues, other problems can also be identified: these relate to the very nature of all natural languages, which are characterized by ambiguity and vagueness.[9]

EU linguistic policy aiming at equality of languages presupposes equivalence of language versions. Yet, equivalence – understood as identity – is an illusion. At best, legal translation – just as any translation – is only approximation.[10] Within the legal context, however, the basic assumption of modern translation theory – that all translation is only an attempt to present information about the source text – has not been fully accepted.[11]

Indeed, the imperative of equality among citizens as well as Member States in the EU context is often referred to as the guiding principle of legal translation. Certainly, translation may be regarded as a means of assuring equality between those concerned by a legal text (be it a statute, a judgment, a contract, or some other type of legal text): translations give access to legal documents to those who would otherwise not have access to them. In the context of EU law, translation forms a prerequisite for direct effect.

In legal translation, it is now commonplace to emphasize the importance of striving for a translation that achieves the intended legal effects and therefore

---

4 Bengoetxea 2011a: 2.

5 Glanert 2008: 164. For a general account of legal languages: Mattila 2006.

6 Šarčević 1997, Gémar 1995: 143–154. See also Garzone 2000: 3 *et seq.*

7 See generally for a critical approach to the translatability of law, *e.g.* Glanert 2008, Legrand 2008.

8 See *e.g.* Cao 2007a, Kjær 2008b.

9 For a comprehensive account of the particularities of legal language in a comparative perspective, see Mattila 2006. Naturally, the same can be said of language in general. Language is essentially open-ended: it forms a flexible means of communication.

10 Gémar 1995: 154. See also Gémar 2002: 169. He notes that in the final analysis, equivalence remains a compromise.

11 Šarčević 1997: 71.

the intended meaning in practice.[12] On this understanding, while legal translators are not expected to produce texts that are equal in meaning – due to the illusory character of equivalence understood as identity – they are expected to produce parallel texts that are equal in legal effect. That is, these parallel texts are expected to be interpreted and applied in the same way irrespective of the legal systemic context.[13]

However, it seems unclear how translators can assure equal legal effect: prejudices and culture affect the way legal texts are interpreted so that each interpretation forms in and of itself a translation too.[14] From this viewpoint, it appears rather difficult to imagine a situation where the translator would be able to ensure that the source text as well as the target text would be interpreted and applied in the same way irrespective of the language and legal system in which the interpreter is situated.[15]

Put differently, EU law forms an amalgam of different systems that have evolved separately and that are generally confined within national and linguistic boundaries. For a translator, this highlights the following problem: how can equivalents be found for culture-bound terms? Indeed, such systemic diversity is often given as another argument for the particular difficulties inherent in legal translation.[16] Nonetheless, looking at legal language from the point of view of translation theory, these characteristics do not make legal translation *per se* particularly difficult: natural languages form an open-ended means of communication acquiring meaning in context, in use.[17] Terminological difficulties, often held to be of particular importance in the context of law too, are present *inter alia* in many other areas of special-purpose translation.[18]

Nonetheless, while the recent trend in translation studies has been to undermine the importance of equivalence and concentrate, *inter alia*, on the communicative function of translation, EU linguistic policy – at least in relation to EU legislation

12 Šarčević 2000: 5. It seems important to note that the idea of 'intention' is problematic in this context. That is, whose intended meaning are we talking about?

13 Šarčević 1997: 88.

14 Steiner 1998: 293–294.

15 In the context of comparative law, Pierre Legrand famously argues that legal transplants are a conceptual impossibility given the divergence of legal cultures, Legrand 1998. For an opposite view: Watson 2000. In the context of uniformization of European law, Simone Glanert suggests that language resists uniformization in the process of translation; see Glanert 2008.

16 Harvey 2002: 180. He relativizes the argued uniqueness of legal languages by noting that while law is certainly unusual in being system-bound, it is not unique in this respect: religion and political science, which are historically related to law, are also inseparable from the notion of systems.

17 Kjær 2008a: 257.

18 These include *inter alia* translation of technical and medical texts. See similarly Šarčević 1997, who sees legal translation as a special field where translation should, according to her, be based on a receiver-oriented approach.

– is based on the presumption that different language versions are equivalent.[19] Similarly, the idea that source and target texts are equivalent (at least in effect) remains the underlying presumption in legal translation in general.[20] Although it might appear plausible to say that striving for equivalence is necessary for assuring equal treatment before the law, achieving it, *in concreto*, in the EU seems less clear. Indeed, the equivalence relation is presupposed to exist not only with the source text but also with the other language versions: all language versions convey the same meaning. For the purposes of equality, exact equivalence is a necessary fiction.[21]

Despite the equal value of official language versions in judicial interpretation, equivalence is sometimes reduced to mere visual equivalence. Arguing that official discourse concerning multilingualism is far from reality, Anthony Pym stresses the symbolic role of translation in the EU. According to Pym, official discourse on translation is produced mainly to 'keep the masses and academics happy'.[22] Equivalence is symbolic. This trait becomes visible when one considers how directives and other EU legislative instruments are drafted: the number of paragraphs has to match, and headings and subheadings have to be located in the same place as in other language versions. In fact, the policy of linguistic equality reduces translation to literal rendering and consequently equivalence to linguistic correspondence.[23] Taking account of the visual constraints in EU translation, what is of particular importance is that the language versions *look* identical.[24]

In a nutshell, translation of EU legislation is not intended to communicate a message to a particular interlocutor, but rather to *produce law*. In other words, translated EU legislation aims at producing a textual representation for norms resulting from the law-making process, without a clearly defined communicative function. Translated EU legislation simply *constitutes* law so that translations *are* law.[25] These translated texts govern legal practice and function as the basis for the production of other texts, such as the Court's judgments in which law created by means of translation is interpreted and applied.[26] After being translated into all

19 Carmen África 2005: 262–264 on recent developments in the field of legal translation.

20 Koskinen 2000: 84. Cf. Šarčević 2000: 1–5. See also *e.g.* Ajani and Rossi 2006: 81, who note that a widespread conviction exists that every law can be translated from one language to another. See also Glanert 2008: 163 for a similarly critical view of the translatability of law.

21 Cf. Cao 2007a: 35. Noting that while in reality no exact equivalence or complete identity of understanding can be expected, it might be that such equivalence is not even necessary.

22 Pym 1998.

23 Koskinen 2000: 85.

24 Koskinen 2000: 85.

25 Kjær 2000: 139. Cf. Kinnunen 2006: 81.

26 See Kjær 2000: 139–140. Kjær makes a useful distinction between three types of legal texts. Legislative texts are constitutive: they include statutes, executive orders, rules,

official languages, these translated texts become legislation: legal texts in their own right.

To problems concerning system- and culture-bound terminology in law can, in the EU context, be added creation of a new variant of all official languages, which adds further problems to the equation: this so-called 'Euro-speak' has moulded structures and created new words in each language.[27] Indeed, even when we are talking about concepts belonging to the autonomous sphere of EU law, some confusion as to their meaning (intention and extension) may nonetheless exist when 'imported' into the national context by national judges and authorities. These concepts, which are situated at the very core of EU law, include, *inter alia*, supremacy, effective judicial protection, direct effect, regulatory acts, legitimate expectations, effectiveness, measures having equivalent effect, mandatory or overriding requirements and direct and individual concern. In this sense, legal terminology used and interpreted in different legal systems reflects profound differences existing between various systems as well as legal conceptions of lawyers in each of these systems.[28]

Clearly, therefore, even if we translate – to the best of our abilities – terms such as direct effect, effective judicial protection, legitimate expectations, and regulatory act into different languages, it might be that these terms will not convey the same meaning to lawyers in different legal systems if no shared theory exists of, for instance, regulatory acts. Importantly, therefore, no matter how well terminology itself is translated, it will not necessarily mean that the legal effect is the same in different legal systems.[29] Additionally, the conceptual autonomy of EU law adds another challenge to this uneasy relationship: in the context of EU law, terms conveying a specific meaning in domestic law – if they indeed exist in the domestic framework – may refer to altogether different concepts when used in the EU context.

Indeed, divergence from one language version to another may be expected for at least three reasons, as explained by Solan.[30] First of all, people in different cultures speaking different languages carry different experiences; these experiences are reflected in words that appear to be translations of each other but really are not,

---

and regulations. These texts establish the law. Other legal text types include descriptive and reproductive texts. The former category includes texts such as legal text books and academic articles: these are legal texts produced by an individual author for the purposes of communicating a message to a specific group of readers. Reproductive texts, then, are used for applying the law. These texts are written in legal practice and include judgments. In these texts, the law is performed and practised with the aim of applying the reproductive text to a specific case. In other words, in the legal field constitutive texts lay down legal rules, reproductive texts apply legal rules and descriptive legal texts describe the two first-mentioned types of texts.

27 Koskinen 2000: 84.

28 Bengoetxea 2011a: 22.

29 Cf. Šarčević 1997.

30 Solan 2009b: 18.

as a result of different semantic fields (*i.e.* false friends). Secondly, languages express concepts differently from each other in small ways to the extent that the Whorfian hypothesis, according to which the concepts of one's language influence thought, can to a certain extent be accepted.[31] Thirdly, keeping in mind that people conceptualize the surrounding world idiosyncratically even when they share both experiences and cultural norms, it comes as no surprise that pinning down the meaning of the law is no easy task for the interpreter.[32] Following Hermans, in our 'de-centred and polycontextual world [...] there is no single privileged way of attributing or processing meaning'.[33]

Not only is translating EU legislation conditioned by these micro-level factors, it also involves 'institutional' problems. Drafting and translating EU legislation do not form a linear process. These two elements, which form the linguistic landscape for the EU law-making process, are intertwined and often overlapping: the final product is a result of a 'collective enterprise'.[34] It proceeds in committees, working groups, teams. There may be several translators of the same document, even with the same target language text. In this sense, translation gets lost in the institutional arrangements: there is no way of clearly separating law drafting from translation. EU law-making is a process where texts rotate and develop in a circular manner so that versions are redrafted and retranslated several times.[35]

In this sense, problems related to legal translation are topped with difficulties that stem from the overall process in which EU law evolves.[36] It is possible to argue that even the preparatory stages of law-making – that is, negotiations carried out by Commission officials, national representatives, the Council and the Parliament – as well as COREPER, the Committee of the Regions of the European Economic and Social Committee – are the result of complex translation processes.[37] As opposed to policy and consultation documents – such as Green and White Papers – generally available in English or French, but also occasionally in German, Spanish or Dutch, a draft regulation, directive and a generally applicable decision initiated in an English or French draft can receive feedback from Member State delegations. This feedback may require additional translation in different directions.[38] More stages of translation and (both linguistic and political) revision

31 Glanert 2008: 11. See also Whorf 1956.

32 Watson 2000: I.

33 Hermans 1999: 150.

34 Koskinen 2000: 88–89. See also Glézl 2007: 3 and Bobek 2007–2008: 10–12 for problems that result from the need to translate the whole *acquis* into new official languages.

35 Bengoetxea 2011a: 5.

36 For the role of the different institutions, see *e.g.* Mathijsen 2010: 61–84 (EP), 90–105 (Council), 106–124 (Commission).

37 Generally on the legislative process, see European Parliament document 'Codecision and Conciliation: A Guide to How the Parliament Co-legislates under the Treaty of Lisbon'.

38 Bengoetxea 2011a: 5. See also Dragone 2006.

form part of legislative processes in the Council and the Parliament.[39] Interestingly, the proposal itself may originate from a draft elaborated by lobbies functioning outside the Commission.[40]

Not surprisingly, the final version in each of the official languages carries traces of earlier phases of the process. All the elements of translation and text production are multiplied. As highlighted above, official language versions are usually collective products: the source text does not remain stable throughout the process, but gets rewritten by new authors, then retranslated by the same translator or possibly someone else. It is not uncommon that the source language changes during this process so that 'this pendulum like movement of source texts and their translations takes place simultaneously in all the official languages'.[41] Due to these particularities, no 'original' text exists that could function as the reference text for judicial interpretation by the Court.

While problems concerning symbolic equivalence and diverging language versions are very real in the context of EU law, it is necessary to underline that exact equivalence between different texts remains a fiction due to the very nature of natural languages. Language is a living tool of communication: it is open-ended and its meaning changes depending on, among other things, the context in which it is used and interpreted. This is so in relation to legal language too.[42] It follows that indeterminacy forms an integral part of legal practices such as law-making and adjudication, even when law is expressed in one single language.[43]

Uncertainties in language and law

Approximations, translated official language versions, can at best be described as more or less equivalent in form and content. However, translation is not the only challenge. As flexible means of communication, all natural languages are indeterminate. Linguistic uncertainties are omnipresent in the language of the law, be it mono- or multilingual. Raymond nicely captures the problem faced by lawyers by noting that although they 'constantly take pains to squeeze the ambiguity out of natural language [...], they are doomed to failure, doomed to having the courts intervene to determine what the statute or the contract *really* means'.[44]

To this end, it is possible to distinguish between 'legal' and 'linguistic' indeterminacy.[45] The former refers to situations where a legal question has no

39 See for an overview, *e.g.* Gallas 2006, Guggeis 2006, Ricci 2006, Hakala 2006.

40 See in this respect Bengoetxea 2011a: 5.

41 Koskinen 2000: 88. Cf. Dragone 2006: 100–101, Guggeis 2006: 114, Hakala 2006: especially 156–161.

42 MacCormick and Summers 1991: 517–518.

43 Tamanaha 2004: 89–90 on how indeterminacy is controlled through legal tradition.

44 Raymond 2000: 5. See also Newmark 1982.

45 See for different aspect of legal indeterminacy and their logical analysis, Moreso 1998: 56–90.

single right answer. In other words, it means that laws do not always determine the answer to a legal question.[46] The latter, then, refers to uncertainty in the meaning of linguistic expressions that may lead to legal indeterminacy.[47]

Linguistic uncertainty takes different forms: it refers to such properties of natural languages as linguistic ambiguity, vagueness and generality.[48] Firstly, even the most simple of words, such as 'break', is ambiguous. It conveys many possible meanings: it can refer to interruptions, pauses or even to good luck. Additionally, a sentence may be structurally or syntactically ambiguous. This type of ambiguity is manifest in the following sentence interpreted by the Court in *Paterson v Weddel*:[49] 'transport of animal carcases or waste not intended for human consumption'. Here, the question is whether 'not intended for human consumption' refers to waste or both carcases as well as waste (*i.e.* whether an exemption provided for in an EC regulation concerns only carcases not intended for human consumption, or all carcases).

Similarly, in *Able UK*[50] the Court was asked to rule on the meaning of the expression 'when such forces take part in the common defence effort' of Article 151(1) (c) of the VAT Directive.[51] More specifically, the issue was whether those words were to be taken to qualify only the part of the sentence immediately preceding them, namely 'the supply of goods or services for supplying their messes or canteens' and not as qualifying the provision in question as a whole. The ambiguity of the sentence emerged from the absence, in certain language versions (such as the English and French versions), of a comma before the said clause.

Secondly, a linguistic formulation reveals its vagueness when it admits of borderline cases in actual use. Many sentences are relatively vague; others relatively precise. While broad consensus exists that a 'car is a vehicle', there are many borderline cases including skates or even war memorials and children's prams. In law, this may be of particular relevance: what really does count as a vehicle within the context of a particular legal rule?[52] Although perfect precision is often presented as a theoretical ideal, it appears unlikely that any natural language could even begin to meet it: even basic observations such as 'this is blue' admit of borderline cases (at least in the purples and greens), since no clear rule exists whether the concept applies in a given situation or not.

---

46 Hart 2012: 126. See also Maxeiner 2006–2007: 543. Cf. Raymond 2000: 1, who notes that language of the law is 'rotten with ambiguity'. But this could be said about natural languages in general too. This is captured by AG Kokott in the case C-243/11, *RVS Levensverzekeringen*, not yet reported, paras 34–36.

47 Endicott 1996: 669.

48 See Cao 2007b: 70.

49 Case 90/83, *Paterson v Weddel* [1984] ECR 1567.

50 Case C-225/11, *Able UK*, not yet reported.

51 Council Directive of 28 November 2006 on the common system of value added tax (OJ 2006 L 347, p. 1).

52 Cf. Schauer 2008, who discusses the so-called Hart and Fuller debate in great detail. See also Chapter 3.

It is commonly accepted that legal language contains a wide array of vague concepts such as 'reasonable', 'proportionate', and 'legitimate'.[53] In *Geltl*,[54] the Court was asked to determine the meaning of several vague expressions contained in Directives 2003/6/EC and 2003/124/EC.[55] These included: 'precise information', 'circumstances or an event which may reasonably be expected to come into existence or occur' and 'may reasonably be expected'.

Thirdly, then, an expression is general when it may be applied to a number of different things. What is important in the legal context is that the above features of natural languages that cause uncertainty can be distinguished, but they are also relative and may often overlap.[56] In *A Oy*,[57] the referring national court was unsure about the meaning of the expression 'operating for reward on international routes'. Taking account of the purpose of the text at issue, the Court came to the conclusion that this expression also encompasses international charter flights within the specific context of VAT exemptions under the Sixth Directive.[58] As is clear from the examples given, lawmakers often use imprecise laws because precision is not desirable. This is particularly so because the law of a given community must be able to govern a wide variety of human activities in a general way with abstract standards. Abstract standards – whether a law enacted by a Parliament or a contract concluded between two parties – that guide action tend to be indeterminate.[59]

Moreover, while legal obligations and rights under various legal instruments can be expressed in precise language, precise linguistic formulations do not necessarily result in precise law: legal effects depend on the way those linguistic formulations are interpreted in a particular factual situation under the constraints of case law that conditions subsequent interpretations.[60] Judges' evaluations concerning the meaning and purpose of the provision in question affect the legal effects of that text.

Importantly, law's own techniques (such as proportionality, the right to effective judicial protection, effectiveness, equality and non-discrimination in the EU context) may also give vague effect to even the most precise of semantic

53 Harvey 2002: 182. Also Endicott 2005 on the value of vagueness in law.

54 C-19/11, *Geltl*, not yet reported.

55 Respectively Directive of the European Parliament and of the Council of 28 January 2003 on insider dealing and market manipulation (market abuse) (OJ 2003 L 96, p. 16) and Commission Directive of 22 December 2003 implementing Directive 2003/6 as regards the definition and public disclosure of inside information and the definition of market manipulation (OJ 2003 L 339, p. 70).

56 Cao 2007b: 70. See also Solan 2005 for this overlap.

57 Case C-33/11, A Oy., not yet reported.

58 Council Directive 77/388/EEC of 17 May 1977 on the harmonization of the laws of the Member States relating to turnover taxes – Common system of value added tax: uniform basis of assessment (OJ 1977 L 145, p. 1).

59 Raudenbush Olmsted 1991: 7.

60 Ojanen 1998: 19–20. See also Dworkin 1986: 228–239 on judges as authors of 'a chain novel called "law"'.

formulations. Endicott gives a telling example: it is possible to imagine a situation where a lawmaker sets out to control traffic at an intersection by requiring cars to stop at a stop sign or at a red light. There is nothing unclear about how such signs should be interpreted. However, judges hearing a case may find resources in law that excuse the driver that has not followed those precise and clear traffic rules. These resources include principles that are based on vague evaluative and normative considerations.[61]

In *Poland v Council*,[62] AG Maduro argued for an expansive reading of a precise time-limit. In this case, the Council had raised a plea of inadmissibility, since the action for annulment brought by Poland had been lodged out of time. According to Article 230 EC, proceedings 'shall be instituted within two months of the publication of the measure [...] or, in the absence [of such publication], on the day on which it came to the knowledge of the [plaintiff]'. Even if it was clear that under traditional rules for computing time-limits, the applicant was time-barred, AG Maduro nonetheless considered that certain fundamental principles of the EU legal order, in particular the principle of the right to effective judicial protection, militated in favour of giving precedence to a more flexible reading of the conditions concerning admissibility of actions for annulment.[63] The Court, while not expressly addressing the issue of admissibility of the action at issue, followed the approach proposed by the Advocate General by holding that it was 'necessary to rule at the outset on the substance of the case'.[64]

Here, it is important to underline that the reasons for indeterminacy are not related to indeterminacy of road signs (as a sign system) or time-limits for bringing an action for annulment (although admittedly, even the precise scope of a two month time-limit can be problematized), but to resources inherent in law, in *legal* indeterminacy. Hence, even the most precise formulation (for example, in the form of speed-, emission- or time-limits), which induces no interpretive problem concerning its meaning *in abstracto*, does not make legal indeterminacy disappear because law's own mechanisms (such as principles) make even precise provisions open-ended when interpreted in a given context.[65] Following Endicott, while precision offers certain benefits from the viewpoint of the rule of law because it contributes to reducing doubt and disagreement in a legal system, even precise law may incur arbitrariness in virtue of its precision.[66] Flexibility can be considered a virtue in law.

Hence, determining the meaning of a legal text – word, expression, sentence and so on – and applying it to specific circumstances in a particular case involves interpretation. Context-dependent, a legal text alone appears to offer courts only

61 Endicott 2001: 381.
62 Case C-273/04, *Poland v Council* [2007] ECR I-8925.
63 See in particular paras 27 *et seq*. of AG Maduro's opinion.
64 Case C-273/04, *Poland v Council* [2007] ECR I-8925, para 33.
65 Raymond 2000: 2.
66 Endicott 2001: 380.

limited guidance in finding an answer to legal questions they are faced with.[67] Therefore, not only the inherent indeterminacy of natural languages topped with problems of translation in the EU context but also the contextuality of language and adjudication implies that the meaning of legal texts is 'potentially *ever-changing*'.[68]

In the first instance, this character of legal texts relates to the contextuality of language: it is difficult to envisage a situation where meaning could be attached to individual words without taking into account the context in which they are used. Words and sentences (as well as paragraphs and so on) are interpreted by reference to other words, sentences and phrases.[69] Here, we are talking about *textual* context: that is, the meaning of a particular text is conditioned by its broader textual context, its textual surroundings.[70]

In the second instance, in order for legal texts to gain meaning they must be interpreted and applied. Judicial interpretation takes place in *context* too. In addition to the textual context of the legal text taken into account in judicial interpretation, context in relation to judicial interpretation refers not only to the circumstances of the case at hand but also to the legal context. In this respect, judicial interpretation builds on interplay between legal materials, comprising both legislation and previous case law, and the particular circumstances of the case at hand. Facts and law thus form inevitable aspects of judicial interpretation.[71] In reality, legal norms condition judicial understanding about facts and vice versa: picking the material facts is not an exercise that comes before choosing relevant legal norms. Rather, deciding on material facts is intertwined with choosing appropriate legal norms: this circular, hermeneutic process weaves 'together a description of the circumstances and a concretization of general norms'.[72]

Emphasizing the contextuality of judicial interpretation and indeterminacy in law relates closely to American legal thinking where the slogan 'we are all realists now' is widely accepted.[73] In its most extreme form, realism contends that law does not determine the outcome in adjudication.[74] Adhering to the idea of legal

67 Cf. Moreso 1998: 159. Lindroos-Hovinheimo 2012. In her book, she addresses the issue of ethical responsibility of judges in interpreting legal texts and highlights the situational character of any instance of interpretation.

68 Ojanen 1998: 25.

69 See *e.g.* MacCormick and Summers 1991: 513.

70 Endicott 1996: 686.

71 Ojanen 1998: 23. See also Bix 1993: 5. In reality, difficulties related to determining the meaning of words in the context of judicial interpretation often turn on the issue of whether, in a specific context, certain rules apply to a set of facts.

72 Habermas 1998: 218.

73 Maxeiner 2006–2007: 543.

74 Maxeiner 2008–2009: 33, who notes that 'we are all realists now', is the 'American credo'. In fact, Oliver Wendell Holmes already identified in law 'a longing for certainty' that remains, in most cases, illusionary. See Holmes 1987: 466. See also Posner 2008 for a moderate account of legal indeterminacy. If my reading of Posner is correct, he seems to

indeterminacy means that legal decisions are seen as necessarily uncertain.[75] To that end, Smith notes that in North America, the 'unstated working assumption of most legal academics is that judicial explanations of a judgment tell us little if anything about why a case was decided as it was'.[76]

Clearly, the above may be seen as both an expression of scepticism *vis-à-vis* legal determinacy but also as a criticism concerning the way judgments are justified. In our European perspective, this view may appear overly pessimistic.[77] However, it captures well the problem of indeterminacy in law, an issue closely related to and sometimes a result of linguistic indeterminacy. Indeed, if applying a rule requires discussion about its meaning, it seems correct to say that the text of the norm does not guide action in a way that commitment to legal certainty as predictability seems to require.[78]

Unstable basis of judicial interpretation

Multilingualism based on the official EU policy of linguistic equality adds to intra-lingual uncertainty the problem of inter-lingual uncertainty when EU law is interpreted. That is, additional uncertainty concerning the meaning of a text may become relevant for interpretation when considered across several languages.[79] Not without reason has the multilingual EU been described as a modern Tower of Babel.[80] Parallels have also been drawn with the Greek myth of the translators of the Septuagint.[81] According to this myth, seventy-two rabbis guided by divine inspiration translated the Old Testament in complete isolation. As a result, they all produced identical translations. Following Koskinen, a similar inbuilt illusion of equivalence also forms the cornerstone of translation practice at the Commission: similarly to their biblical colleagues from ancient Greece, EU translators are

---

argue in favour of indeterminacy in adjudication that is to a certain extent controlled by inter-subjectivity. Cf. Tamanaha 2010, who attempts to reconcile the formalist and realists strands of American legal thought.

75 Leiter 2007: 15–17.

76 Smith 2000: 247.

77 Cf. Klatt 2008.

78 See in similar vein Dorf 2003: 876–877.

79 Cao 2007b: 71. See also Solan 2009a: 46. Solan argues that in situations where, for instance, one of the language versions contains a syntactic ambiguity allowing for multiple interpretations, whereas other versions do not, the Court may relatively easily unmask the common meaning of the language versions by ruling out the version containing the syntactic ambiguity. However, when uncertainty stems from subtle differences in the meaning of individual words, the Court's task is much more difficult.

80 Generally on the topic of linguistic reasoning at the Court and reference to Babel, see Van Calster 1997. See also Bobek 2006–2007, Bengoetxea 2011a: 6–7.

81 Pym 1992: 154–155, Koskinen 2000: 84.

expected to miraculously produce identical versions of EU legislation in all official languages.[82]

These metaphors accurately describe institutional and systemic factors affecting legal translation forming part of EU law-making processes. Yet another fitting analogy might be found in the well-known game of Chinese Whispers. In this game, each player whispers to the next player a phrase whispered to them by the preceding participant. The idea is that cumulative errors from mishearing generally result in a situation where the words heard by the last player bear only a remote resemblance to those uttered by the first player. Just like players of the game of Chinese Whispers, EU translators work on draft texts that undergo extensive examination and revision.

Importantly, this hybrid-like political process of creating EU legislation – comprising political negotiations, translation and interpretation – often requires that the final text adopted is fuzzy and vague so that it can cater for different political interests present in the law-making process.[83] However, the inherent textual uncertainty of EU law is not only a result of political bargaining that leads to intentionally vague texts. One can even say that the final product of the political process that takes shape in the form of EU legislation is an agreement reached on the basis of different normative assumptions and expressed by means of translation.

Put differently, changes are often made for policy reasons: sometimes translators even have to take into account that texts are intentionally left vague for political purposes. Undoubtedly, EU legislation is often a result of difficult political compromises and several rounds of revisions resulting in a political agreement based on the fuzziness of the final text so that it can be accepted irrespective of political interests.[84] Indeed, in some cases such agreement is never reached (nor ratified on the national level). The Constitutional Treaty offers a paradigmatic example in this regard. When agreement is finally reached and a text is adopted, political compromises between conflicting interests nonetheless remain inherent in the law.[85] While the actual textual representation of the norm may in certain cases appear clear, it may be the case that no consensus exists regarding the underlying societal model and purpose.[86]

Instead of 'merely' being a mediating process between text producers and addressees, EU translation thus forms part of a complex and multifaceted text production process that does not follow the classic distinction between text production and translation as two separate entities. In fact, in a multilingual

82 Koskinen 2000: 84. See also Coulmas 1991 on problems of EU translation.

83 Koskinen 2000: 86, similarly Gallas 2006: 124, Maduro 2007: 9.

84 Maduro 2007: 9. See also Cao 2007b: 72, Gallas 2006: 123, Koskinen 2000: 86.

85 For changes in EU environmental regulation entailing a shift of focus from prescriptive legislation to framework norms and emphasis on implementation, see Korkea-aho 2011.

86 Van Hoecke 2002: 61.

institutional setting such as that of the EU, the process of translation stays hidden or masked. Essentially, instead of remaining separate actors working independently from the actual text production process, EU translators form an organic but invisible part of law-making in the EU.[87]

Officially, these parallel, translated originals are produced simultaneously so that none of them represents the original in its own right. Yet, no matter how invisible translation is, the translated originals on the basis of which the Court adjudicates remain an expression of how the translator understands the text in question.[88] This view becomes law, since no source text can be identified as a result of the policy of linguistic equality and equal authenticity of language versions in judicial interpretation.

The described process of EU law-making comprising political negotiation, translation as well as interpretation raises fundamental questions about understanding norms. This process necessarily induces discrepancies between linguistic versions: the final official versions of EU legislation are not identical in meaning.[89] In addition to difficulties of translation, the EU law-making process is characterized by different political agendas as well as institutional complexities.

Discussing the problem of authentic texts in the multilingual EU context, Glétzl notes that 'translations are statistically bound to contain mistakes and the translation of a document into another language may cause the fact that a different meaning will be given to the translation (or its part) than to the original document'.[90] This recurrent claim appears to rest on a fallacy. While it is clear that translation errors occur, it is less clear where such an 'original document' can be found. If no version can prevail over the others, what, then, is the Court's interpretation based on?

Instead of being based on one single authoritative text, the Court works without such a 'stable' textual basis. As a result of complexities in the EU law-making process, coupled with the imperative of equal authenticity of language versions, in principle no language version exists that the ECJ could resort to in case of doubt.[91] Given these institutional and linguistic constraints, identifying a singular

87 See in more detail Koskinen 2008 for institutional constraints related to translation at the Commission.

88 This is so no matter how much translation scholars emphasize the legal translator's task to understand the source text but 'not to interpret it in the legal sense'. See *e.g.* Šarčević 2000: 5. Cf. Koskinen 2000: 85, who criticises the Commission Translation Services for a very narrow conception of equivalence whereby translating is reduced to linguistic correspondence and literal rendering.

89 This view, taken from a purely translational perspective, is self-evident; there is no way of creating equivalence because of the differences in language systems.

90 Glézl 2007: 3.

91 Cf. case C-364/11, *Abed El Karem El Kott and Others*, not yet reported, paras 29–30 of AG Sharpston's opinion. Here, she undertakes a comparative analysis of two versions, namely English and French. This is because the EU text requiring interpretation (Article 12(1)(a) of Council Directive 2004/83/EC) is based on the wording of the Geneva

'legislative intent' as expressed in one or several authentic versions becomes problematic. Nor is it feasible to speak of *authentic* interpretation. Indeed, it might even be impossible to trace the original drafting language.

Nonetheless, Šarčević contends that 'the translator's first consideration is no longer fidelity to the source text but rather fidelity to *the uniform intent* of the single instrument, i.e., what the legislator or negotiators intended to say'.[92] Indeed, in domestic legal systems in particular, it is commonplace to speak of legislative intent as the starting point of interpretation.[93] But where can this intent be found? Whose intent or will are we talking about? And more specifically, where can the Court look for it? Indeed, within the multilingual and pluralistic EU context, it seems realistic to argue that no clearly definable legislator exists to whom such an intent or will can be traced back or attributed.[94]

Unlike in monolingual legal systems where it certainly appears somewhat more plausible to speak about legislative intent – to the extent that the legislative process is less complex – EU legislation is not drafted in any particular language: it is a result of a mixture of language and politics. Complexities abundant in the legislative process as well as its cumulative and successive nature make referring to a particular legislative will or intent impossible. What is more, the legislator expresses itself through translators (and interpreters) whose input in drafting law is considerable. In such a context of confusion, it is not surprising that the Court appears to deploy legislative intent in its reasoning with caution.

Taking account of these complexities, multilingual law only brings to the fore the question that lies at the heart of all judicial interpretation: what is judicial interpretation really based on? Be it mono- or multilingual, law is an unstable discipline that cannot be broken down into clearly definable elements, but instead relies on vague and ambiguous notions such as 'proportionality' and 'fair trial'. As a result, legal discourse constantly fluctuates: its meaning may change depending on the language in which it is expressed and even depending on the interpreter.[95] In the EU context, official language versions offer multifaceted, sometimes contradictory and ambiguous, raw material which functions as the starting point of the Court's interpretive enterprise.[96]

Convention of 28 July 1951 relating to the status of refugees. This provision, in turn, only exists in the above-mentioned equally authentic language versions.

92 Šarčević 1997: 112.

93 Generally on statutory interpretation and arguments used in judicial interpretation see *e.g.* MacCormick and Summers 1991. Cf. Scalia 1997, who favours the so-called 'originalist' method of statutory interpretation according to which judges ought to interpret statutes and the (US) Constitution according to how their authors intended them to be. See also Conway 2012 for a similar claim in the EU context.

94 See Bengoetxea 2011a: 9. Also Bix 2003: 292 on problems related to legislative intentions.

95 Harvey 2002: 182.

96 See Kjær 2010 for an interesting analysis of EU legislation that she describes as 'nonsense'. In a nutshell, she argues that through its judgments the ECJ plays an important

Tentatively, it could be argued that no unequivocally identifiable norm – expressing the EU legislature's (subjective) 'intention' or in more objective terms, 'legislative will' – underlying its textual representations in official languages exists. Consequently, EU legislation – official and equally authentic in all official languages after being drafted and translated on the basis of differing normative assumptions and after several stages of negotiation and translation – forms a rather uncertain and unstable basis on which to build judicial interpretation. As Sankari points out, 'there may be as many probable intentions [...] of the "drafter" as there are drafters. In any case, the intentions remain largely secret. Even with secondary law, intentions can only be followed as an interpretative guideline when [...] they can be recognised. In this sense, most EU law notoriously suffers from a lack of public *travaux préparatoires*'.[97]

In such a context of linguistic as well as political uncertainty as to norms underlying EU legislation, the Court's role in defining the content and the meaning of multilingual legal texts is of key importance. In short, the Court works on the basis of different language versions to construct an interpretive meaning taking into account the factual circumstances (context) of the case as well as systemic and teleological considerations.[98]

Architecture of judicial interpretation at the Court

As the above suggests and contrary to what is often taken to form the kernel of statutory interpretation, it appears realistic to argue that textual representations of rules cannot lead the Court straight to some predetermined meaning, a norm underlying all official language versions. Multilingual EU law does not contain 'one' unequivocal meaning that the interpreter can 'discover'. Instead, the Court as interpreter adds meaning to EU legislation, using the formal elements of the text only as a springboard. Since rules are not self-explanatory, the ECJ has to adapt the content of the text it is called on to interpret not only to the legal surroundings (legal texts and case law) but also to the concrete situation in which the text should be applied. If rules contained in EU legislation are contradictory, hiding beneath their surface different political agendas, normative assumptions and translation problems, then what exactly are the Court's judgments based on?

A fundamental difference which separates supranational law-making and adjudication can be identified: whereas drafting is the field of negotiation and compromise, often best achieved by deliberately fuzzy linguistic utterances and characterized by translation problems, adjudication ideally aims at establishing determinate, unambiguous meaning across languages and at resolving ambiguities

---

role in making sense of the nonsense of multilingual EU legislation.

97 Sankari 2011: 70.

98 Cf. Twining 2008: 162–165 on American Legal Realism and the distinction between 'paper rules' and 'real rules'.

left in the legal instrument due to policy considerations.[99] In a situation where translation forms an integral part of EU law-making, the Court's role in defining the content and meaning of multilingual legal texts is of central importance. At the same time, however, especially in the preliminary ruling procedure governed by Article 267 TFEU, the ECJ may itself opt for vagueness, leaving certain questions unanswered or to the discretion of national courts, thus choosing the road of judicial minimalism and self-restraint.[100]

As long as the law-making process is not itself capable of reconciling different political as well as normative assumptions during the actual law-making process, these incomplete decisions on the content of law are bound to lead to delegation of law-making power to the Court in order to make a final decision on issues that have not been agreed on during the actual political process.[101] Therefore, the ECJ often gives a legal answer to issues involving broad political importance that have not been decided in the political process itself. Certainly, delegating legislative powers to institutions that have not been elected in a democratic process may be argued to create problems from the viewpoint of democracy and democratic deliberation.[102]

Indeed, with regard to the institutional constraints of law-making related to the role of both translation and political bargaining, the Court could be characterized as mediating between lawmakers and national courts and authorities applying EU legislation in national contexts. In this sense, the Court negotiates a solution to legal as well as political questions by reconciling the expectations of the EU legal community with the legislative text.

The Court therefore also assumes the role of a translator: it acts as mediator between text producer (the EU legislature) and text addressees (other courts and other authorities applying EU law). In this respect, the Court in fact translates EU legislative texts into a new judicial language that reflects its perception of the underlying normative foundations of the EU legal system.[103] As will be argued in the following, the teleological approach employed by the Court in interpreting EU law can be seen as a specific expression of the way the ECJ perceives the normative foundations of the EU legal system whereby EU legislation is interpreted in accordance with the aims and objectives of that legislation.

Distinguishing between discovery and justification in legal adjudication is helpful in this context.[104] Undoubtedly, reasons for reaching a given decision can vary considerably from case to case. Reasoning, the act of justifying a ruling and

99 Cao 2007b: 72.

100 Sarmiento 2012. For judicial minimalism in the US, see Sunstein 1999.

101 Cartabia 2007: 3. See similarly Maduro 2007: 9.

102 See *e.g.* Weiler 1999: 363 for the Court's role in arbitrating delicate social choices and reconciling trade with competing social policies. See also Avbelj 2004: 14–15, Korkea-aho 2011.

103 Maduro 2007: 9–10.

104 Bengoetxea 1993: 112–122, Bengoetxea *et al.* 2001: 48–50.

the interpretive choices involved, constitutes part of this judicial decision-making process, the part of judicial interpretation that is visible to the external eye. In other words, reasoning can be deduced from the judgment itself. However, no way exists to control that reasons for reaching a particular decision correspond to those given to justify the decision in question.[105]

Judicial reasoning includes arguments that the Court both explicitly and implicitly refers to in its judgment. In the words of Moral Soriano, 'legal reasoning is a matter of justification [...], to justify is the activity of supporting a particular statement with good reasons'.[106] In essence, judicial reasoning constitutes a process that aims at justifying a claim, a decision, or a particular outcome by means of different arguments (reasons). In this sense, judicial reasoning is the *explicit* part of justification.

Importantly, justification takes place in *discourse*: no such thing exists as justification in the abstract. Justifying a judicial decision consists in a discursive activity aiming at giving legally 'good' or 'correct' reasons to a given audience. Interpersonal and communicative, legal justification is ingrained in discourse. Discourse, then, may be taken to refer to the context where reasoning takes place. Indeed, justification occurs within a given discourse, since justifying a judicial decision requires giving arguments that as a whole form judicial reasoning.[107]

Hence, in justifying its decisions the ECJ is bound by the constraints of judicial reasoning accepted in the EU legal system: it may only use interpretive criteria considered as acceptable in legal argumentation in the particular context of EU law. Additionally, the Court needs to adhere to systemic constraints of coherence and consistency in interpreting EU law.[108] In the following, we explore explicitly stated arguments used by the Court in its judgments.

Reconciling language versions by way of interpretation

The Court lies at the heart of any task aiming at reconciling language versions that have emerged in a process characterized by multiple interpretations in different directions and at different stages of the law-making process. In deciding individual cases on the basis of multilingual EU legislation, the Court resorts

105 See *e.g.* Posner 2008 for a critical account of the reasons that in reality affect judicial decision-making. Indeed, although Posner discusses judicial decision-making in the US, certain similarities may nonetheless be said to exist between the Court and the model of judicial decision-making put forward by Posner. Just as may be said to be the case with the Court, Posner argues that in non-routine cases judges take on an active role. In this respect, judges may be said to be legal pragmatists that base their decisions on policy considerations concentrating on consequences in a forward-looking manner.

106 Moral Soriano 2003: 308.

107 Bengoetxea 1993: 141–142. He differentiates between legal argumentation and legal reasoning while noting that they are closely related.

108 Maduro 2007: 10.

to interpretation. In the wide sense of the term, 'interpretation' referring to understanding of a particular text is an unavoidable feature of applying the law; indeed, any apprehension of meaning involves interpretation.[109]

However, for present purposes, a narrower conception of the term 'interpretation' is more useful in the context of analyzing judicial reasoning.[110] In the strict sense, interpretation occurs only when doubt exists as to the meaning of a text: interpretation resolves doubt through reasons supporting the way the interpretive question is decided. Reflective elimination of doubt must be distinguished from unreflective understanding that does not include meditation as to how a word or sign should be interpreted.[111]

Judicial interpretation can be described as the act performed to deduce a legal norm from a legal text.[112] Interpretation is therefore an act 'that begins with a question and ends with a choice between different possible constructions'.[113] The choice, then, is made by means of judicial reasoning. Alexy formulates the connection between interpretation and argumentation in law as follows: 'interpretation is argumentation'.[114] The idea of dividing interpretation into unreflective understanding and conscious decision-making is connected to the distinction between hard and easy cases ('clear cases') in which a sufficient degree of determinacy is presupposed as to meaning of legal provisions.[115] According to this dichotomy, 'easy cases' require no interpretation since the legal answer to a specific question is obvious or not problematized.[116] Following MacCormick's description, a 'hard case is now understood as a case where some difficulty in interpreting the law has arisen, where there are strong arguments for each of the rival understandings or interpretations of the law put forward by or on behalf of the parties'.[117]

However, from a hermeneutical viewpoint, no way of clearly distinguishing between hard cases and easy cases exists. In hard cases, interpretive choices come clearly into play, whereas easy cases simply require applying the relevant provision to the case in question.[118] Nonetheless, classifying a case as easy or clear already includes an interpretive evaluation of the case in question: a case

109 See Schauer 1991: especially 207 *et seq.* for an interesting account of rule-based behaviour and interpretation of rules.

110 MacCormick 2005: 121.

111 See also Van Hoecke 2002: 128–129 who makes a helpful distinction between *prima facie* meaning and methodologically determined meaning.

112 Lindroos-Hovinheimo 2012: 6.

113 Klatt 2008: 4, Alexy 1995: 73.

114 Alexy 1995: 78.

115 Endicott 2000: 8–11. See also Bix 1993: 63–70 on the idea of easy or clear cases. See also Schauer 1991: 207–208.

116 See Bix 1993: 76, also Bengoetxea 1993: 221.

117 MacCormick 2005: 50.

118 The term 'easy case' is generally associated with Ronald Dworkin, see Dworkin 1977: 337.

is considered an easy or routine case only after it has been interpreted (perhaps even unconsciously) as belonging to that category of cases.[119] Indeed, a further distinction can be made: not all clear (problematized) cases are easy.[120]

This last distinction aside, it seems that both terms are generally used interchangeably to mark cases that can be decided on the basis of deduction in accordance with syllogistic reasoning. These are unproblematized cases where the formulation of premises proceeds in a straightforward manner.[121] Yet, the majority of cases decided by the Court in the preliminary ruling procedure – our main interest here – are hard.[122] Arguably, the multilingual character of EU law implies that classifying a case as clear might be more difficult when divergence between language versions is detected. As Bengoetxea observes, empirical evidence suggests that this distinction is also implicitly recognized by the Court: cases that are considered clearer are assigned to chambers of three judges whereas harder cases are decided by chambers of five judges or the grand chamber (in rare cases, the full Court). If the assigned chamber so requests, the case can also be reassigned to a formation composed of a greater number of judges.[123] In addition, whether or not the Court's judgment is accompanied by an AG's Opinion can serve as an indication that the case is not considered to constitute a clear case.

Another useful way of looking at judicial interpretation is to apply a distinction between interpreting *in abstracto* as opposed to interpreting *in concreto*. Interpreting *in abstracto* refers to the act of giving a general account of the meaning of a legal text without considering it in connection with a specific case (to which the result of interpretation is applied). The result is an abstract legal norm, a *prima facie* applicable norm.[124] Interpreting *in concreto*, then, refers to an act of interpretation whereby meaning is attached to a legal text in the context of an actual case. The result offers us a concrete legal norm or the most appropriate norm with regard to the factual situation at hand.[125] Judicial interpretation *in concreto* relates to the above-discussed issue of context: an act of interpretation *in concreto* is conditioned by its context, the factual as well as legal circumstances of the case in question.

Here, the juxtaposition between *semantic* and *pragmatic* meaning comes into play.[126] Judicial interpretation cannot be reduced to explicating the semantic meaning of a particular legal text, but rather its meaning is determined in judicial

119 Tontti 2004: 177. See also Bengoetxea 1993, Posner 2008, for a distinction between decision-making in easy and hard cases.

120 MacCormick 2005: 50–52.

121 Bengoetxea 1993: 183–207, Bengoetxea *et al.* 2001: 49. MacCormick 2005: 51. See also Sankari 2011: 82 for a reconstruction of Joxerramon Bengoetxea's (Bengoetxea 1993) analysis of the division between clear and hard cases.

122 Bengoetxea *et al.* 2001: 50.

123 Bengoetxea 1993: 195–196. See also Chapter 2 of the Rules of Procedure of the Court of Justice (OJ 2012 L 265, p. 1).

124 Habermas 1998: 217.

125 Habermas 1998: 217–218. See also Endicott 1996: 681, Ojanen 1998: 24.

126 See Lindroos-Hovinheimo 2006: 56.

interpretation and application.[127] This pragmatic approach, which complements a more restrictive view on semantic meaning, offers an explanation of judicial interpretation according to which meaning develops in use and is determined by use.[128] While not resolving the problem of meaning, it takes as its starting point the idea that meaning can be re-determined. For example, Kinnunen describes judicial interpretation as a concretization process whereby norms gain a linguistic meaning: their meaning is only determined when a norm sentence is interpreted and applied in the concrete circumstances of a given case.[129]

According to Bengoetxea, it is possible to distinguish between 11 phases in the ECJ decision-making process in the framework of the preliminary ruling procedure.[130] Some of these steps belong to the above-mentioned context of discovery, but some are set in the context of justification. These steps include at least the following moments which are characterized by discretion on the part of the Court: deciding on the need for a preliminary ruling, categorizing the legal problem, choosing applicable provisions, deciding on the need to interpret the provisions in question, deciding on the validity of applicable provisions, interpreting the chosen provisions, formulating the norm governing the dispute, establishing the facts and deciding on evidence, qualifying the facts and deciding on their classification, choosing among consequences, and deciding on mitigation of the consequence chosen.[131]

Undoubtedly, all of the above logical moments of discretion affect the final outcome of the case as well as the meaning attributed to specific provisions in the context of a particular case. In this sense, they all constitute judicial interpretation in the broadest sense of the term. Here, however, interpreting the chosen provisions forms the moment of discretion that carries particular significance. Interpretation understood in the strict sense is generally argued to function as the classic domain for discretion. It may be described as a process whereby the selected provision is constructed into the applicable norm.[132]

This process is not governed by any procedural or substantive legal rule: it depends *inter alia* on legal culture and ideology as well as on institutional practices.[133] In this respect, whenever uncertainty with regard to the meaning of a chosen provision or a set of provisions is identified, the ECJ must resort to interpretation *stricto sensu*. While the Court may freely choose one plausible interpretation of the law amongst various possibilities (that depend, *inter alia*, on choices made in previous steps of judicial decision-making charted above but also

127 Kinnunen 2006: 115. See also Sperber and Wilson 1995.

128 Christensen and Sokolowski 2002: 66–69.

129 Kinnunen 2006: 115.

130 Bengoetxea 2007: 56. See also Bengoetxea *et al.* 2001: 51–60.

131 See Bengoetxea 2007 for a more detailed analysis of these moments of discretion that are present in judicial decision-making at the Court.

132 Bengoetxea 2007: 59.

133 Bengoetxea 2007: 59.

on previous case law in the field), it nonetheless needs to justify this choice by resorting to interpretive arguments and different categories of arguments.[134]

In this respect, choosing one category of arguments rather than another as well as choosing one argument over another depends on whether, at any given moment, the Court uses its discretion in order to further certain values. Therefore, the Court may choose to deploy – when available – soft law instruments, including recommendations, opinions and guidelines as well as *travaux préparatoires*, to support an interpretation it has reached using the different arguments available. Naturally, making recourse to these additional sources of interpretation also involves discretion.[135] What is of importance in this context, however, is how these choices are *justified.*

While having many characteristics in common with interpreting texts in general, judicial interpretation also possesses specific features. This is due to its normative and institutional character.[136] Firstly, its normative features are a result of the claim to correctness included in every interpretation. Secondly, its institutional features stem from the authoritative objects of interpretation (legal sources) and the authority of those who interpret these texts (judges). Here it is useful to distinguish between interpretive arguments and categories of arguments. Categories of arguments refer to what must be looked at: for example, language, context, or functions. Interpretive arguments, then, answer the question of how each of the categories should be used in interpretation.[137]

Types of argument used by the Court

Here we stand in the realm of hard cases where the interpretive question has been problematized. In this context, three primary categories of interpretive argument, although often intertwined and overlapping in actual judgments, may be deduced from the Court's case law: semiotic or linguistic arguments, systemic or contextual arguments, and dynamic arguments.[138] Linguistic arguments employ the linguistic usage of a text; systemic or contextual arguments relate to both the position of the norm sentence or a single word in a wider legal context, that of the wider legal text or the legal system as a whole, but also to the temporal context; and

134 See Bengoetxea 1993, who analyzes and categorizes arguments and categories of interpretation rationally reconstructed from ECJ case law.

135 Bengoetxea 2007: 60.

136 Klatt 2008: 4. Cf. Lindroos-Hovinheimo 2012: 161, who argues that ultimately what distinguishes legal interpretation from other interpretive practices is the demand for justice.

137 Bengoetxea *et al.* 2001: 57.

138 See *e.g.* Bengoetxea 1993: 233–262, Schermers and Waelbroeck 2001: 10–27, McLeod 2004.

finally, dynamic arguments consider factors such as the purpose, aims, goals, and consequences of the text that is to be interpreted.[139]

From the standpoint of justification, it is irrelevant how the Court arrives at choosing certain arguments to support a specific decision: rather, one needs to ask whether the chosen interpretation is meaningful and whether the ECJ provides good reasons for it.[140] Importantly, the interpretive process closely relates to what is seen as valuable in a particular legal system: it rests on intricate questions of value and principle in a specific legal community.[141]

Following the distinction between different categories of arguments, the Court's reasoning is generally said to be based on the above three categories; that is, on 'the spirit, the general scheme and the wording' of the provision in accordance with the early judgment in the seminal *Van Gend en Loos* case.[142] Also of particular significance here is the landmark *CILFIT*[143] case in which the Court not only formulated the *acte clair* doctrine but also expressed the requirement according to which interpreting a provision of EU law necessarily involves comparing different language versions.[144] However, the Court does not systematically compare official language versions of the law it applies. Only occasionally – typically on the initiative of the parties – does the Court resort to comparison of language versions.[145]

After comparison – if language versions are compared at all – the provision is as a rule placed in its broader context and interpreted in the light of one or several identified purposes that possess a linkage with the provision at hand. In particular, as the Court already noted in *CILFIT*, the *state of evolution* of EU law (at the time the provision in question is applied) needs to be taken into account.[146] Context, therefore, has a considerable impact on interpreting EU law: not only the textual and factual context, but also the temporal context play a role in determining the meaning of EU law provisions. This last-mentioned temporal aspect of contextuality is interesting because it highlights the dynamic and continuously evolving character of EU law, tying contextual arguments closely to those possessing a

---

139 MacCormick and Summers 1991. See also Bengoetxea 1993: 233–234, Alexy 1989: 234–244, who further distinguishes between genetic, historical, and comparative arguments. Some confusion exists between dynamic and teleological arguments. The first-mentioned category of arguments is often referred to as teleological arguments although, for instance, Bengoetxea categorizes teleological arguments as a subcategory of dynamic arguments. See also Maduro 2010: xvii–xviii.

140 Bengoetxea *et al.* 2001: 57.

141 Bengoetxea *et al.* 2001: 57.

142 Case 26/62, *Van Gend en Loos* [1963] ECR 1.

143 Case 283/81, *CILFIT v Ministère de la santé* [1982] ECR 3415.

144 Case 283/81, *CILFIT v Ministère de la santé* [1982] ECR 3415, para 18. See also Stone Sweet 2012 for a reconstruction of *CILFIT* from the viewpoint of judicial authority.

145 Bengoetxea 2011a: 1.

146 Case 283/81, *CILFIT v Ministère de la santé* [1982] ECR 3415, para 20.

dynamic character.[147] This point is neatly summarized by Ojanen, who observes that 'as with the interpretation of the law generally, the interpretation of [EU law] is a matter of contextual, moment-to-moment construction'.[148]

In sum, the Court has repeatedly held that not only wording but also contextual and teleological considerations have to be taken into account in interpreting EU law: in this respect, it employs different criteria of interpretation regarded as acceptable in the EU legal system. The criteria of interpretation used in ECJ case law and the values associated with them may be described in Figure 1.1.[149]

In fact, the model adopted by the Court for interpreting EU law can be traced back to the Vienna Convention on the Law of Treaties. Article 31 of the Convention gives the general rule for interpreting international treaties. In that Convention, the starting point is the ordinary meaning of the Treaty text followed by context and other interpretive methods. In fact, the Court seems to have inversed the order of interpretive methods provided in the Convention so that the purpose of the text in question is followed by systemic, contextual and, lastly, linguistic considerations.[150] However, according to Arnull, no fixed hierarchy among arguments employed by

Linguistic	Systemic	Dynamic
• Arguments: language versions; ordinary meaning; EU law meaning • Values: certainty; rule of law	• Arguments: quasi-logical arguments such as *a fortiori*, *a pari*, analogy, *a contrario*, antinomy solution criteria; competence criteria; *ratio legis* • Values: systemic values of autonomy, integrity and consistency	• Arguments: teleological; functional; consequences • Values: integrity coherence; innovation; reflexivity

Figure 1.1 Interpretive criteria used by the Court

147 Cf. Tontti 2004: 101 *et seq*. on dialectics of past, present and future in law.

148 Ojanen 2003: 203.

149 This figure is based on categorization proposed by Bengoetxea. See *e.g.* Bengoetxea 2007: 59.

150 Sankari's analysis distinguishes between different opinions expressed in legal scholarship as to the method of interpretation used by the Court. It seems that the majority of scholars ascribe special importance to teleological traits in the Court's reasoning. Sankari 2011: 65–68.

the Court can be deduced from the case law. Rather, 'the Court simply selects those it considers most appropriate in the circumstances'.[151]

Whatever their internal ranking order, considerations are deployed to pin down the meaning of EU law published in over 20 languages that, according to the Court, uses terminology that is peculiar to EU law in that it is not based on domestic law unless expressly mentioned.[152] Thus, as we will see in the following, linguistic comparison of authentic versions or indeed, use of semantic arguments, can only offer the starting point for EU judicial interpretation and must be complemented by contextual, systemic and teleological considerations.[153]

In fact, it can be said that the need to consult and compare language versions forms a logical corollary of the idea that each version contributes to the meaning of the provision.[154] Importantly, however, even the most recent enlargements, and consequently, the exponential growth in the number of official languages, have not led the Court to officially reconsider its position on the need for (and usefulness of) comparison; instead, comparison remains one of the techniques employed by the Court to justify its judgments.

Comparison of language versions also relates closely to the special emphasis the Court places on the need for uniform interpretation of EU law: comparing language versions is understood as ensuring uniform interpretation. Stressing the need for such interpretation and application across Member States, the Court has also stated that it is impossible to consider EU law provisions without also taking into consideration the intention of the author or, in other words, the aims of the legislative text at issue. Thus, the Court rarely draws any direct legal consequences from comparison and instead emphasizes the need for interpreting the provisions at issue in the light of the purpose (*telos*) and general scheme (system) of the provision.[155]

---

151 Arnull 2006: 617. See also Rosas 2006: 488.

152 Recently, case C-376/11, *Pie Optiek,* not yet reported, para 33.

153 Case C-236/97, *Skatteministeriet v Aktieselskabet Forsikringsselskabet Codan* [1998] ECR I-8679, para 25 and case 283/81, *CILFIT v Ministère de la santé* [1982] ECR 3415, paras 18–19. For an earlier occurrence, see case 29/69, *Stauder v Stadt Ulm* [1969] ECR 419, para 3.

154 Šarčević 2002: 248. For criticism of the *CILFIT* criteria, Bobek 2007–2008: especially 10–14, 34. Bobek argues that in reality, adhering to ECJ guidelines on comparing language versions in national courts is a 'mission impossible'. Similarly, see Derlén 2009: 352.

155 Case 6/74, *Moulijn* [1974] ECR 1287, paras 10–11, case 30/77, *Bouchereau* [1977] ECR 1999, para 14. See also case C-149/97, *Institute of the Motor Industry* [1998] ECR I-7053, para 16, case C-187/07, *Endendijk* [2008] ECR I-2115, para 23, case C-239/07, *Sabatauskas and Others* [2008] ECR I-7523, para 38, case C-279/09, *DEB* [2010] ECR I-13849, para 32 and case C-179/11, *CIMADE and GISTI,* not yet reported, paras 42 and 56. For recent cases where the issue of restrictions on fundamental rights have been discussed, see case C-28/05, *Dokter and Others* [2006] ECR I-5431, para 75, case

It is therefore no surprise that the Court's method of interpretation is generally described as teleological.[156] Indeed, while for instance both functional arguments (such as effectiveness, recourse to the *effet utile* of provisions) as well as arguments related to consequences (internal and external to the legal system) theoretically form distinct groups of dynamic arguments, they might nonetheless be said to be closely connected to teleological considerations: namely, in order to ensure that a certain aim or objective is achieved, account must be taken of possible consequences (both in terms of repercussions as well as juridical consequences) of the interpretation. Characteristically teleological arguments are thus frequently employed to deduce the meaning of the EU law text in question in a particular case. The interpretive context of specific EU law provisions is construed – depending on the case – on the basis of the aims and objectives of secondary legislation at issue or the EU legal system as expressed in the Treaties.

For this reason, it is often argued that systemic, contextual, and teleological arguments rank highest on the list of arguments used by the Court in its reasoning.[157] In practice, these arguments are often intertwined and, depending on one's viewpoint, they may be categorized in different ways. For example, Lasser reads the Court's case law as attesting a (meta)teleological stance driven by systemic considerations: the 'ECJ deploys prototypically systemic, meta-teleological arguments'.[158] For Itzcovic, consequentialist interpretation overlaps with systemic interpretation, when 'consequences that are taken into consideration are not the practical effects "out there," in the world, but are the internal legal effect in the system'.[159] Or, inevitably, as Sankari puts it, 'the borderlines between such closely linked groups of interpretive criteria can hardly always remain clear'.[160]

In addition, fundamental rights arguments continue to grow in importance in the Court's reasoning.[161] The use of broad principles can be tentatively posited in the group of systemic arguments, although the line between legal and policy

C-394/07, *Gambazzi* [2009] ECR I-2563, para 29 and case C-317/08, *Alassini and Others* [2010] ECR I-2213, para 63.

156 See *e.g.* the classic case, 43/75, *Defrenne v Sabena* [1976] ECR 455 for how different types of dynamic argument are often intertwined in reasoning. See in this respect Bengoetxea *et al.* 2001: 58.

157 Lasser 2004 and McLeod 2004.

158 Lasser 2004: 232.

159 Itzcovic 2009: 555.

160 Sankari 2011: 69.

161 For an assessment of the Court's case law in placing fundamental rights at the core of the European project, see Defeis 2007. In fact, fundamental rights made their first appearance in ECJ case law early on. At the time, they were referred to as general principles of Community law reflecting the constitutional traditions of the Member States: see *inter alia* case 9/69, *Stauder v Stadt Ulm* [1969] ECR 419, para 7, case 11/70, *Internationale Handelsgesellschaft* [1970] ECR 1125, para 3 and case 4/73, *Nold v Commission* [1974] ECR 491, para 13. See also Dehousse 1998: 64 and more generally on this development, see Ojanen 1998.

considerations can be somewhat blurred.[162] They tie the Court's reasoning to a broader legal context, not only to primary EU law but also to pan-European law of fundamental rights. Indeed, at the current state of evolution of EU law, protection of fundamental rights, while an undeniable source of substantive rights through the application of the EU Charter, also forms a general principle guiding interpretation in EU law, thus influencing the choice between conflicting interpretations.[163] Indeed, it appears that although traditionally the number of cases touching on fundamental rights has been limited, the role of fundamental rights will only increase in this respect given that in accordance with Article 6 TEU, the EU Charter now possesses the same legal value as the Treaties as a result of the entry into force of the TFEU.

In particular, this relates to the need to interpret EU law in accordance with the European Convention of Human Rights (ECHR), since according to Article 52(3) EU Charter, the ECHR forms a minimum level of protection for corresponding rights referred to in the EU Charter: 'the meaning and scope of those rights shall be the same as those laid down by the said Convention. This provision shall not prevent Union law providing more extensive protection'. According to the formula already expressed by the Court in the *ERT*[164] case:

> 41. Fundamental rights form an integral part of the general principles of law the observance of which the Court ensures. For that purpose, the Court draws inspiration from the constitutional traditions common to the Member States and from the guidelines supplied by international treaties for the protection of human rights on which the Member States have collaborated or to which they are signatories. [...] The ECHR has special significance [...].

Importantly, while in principle the ECHR and the case law of the European Court of Human Rights (ECtHR) are not binding on the EU, the Court has come to consider both as obligatory points of reference in dealing with cases involving fundamental rights.[165] Hence, the ECHR and Strasbourg case law forms a compulsory guideline occupying a central position in interpreting EU law.[166] Although the Court has been criticized for its 'utilitarian' approach towards fundamental rights (meaning that its reliance on fundamental rights has expanded its influence over Member

162 Reich 2005: 24–34, who speaks about principle orientation in the Court's reasoning. See also Sankari 2011: 65–66.

163 See *e.g.* Ojanen 1998: 133–138. See also Ojanen 2009: 1117, Ojanen 2008 for the role of fundamental rights in the current state of evolution of EU law.

164 Case C-260/89, *ERT* [1991] ECR I-2925. See also case C-402/05 P, *Kadi and Al Barakaat International Foundation v Council and Commission* [2008] ECR I-6351, para 283 and C-571/10, *Servet Kamberaj*, not yet reported, paras 60–61.

165 See case C-238/99 P, *Limburgse Vinyl Maatschappij and Others v Commission* [2002] ECR I-8375, paras 273–274. See also Rosas 2003: 97–98.

166 Morijn 2006: 18.

States), it seems accurate to say that the ECJ has been not only willing to adjust its own case law to match requirements set in the ECHR but has also elevated fundamental rights to the core of EU values.[167] To be sure, fundamental rights – as expressed in the ECHR and relevant case law – set constraints on the way in which EU law can be interpreted.

Lastly, linguistic (semantic) arguments, which are based on the meaning of individual words or expressions, indicate the Court's willingness never to wholly abandon the text. This is so even though multilingualism constitutes a challenge for judicial interpretation because of *inter alia* divergences in language versions that result from different ways of conceptualizing the surrounding world.[168] Importantly, linguistic reasoning is problematic in any legal system, not only in a multilingual legal system such as that of the EU, since it offers no conclusive answer to the question of meaning.[169] It is argued in the following that the multilingual nature of EU law makes linguistic reasoning even more problematic than in mono- or bilingual legal systems. Next, we will discuss problems encountered in comparing language versions and linguistic reasoning in the context of EU law.

Comparing and justifying with language

The 'ordinary meaning of words' argument is perhaps the most important among linguistic arguments employed by the Court, since it is commonly accepted that wording should form the basis of statutory interpretation.[170] The underlying rationale is that if the meaning of a provision is clear, intelligible in ordinary or technical language, then there is no need to look further.[171] In the EU context, this intimately ties to the imperative of comparison expressed in *CILFIT*[172] because comparative analysis is often used by the Court to confirm the existence of divergences between language versions.

However, closer examination of the *CILFIT* criteria reveals the shortcomings of comparative analysis: taking account of the characteristics of the process in

167 For criticism, see Coppel and O'Neill 1992. Cf. Tridimas 2011: 102–103. Case C-94/00, *Roquette Frères* [2002] ECR I-9011.

168 See *e.g.* Derlén 2007 for a detailed analysis of the challenges the multilingual character of EU law poses, particularly on the national level. The Court has admitted that the multilingual nature of EU law involves problematic aspects in the context of judicial interpretation. See *e.g.* case 29/69, *Stauder v Stadt Ulm* [1969] ECR 419, para 3. See also generally on problems related to literal interpretation Lindroos-Hovinheimo 2006: 61 *et seq*.

169 Lindroos-Hovinheimo 2012.

170 MacCormick and Summers 1991: 516–517. See also case C-190/10, *Génesis*, not yet reported, paras 46–47, case C-559/10, *Deli Ostrich*, not yet reported, para 27.

171 Itzcovich 2009: 550. Cf. Klatt 2008: especially 15–20. See also Conway 2012: 144 *et seq*. In essence, he argues for interpretative restraint in the context of EU law and for a return to originalism.

172 Case 283/81, *CILFIT v Ministère de la santé* [1982] ECR 3415.

which multilingual EU law comes into being together with the constraints set on that approach by language in general terms, genuine comparison is not possible.[173] Reconstructing the *CILFIT* guidelines in the EU of over 20 Member States, Bobek argues that taking multilingualism seriously would mean the following for interpreting EU law. (a) Since all language versions are equally authentic, they cannot be read in isolation. This means that interpreting any one piece of EU legislation involves reading all versions in parallel. (b) Choosing 'majority meaning' from a number of confluent language versions is not possible because of linguistic equality, and in addition to comparison, (c) other methods (context, system and *telos*) must be taken into account.[174] Bengoetxea adds to these requirements that of revealing a common denominator among language versions, or in other words, the imperative of searching for a meaning that is not incompatible with any particular language version.[175]

The fictional nature of comparison of the kind formally required by *CILFIT* is revealed with ease, as true comparison across official languages would require an 'ability to spot ambiguities, to recognise vagueness, to identify the emotive pull of a word and to make appropriate allowances for it, and to analyse and elucidate class words and abstractions'.[176] Keeping this in mind, the criteria set by the Court for interpreting EU law undoubtedly form an unreasonable requirement (for national judges): possessing such skills in one language may be difficult enough.[177] Additionally, requiring that comparison should aim at revealing the common denominator and disregarding a majority interpretation might also be problematic: precisely by comparing language versions, linguistic differences may be unmasked and used to orient interpretation.[178] This is why Maduro's reading of *CILFIT* appears particularly workable. He frames the core of the *CILFIT* doctrine as requiring that 'decisions of national courts applying EU law must be grounded in an interpretation that could be applied by any other national court in similar situations'.[179]

173 See Kjær 2010: 303–304. She notes that comparing language versions results in a vicious circle whereby the meaning of the parts is dependent on the whole and vice versa so that the meaning is, in fact, somewhere in between. It is for the interpreter to discover this inbetween-ness.

174 Bobek 2007–2008: 3. See also Van Calster 1997: 378 *et seq.*

175 Bengoetxea 2011a: 21. See also Solan 2009b: 16–18.

176 Twining and Miers 1999: 197. See also Bobek 2007–2008: especially 10–13, Kjær 2010.

177 For consequences of this approach in the national setting, see Derlén 2009.

178 Solan 2009b: 18. Cf. Van Calster 1997: 378, 384. He addresses problems related to majority reasoning and looking at the minimum common denominator in language versions, noting that this will result in 'territorial subdivisions of applicability' of EU law. See for case law, case C-509/10, *Geistbeck and Geistbeck*, not yet reported, para 28.

179 Maduro 2009: 18. See also Sarmiento 2012: 313 *et seq.* on the need to adapt the *acte clair* doctrine to current difficulties in constitutional dialogue so that they would serve as an interpretive presumption in favour of national courts.

With regard to comparison at the Court, Solan puts forward an interesting argument which seems helpful in understanding how comparison can contribute to revealing the common meaning of all language versions (but also, conversely, their divergence). In cases where, for instance, one of the language versions contains a syntactic ambiguity allowing for multiple interpretations[180] whereas other versions do not, the Court may relatively easily unmask the common denominator in the language versions by ruling out the version containing the syntactic ambiguity. However, when uncertainty stems from subtle differences in the meaning of individual words or expressions, the Court is faced with a much more delicate task.[181] This is so because EU legislation cannot escape from the open-endedness and context-sensitivity that characterize all natural languages. While this argument certainly seems well founded, it must be observed that because of linguistic equality as well as equal authenticity, the Court remains rather reluctant to openly choose a majority meaning although it might choose such an interpretation on the basis of other arguments and deploy the meaning of the majority of the language versions to support this view.[182]

As observed above, the Court does not itself systematically resort to comparison in accordance with the guidelines formulated in *CILFIT*: in this respect, the Court can be described as a multilingual institution essentially resorting to monolingual reasoning in French.[183] To be sure, taking account of the difficulties outlined above, comparison forms at most a useful tool for confirming an interpretation reached by other means. In this respect, Bengoetxea suggests that the test for evaluating the usefulness of comparing language versions could include looking at whether comparison adds any real value to reasoning, or whether it instead only functions as a prerequisite for procedural justice requiring the Court to address points raised by the parties, thereby satisfying a rather formal role in judicial reasoning.[184]

Put differently, comparing different language versions can, at best, be used as a point of orientation in interpreting EU law, but not as a decisive argument.[185] The Court deployed the results of linguistic comparison in this manner in *Nowaco Germany*.[186] In addition to linguistic comparative analysis, it makes use of systemic and teleological arguments to explicate its understanding of the law:

> 41. It should first be pointed out that that uncertainty follows essentially from divergences between the different linguistic versions of Article 7 of Regulation

180 See *e.g.* case C-225/11, *Able UK*, not yet reported.

181 Solan 2009a: 46. See similarly Gallas 2006: 123.

182 Case C-289/05, *Länsstyrelsen i Norrbottens län* [2007] ECR I-1965, paras 18–20.

183 Bengoetxea 2011a: 15.

184 Bengoetxea 2011a: 17.

185 See in this respect, T-22/02 and T-23/02, *Sumitomo Chemical Co. Ltd and Sumika Fine Chemicals Co. Ltd v Commission of the European Communities* [2005] ECR II-4065, especially paras 41–47.

186 Case C-353/04, *Nowaco Germany* [2006] ECR I-7357.

No 1538/91. The German version of that provision, which contains the term 'Fertigpackung' (prepackage), is inconsistent with the other linguistic versions of that provision, in particular the Spanish ('unidad'), Danish ('emne'), Greek ('μονάδα'), English ('unit'), French ('unité'), Italian ('unità'), Dutch ('produkt'), Portuguese ('unidade') Finnish ('yksiköt') and Swedish ('enhet') versions. In such a case, according to settled case-law, the need for a uniform interpretation of Community law makes it impossible for the text of a provision to be considered in isolation; on the contrary, it requires that it be interpreted in the light of the versions existing in the other official languages [...].

42. Apart from a comparison of the wording of the different linguistic versions of Regulation No 1538/91, an analysis of the structure and history of that Regulation also shows that use of the term 'unit' in the Table in Article 7(3) thereof is preferable. It should be recalled that it is Article 8 of Regulation No 1538/91 which concerns prepackages and that the German version of Article 7 of that Regulation, before its amendment by Article 1(4) of Commission Regulation (EEC) No 2891/93 of 21 October 1993 (JO 1993 L 263, p. 12), did not mention prepackages. It is beyond doubt that that amendment concerned only tolerance margins and not the products concerned.

43. Second, even if it were necessary to read in Article 7 of Regulation No 1538/91 the term 'prepackage' instead of 'unit', that is, to accept a wording according to which the tolerance margins laid down relate to prepackages, it is appropriate to apply the analysis of the referring court and that of the Advocate General set out in paragraphs 45 and 46 of his Opinion, according to which those tolerance margins should also be applied by analogy to non-prepackaged products. If such tolerance margins apply where poultrymeat is intended for consumers, that is for those most deserving of protection, it seems logical to also make them applicable when that meat is sold to intermediaries.

If language versions are indeed compared, some conclusions need to be drawn from the wording of compared language versions.[187] Interestingly, however, comparison often confirms the existence of difference so that it is not uncommon for the Court to proceed directly – without more profound analysis of the differences observed – to contextual, systemic and teleological arguments.[188]

While, admittedly, a linguistic approach does not generally assume a conclusive role in ECJ judicial reasoning, linguistic arguments undoubtedly form part of the

187 In case C-243/11, *RVS Levensverzekeringen*, not yet reported, comparison of Dutch, German, English and French language versions led AG Kokott to conclude that the wording of the text at issue is not helpful for the purposes of the case at hand and to resort to systemic and teleological analysis of the situation. See especially paras 37 *et seq.*

188 C-19/11, *Geltl*, not yet reported, paras 42 *et seq.* See also case C-245/01, *RTL Television* [2003] ECR I-12489, paras 97–99.

criteria employed by the Court.[189] It is therefore necessary to briefly discuss the use of language as a means of justifying judicial decisions. Ultimately, if language is used as justification, we should in fact be able to pin down the 'true' meaning of the text.[190] And even more importantly, what does clear or ordinary meaning actually refer to in a multilingual legal system comprising a plurality of languages? Where is the norm that these language versions are supposed to convey?

Firstly, the so-called ordinary meaning of words argument may generally refer to the meaning that a member of a particular linguistic community would attribute to a word or expression in a given context: it is the ordinary meaning of those words in a particular language in general. The ordinary meaning of a word may also refer to the meaning a lawyer attributes to a word or an expression: it is the ordinary meaning of those words in a particular legal language.[191] As such, legal usage cannot be clearly distinguished from the systemic meaning of the provision, its meaning in a particular legal system. In this sense, linguistic and systemic criteria often overlap.[192] In the legal context, meaning of legal concepts is often subject to controversy. Certainly, law is argumentative in that it allows for continuous competition among interpretations.

Secondly, linguistic reasoning in the present context is particularly problematic because of the multiplicity of official language versions. In a context of linguistic plurality, referring to the ordinary meaning of words as an argument to justify a particular legal outcome means that instead of only two (general and legal) 'ordinary' meanings, several such meanings exist, raising important interpretive questions. The Court must choose among these different possibilities. Indeed, due to the policy of linguistic equality, the Court cannot in principle rely on any particular language version of the provisions it interprets. For example, in *EMU Tabac*,[193] it held that all the language versions must be recognized as carrying the same weight. Additionally, relying on the underlying principle of equality, it noted that EU law does not define concepts on the basis of one or more national legal systems unless an express provision points to that effect.[194] The Court therefore typically rejects the idea that any definitive conclusion could be based on one or more versions and justifies the use of systemic and teleological reasoning in the following lines:

---

189 Case C-190/10, *Génesis*, not yet reported, paras 42–46. See also case 349/85, *Denmark v Commission* [1988] ECR 169 and case C-135/03, *Commission v Spain* [2005] ECR 6909.

190 MacCormick and Summers 1991: 516–518.

191 Schauer 2008: 1123. See also Lindroos-Hovinheimo 2006.

192 Itzcovich 2009: 550.

193 Case C-296/95, *EMU Tabac and Others* [1998] ECR I-1605.

194 Case C-296/95, *EMU Tabac and Others* [1998] ECR I-1605, paras 30 and 36 and case 64/81 *Corman* [1982] ECR 13, para 8.

> According to settled case-law, firstly, the wording used in one language version of a provision of European Union law cannot serve as the sole basis for the interpretation of that provision, or be made to override the other language versions in that regard. Secondly, the various language versions of a text of European Union law must be given a uniform interpretation and hence, in the case of divergence between the language versions, the provision in question must be interpreted by reference to the purpose and general scheme of the rules of which it forms a part.[195]

Although officially rejecting a majority reading, the general approach employed by the Court appears to be to interpret the provision in a way which is argued to be consistent with at least several, if not the majority, of language versions, although not all language versions are consistently analyzed in reasoning.[196] What does leaving some versions outside the scope of comparison, or simply not comparing language versions, tell us? Does it mean that differences are masked, dormant under the surface of a seemingly calm surface?

Due to the limited justificatory force of linguistic arguments in a multilingual context, it appears well founded to search for meaning with the help of systemic and teleological interpretation.[197] Indeed, to remedy the problem of linguistic reasoning, it is feasible that the ECJ takes into consideration both the normative context to which the provision belongs as well as its purpose, or rather, the purpose of the piece of legislation to which the provision belongs – possibly even the purpose of the legal system as construed in the case at issue.

With regard to the added challenge of multilingualism in interpreting EU legislation, it may be argued that a purposive approach to reasoning lends itself better to interpreting EU law than an approach based on language. This is so in the realm of hard cases because truly multilingual reasoning based on comparing all official languages in all cases before deciding on an interpretation seems an impossible task to fulfil – especially in view of the number of official languages today. Importantly, paying due attention to systemic and purpose-oriented

---

195 Case C-215/10, *Pacific World and FDD International*, not yet reported, para 48.

196 Case C-33/11, *A Oy.*, not yet reported, especially paras 26 and 38. See also joint Cases C-283/94, C-291/94 and C-292/94, *Denkavit Internationaal and others v Bundesamt für Finanzen* [1996] ECR I-5063, para 25; case C-30/77, *Régina v Bouchereau* [1977] ECR 1999, para 13; case C-372/88, *Milk Marketing Board v Cricket St Thomas* [1990] ECR I-1345, paras 15–16; Case C-56/06, *Euro Tex Textilverwertung* [2007] ECR I-4859, paras 23–27. See also Van Calster 1997 who discusses problems related to a method of interpretation whereby only the majority of language versions are taken into consideration. See also for problems related to multilingualism and judicial reasoning in the context of the *CILFIT* guidelines Bobek 2007–2008: especially 3–4, Bengoetxea 2011: 21–24.

197 Case C-56/06 *Euro Tex Textilverwertung* [2007] ECR I-4859, paras 27 *et seq*, case C-332/04 *Commission v Spain* [2006] ECR I-40, paras 52 *et seq*, case C-420/98, *W.N.* [2000] ECR I-2847, paras 21 *et seq* and case C-236/97 *Codan* [1998] ECR I-8679, paras 25 *et seq*. Itzcovich 2009: 551.

considerations is here argued to form an inevitable aspect of judicial reasoning in a pluralistic and multilingual legal system, since multilingualism (as well as pluralism) increases linguistic indeterminacy and the potential for conflicting legal norms.[198]

To understand this claim, we need to shed light on how legal meaning evolves. EU legal meaning fluctuates, unlike in domestic legal systems where the number of participants in the process in which legal meaning is established is limited to a group of specialists – or more specifically, judges – who possess the required authority to decide what legal texts mean. In this sense, legal meaning may be described as agreement among legal actors on the most sensible interpretation of a legal text in a given context.[199]

Within such a framework, legal concepts carry relatively stable meaning, because only a limited number of specialists possess the necessary authority to decide what legal words in that specific legal system mean. As Engberg notes, this does not imply that every person interprets legal texts in an identical manner without communicating with others. Rather, it means that when engaging in communication, nearly all legal actors are convinced by the arguments given in support of interpretive choices made in the judgment in question. As a result, legal actors are convinced of the proposed interpretation so that it can be accepted.[200]

Accordingly, the criterion may be said to consist of whether agreement on legal meaning may be reached among authorized experts in a relatively clear way and not whether everyone would reach the same interpretation in all imaginable situations.[201] This idea seems particularly feasible if one takes into consideration the inherent indeterminacy of natural languages and the importance of context in constructing meaning. Indeed, in EU law the construction of meaning valid across languages requires that the relevant specialists agree on the Court's understanding of the law.

In a multilingual legal system, agreement is based on mutual understanding with regard to the acceptability of an interpretation by specialists speaking different languages and belonging to different legal traditions. This emphasizes the way in which the Court justifies its decisions: acceptance of an interpretation by the legal community is only possible through substantive argumentation which does not 'hide' behind empty linguistic arguments. These include arguments formulated as ordinary meaning or usual meaning in the language versions. These arguments can with relative ease be considered as empty in that no such thing as 'ordinary' or 'plain' meaning exists: words do not have clearly definable boundaries and their meaning is context-bound.[202]

---

198 Maduro 2007: 8.
199 Engberg 2004: 1137.
200 Engberg 2004: 1137.
201 Engberg 2004: 1165.
202 Lindroos-Hovinheimo 2012.

The *OABA*[203] case offers an illustrative example. In this case, the interpretive issue turned on the meaning of the concept of poultry for the purposes of Directive 96/61[204] within the context of integrated pollution prevention and control. The central issue was whether quails, partridges and pigeons are to be regarded as poultry coming within the scope of the Directive, which establishes a prior authorization system for installations intended for intensive rearing of poultry with more than 40 000 places. According to the Court:

> 23. [As] regards the term 'poultry', which is not specifically defined by Directive 96/61, it should be borne in mind that the usual meaning of that word describes all those birds farmed for their eggs or their meat. Quails, partridges and pigeons are species of birds which may be farmed for the consumption of their eggs or their meat.
>
> 24. That interpretation can also be based on the general scheme and purpose of the directive (see, by analogy, Case C-72/95 Kraaijeveld and Others [1996] ECR I-5403, paragraph 38).
>
> 25. In that regard, it must be borne in mind that the purpose of Directive 96/61, as laid down in Article 1, is to achieve integrated prevention and control of pollution by putting in place measures designed to prevent or reduce the emissions, of the activities listed in Annex I, into the air, water and land in order to achieve a high level of protection of the environment.
>
> 26. As the Advocate General states in point 34 of his Opinion, that integrated approach is realised by appropriate coordination of the procedure and authorisation conditions for industrial installations whose potential for pollution is significant, making it possible to achieve the highest level of protection for the environment as a whole, which must in all cases include provisions minimising long-distance or transboundary pollution and ensure a high level of protection for the environment as a whole.
>
> 27. Since the purpose of Directive 96/61 has been broadly defined, it cannot be held that subheading 6.6(a) of Annex I could be interpreted in such a way as to exclude quail, partridge and pigeon.

In this case, if the Court had based its reasoning on purely linguistic (semantic) arguments on the 'usual meaning' of the concept of poultry, it would have amounted to a weak argument with regard to its justificatory force, not least because the birds in question are principally game birds in certain Member States. In this regard, the linguistic argument about the scope of the concept within its 'usual meaning'

203 Case C-473/07, *Association nationale pour la protection des eaux and rivières and OABA* [2009] I-319.

204 Council Directive 96/61/EC of 24 September 1996 concerning integrated pollution prevention and control (OJ 1996 L 257, p. 26).

or in 'common parlance' would not carry sufficient justification.[205] In reality, the need to adopt a broad interpretation of the concept of poultry is only revealed after enquiring into the systemic context in which the term is used, namely that of Directive 96/61 and the purposes of that legal instrument.[206]

In a situation where the indeterminacy inherent in all natural languages may present itself in different parts of the same text interpreted by the Court, it appears realistic to argue that reference to linguistic arguments is rarely – if ever – sufficient to convince the legal community of the interpretation. Nor does it contribute to building a mutual understanding among a multilingual legal community of the legally correct understanding of the law in the context of the case in question. In this respect, reference to linguistic arguments is not in itself sufficient to justify a ruling. The following relatively lengthy extract from the Court's reasoning in *Geltl*[207] illustrates how reference to ordinary meaning would, without appropriate reference to contextual, systemic and teleological considerations, form a highly superficial justification for the Court's understanding of the law:

> 30. Since the terms 'set of circumstances' and 'event' are not defined in that directive, it is appropriate to look at their ordinary meaning.
>
> 31. An intermediate step in a protracted process may in itself constitute a set of circumstances or an event in the meaning normally attributed to those terms.
>
> 32. That finding is supported by Article 3(1) of Directive 2003/124, which gives, by way of examples of inside information the disclosure of which may be delayed under Article 6(2) of Directive 2003/6, situations which are typical examples of intermediate steps in protracted processes, namely negotiations in course and decisions taken or contracts made by the management body of an issuer which need the approval of another body of the issuer in order to become effective.
>
> 33. Moreover, as is evident from recitals 2 and 12 in the preamble thereto, the purpose of Directive 2003/6 is to protect the integrity of the European Union financial markets and to enhance investor confidence in those markets. That confidence depends on, inter alia, investors being placed on an equal footing and protected against the improper use of insider information (see, to that effect, Case C-45/08, Spector Photo Group and Van Raemdonck [2009] ECR I-12073, paragraph 47, and Case C-445/09 IMC Securities [2011] ECR I-0000, paragraph 27).

205 See para 33 of AG Mengozzi's opinion in Case C-473/07, *Association nationale pour la protection des eaux and rivières and OABA* [2009] I-319 for the use of 'common parlance'.

206 Both the Court and AG Mengozzi undertook an analysis of the aims and objectives of Directive before coming to the conclusion that a broad construction of the concept was called for.

207 C-19/11, *Geltl*, not yet reported.

> 34. In that regard, recital 24 in the preamble to that directive states that prompt and fair disclosure of information to the public enhances market integrity, whereas selective disclosure by issuers can lead to a loss of investor confidence in the integrity of financial markets.
>
> 35. An interpretation of the terms 'set of circumstances' and 'event' which disregards the intermediate steps in a protracted process risks undermining the objectives as referred to in the two preceding paragraphs of this judgment. To rule out the possibility that information relating to such a step in a protracted process may be of a precise nature for the purposes of point 1 of Article 1 of Directive 2003/6 would remove the obligation, provided for in the first subparagraph of Article 6(1), to disclose that information, even if it were quite specific and even though the other elements making up inside information, as listed in paragraph 25 of this judgment, were also present.
>
> 36. In such a situation, certain parties who possessed inside information could be in an advantageous position vis-à-vis other investors and be able to profit from that information, to the detriment of those who are unaware of it (see, to that effect, Spector Photo Group and Van Raemdonck, paragraph 48).
>
> 37. The risk of such a situation occurring is all the greater given that it would be possible, in certain circumstances, to regard the outcome of a specific process as an intermediate step in another, larger process.

To conclude, linguistic uncertainty places special emphasis on substantive judicial reasoning in the context of hard cases in which value choices are unavoidable. More particularly, linguistic arguments may be said to constitute 'empty arguments' in that they do not offer the judgment's addressees sufficient insight as to the reasons why a particular case has been decided in a specific way. That is, linguistic arguments do not flesh out the reasons why certain policies, principles or values are taken to be more important than others in a given legal system. Indeed, the wording of a provision does not tie it to other provisions, principles, policies and values that together form the legal system and make adjudication coherent.

Realistically, linguistic arguments – be they based on comparison of language versions or 'ordinary', 'usual' or 'clear' meaning – appear to work best as supporting arguments that confirm an interpretation reached by other means and they do so by clarifying points of interpretation.[208] In this respect, paying attention to purposes and consequences in legal adjudication means that consequences are used 'as an important yardstick to measure a given interpretation's faithfulness to [specific] democratic purposes'.[209]

Even though it is possible to disagree on such policies, principles and values or indeed on their mutual importance, legal adjudication that does not openly express such considerations cannot control and ensure a degree of legitimacy in the context of judicial decisions taken outside the democratically conditioned process of

208 Bengoetxea 2011a: 17.

209 Breyer 2005: 115.

law-making. In this respect, it is argued that teleological reasoning carries special significance in the multilingual EU context: it ties individual decisions together and illustrates the deeper normative choices involved in deciding a particular case: in using teleological reasoning, the Court provides relevant legal actors with a basis for positing a judgment in a wider systemic context.[210]

Virtue of telos

As noted in the previous sections, the Court refers not only to teleological but also to systemic and contextual as well as linguistic arguments. Nonetheless, the Court's approach is here described as predominantly teleological.[211] Following MacCormick, the 'enterprise of explicating and expounding criteria and forms of good legal reasoning has to be in the context of fundamental values that we impute to a legal order'.[212] It is argued that teleological reasoning – appropriately tied to systemic considerations given their inevitable role in constructing meaning in a legal system[213] – offers a tool for making these values apparent in judicial reasoning.

The Court's approach to interpreting EU law has even been described as meta-teleological. In fact, Lasser's analysis suggests that meta-teleology is not only a predominant part of the Advocates Generals' opinions but also a recurring phenomenon in the Court's judgments: this is revealed by the use of a small number of recurring general and abstract purposes (or principles). These include effectiveness of EU law, uniformity of application, legal certainty, and legal protection.[214] These 'umbrella-purposes', which seem to possess particular significance in cases of constitutional importance concerning interpretation of Treaty provisions, may be said to represent a particular understanding of the normative context in which rules are interpreted. Therefore, it might be said that this approach aims at not only ascertaining aims and objectives but also interpreting a provision in the light of the broader context; that is, in the light of the legal system as a whole, in accordance with its systemic *telos*.[215] In this respect, contextual and teleological arguments are often intertwined: it is not only the *telos* of the individual rules that is taken into consideration but also the *telos* of the legal context in which the rules in question exist.

Therefore, teleological reasoning does not exclusively refer to a purpose-oriented interpretation of the relevant legal provisions. It also refers to a particular

210 Maduro 2007: 13, who primarily attributes this role to the Advocates General.

211 Rosas 2006: 487, Maduro 2007 defending use of the teleological method of interpretation. See also Conway 2012 who expresses criticism towards the generality of the Court's teleological reasoning.

212 MacCormick 2005: 1.

213 MacCormick and Summers 1991: 517.

214 Lasser 2004: 211 *et seq.*, Conway 2012: 274.

215 Maduro 2007: 5.

systemic understanding of those rules. In this respect, Maduro suggests that the Court is not only concerned with ascertaining the aim of a particular legal provision, it also interprets that rule in the light of the broader context provided by the EU legal system and its 'constitutional *telos*'. In this respect, a clear connection between systemic (context) and teleological elements in ECJ reasoning may be established.[216]

As the above discussion aims to illustrate, linguistic reasoning cannot alone exhaust the argumentative task of the Court. Its interpretations need further justification. This breach may be remedied with contextual, systemic and purposive arguments as well as deontological – that is, strongly normative – arguments such as principles. However, exigently normative requirements are closely connected to the legal system in which they are applied. Principles that are considered to carry strong normative force may vary from one legal system to another. For instance, in the pluralistic EU legal system – and from the viewpoint of *acceptability* of judicial decisions in particular – it might not be enough to refer to principles alone without reference to the Court's underlying normative understanding of the aims and objectives of the legal system.[217]

Because of linguistic plurality, it is not uncommon for the textual representation of the norm to point towards different directions depending on which language version one examines. Since all language versions possess the same legal value, the Court has to arbitrate these linguistic disputes under different criteria.[218] Multiplicity of languages and legal cultures brings with it conceptual problems of translation referred to above.

An example of how multilingual legislation may potentially affect rights of individuals if language versions are considered in isolation and without due regard to other interpretive criteria is the *García and Choque Cabrera*[219] case. Here, the question put to the Court was whether Member State authorities possess discretion with regard to expulsion of third-country nationals who reside unlawfully in the Member State in question.

In this respect, the Court found a discrepancy between the wording of the Spanish version of Article 11(3) of Regulation (EC) No 562/2006[220] on the rules governing movement of persons across borders (Schengen Borders Code) and that of the other language versions. In the Spanish language version, the provision imposes an obligation on competent national authorities to expel the third-country national (el nacional del tercer país *será* expulsado) from the territory of that Member State if the presumption is not rebutted. By contrast, according to the

216 Maduro 2007: 5.

217 See similarly Paunio and Lindroos-Hovinheimo 2010: 411–412.

218 Maduro 2007: 8–9.

219 Case C-261/08, *Zurita García and Choque Cabrera* [2009] ECR I-10143.

220 Regulation of the European Parliament and of the Council of 15 March 2006 establishing a Community Code on the rules governing the movement of persons across borders (Schengen Borders Code) (OJ 2006 L 105, p. 1).

Court, in all the other language versions, expulsion is expressed as an option, not as an obligation (in English, the expression used is 'the third-country national may be expelled').[221]

According to the Court, the necessity for uniform application and, accordingly, for uniform interpretation of an EU measure makes it impossible to consider one version of the text in isolation; rather, these aims require that it is interpreted on the basis of both 'the real intention of its author and the aim he seeks to achieve, in the light, in particular, of the versions in all languages'.[222] After looking at the objectives of the Schengen Agreement, the Court observed that while the Agreement does not as such aim to guarantee rights to third-country nationals, Member States nonetheless possess discretion in expelling persons residing unlawfully within their territory.[223]

Taking account taken of the constraints of EU law-making, the Court's reasoning with reference to 'the real intention of the author' is certainly open to criticism: it is doubtful whether the Court could in reality reconstruct the 'real' intention of the author with sufficient precision so as to be able to base its understanding on the authority of the intention of the author: indeed, what often emerges from analysis of preparatory documents, for example, is not the will of the legislator, but 'an incoherent and inconclusive plurality of viewpoints and opinions'.[224] As is clear from the Court's reasoning, however, the Court constructs this legislative intention on the basis of its analysis of the aims of the relevant legal provision in its wider systemic context.[225] In this respect, the case highlights the need to enquire into the aims and objectives of the law in the multilingual EU context in order to construe an understanding of the law across languages.

The case also clearly illustrates risks related to looking at language versions in isolation.[226] However, as we have seen, due to institutional as well as linguistic constraints, the Court resorts to genuine comparison of language versions only exceptionally: cases where the ECJ carries out a comparative analysis of language versions are those where the parties have referred to some possible deviations in language versions or have referred to the unequivocal terms of the provision in

221 Case C-261/08, *Zurita García and Choque Cabrera* [2009] ECR I-10143, paras 52–53.

222 Case C-261/08, *Zurita García and Choque Cabrera* [2009] ECR I-10143, para 54. Cf. Bengoetxea 2011: 9 for the use of legislative intent in the Court's reasoning.

223 Case C-261/08, *Zurita García and Choque Cabrera* [2009] ECR I-10143, paras 43 and 66.

224 Itzcovic 2009: 555.

225 MacCormick 2005: 135, Van Hoecke 2002: 149. According to the distinction between subjective and objective teleological methods of interpretation, one could say that ECJ reasoning is here based on objective teleology; the Court bases its interpretation on topical rather than historical purposes.

226 See also case C-340/08, *M and Others* [2010] ECR I-03913 and Case C-56/11, *Raiffeisen-Waren-Zentrale*, not yet reported. See in particular para 27 of AG Jääskinen's opinion.

question.[227] Although comparing language versions may at best help unmask the common denominator in different language versions, thus bringing added value to argumentation, it must be backed up by other arguments.[228] In such a context of linguistic uncertainty, it appears realistic to say that interpretation based on *telos* as well as systemic considerations forms an appropriate approach for interpreting EU law: while by no means sufficient alone without any connection to text, context and system, teleological reasoning may be said to offer a particularly persuasive form of reasoning when tied to systemic arguments.[229]

Recently, in her analysis of a selection of the Court's landmark cases related to Articles 20 and 21 TFEU, Sankari suggested that the Court's reasoning in the field of Union citizenship could best be described as 'systemic, although always taking its cue from and never wholly abandoning the wording'.[230] However, keeping in mind this position and scholarly criticism concerning the Court's judicial activism,[231] it is important to ask the following question: could teleological reasoning coupled with substantive reasons have provided the Court's audience with a more comprehensive picture of the Court's understanding of the law governing this field?

Certainly, it may well be that in cases where the meaning of relevant provisions has not been problematized across languages, the Court does not consider it necessary to expressly state the different steps (language, system and *telos*) on which its interpretive task is based. And depending on the arguments it sees appropriate to employ after deliberation, not all cases carry traces of openly stated teleological arguments so that considerations related to purpose may remain in the context of discovery, not justification.

This is why the nucleus of the claim about the virtue of teleological reasoning in the present multilingual context is normative, not descriptive. Indeed, taking account of the discussion at the beginning of this chapter, it seems realistic to argue that the teleological method of interpretation may be argued to constitute an approach that better guides national courts in their task as 'first instance' EU courts. *Telos* ties the case at hand to the broader *systemic* context of EU law: in this respect, it not only provides a specific legal outcome for the case at hand but offers a broader 'normative toolbox' with which future cases can be decided. In a decentralized legal system, it appears to be of particular importance that the Court justifies its decisions in a way that provides a 'thicker normative understanding' of the content of EU law, reaching in this respect beyond the ECJ judgment in the particular case.[232] Arguably, an approach that departs from strict textuality and presumed 'real' meaning, and instead takes as a starting point the underlying

227 Bengoetxea 2011a: 15.
228 See Solan 2009a: 47. Cf. Bengoetxea 2011a: 22.
229 Cf. Bengoetxea 1994: 79. See also MacCormick 2005.
230 Sankari 2011: 300.
231 See notably Rasmussen 1998: 27.
232 Maduro 2007: 9.

objectives of the text and the legal system, seems better capable of guiding national courts in interpreting and applying EU law in the large majority of cases that never reach the Court. This is of particular relevance keeping in mind the Court's task in the context of the preliminary ruling procedure, as summarized by AG Jacobs before the EU enlargement in 2004:

> The Court's primary task in preliminary rulings is not to decide specific cases on the basis of narrowly distinguished facts, or to solve a problem for the national court in the particular case, but to state clearly and coherently for the benefit of everyone in the Community what the correct understanding of the law is, and to give rulings of general significance. It is only that broader function which justifies the system of preliminary rulings and explains the unique procedure whereby Member States and the Commission are systematically invited to submit observations and indeed why the judgment of the Court and the Opinion of the Advocate General in every case are published in no fewer than 11 languages.[233]

Teleological interpretation might also be argued, as Maduro does, to be more faithful to democratic outcomes than a purely textual approach, since it prevents textual manipulation of legal rules. Indeed, an interpretation considering the goals of a rule, and not simply its wording, might be argued to prevent opportunistic behaviour and minimize the risk of an interpretive manipulation of legislation.[234] In practice, this would mean deriving effects from those rules that were neither wished for nor debated in the political process. In the final analysis, to allow such interpretive manipulations would have a negative impact on mechanisms of political responsibility and democratic control of legislative choices made by the EU legislature.[235]

Nonetheless, critics of teleological reasoning might say that this approach does not necessarily correspond to what was intended by the legislator, nor does it remain within the confines of the (multilingual) text. However, as illustrated above, the complexity of the EU law-making process makes this argument somewhat problematic. Firstly, keeping in mind the institutional-cum-systemic constraints of the legislative process, it is difficult to ascertain the legislator's will with certainty. Nor can we ascertain a pre-interpretive meaning of the (multilingual) text. Secondly, the Court is not a simple carrier of legislative will without autonomous

233 Case C-136/00, *Danner* [2002] ECR I-8147. See para 38 of AG Jacobs' opinion.

234 Maduro 2007: 10. See for similar ideas Solan 2009a: 47. However, Solan argues that purposive reasoning can only work if language versions are close enough to allow only a limited number of possible interpretations: otherwise, the amount of discretion available to the ECJ would be so broad that it would challenge the very idea of a supranational legal system governed by the rule of law.

235 See also Paunio and Lindroos-Hovinheimo 2010 defending the need for purpose-oriented reasoning and questioning the justificatory force of linguistic arguments.

normative preferences or value choices: it actively moulds the legal system with its interpretations.

Indeed, while teleological reasoning favours a debate among alternative normative preferences in interpreting EU law provisions, an appeal to text, to the meaning of words, would hide those alternatives and preclude a debate among them.[236] In this respect, appealing to *telos* means that no claim of absolute correctness is made; rather, the soundness of legal decisions is relative.[237] The claim to correctness applies only in relation to the aims and objectives of the legal system.[238] Given the *temporal* contextuality of EU law, ECJ judgments represent the Court's view of EU law and its underlying purposes and aims at a particular point in time.[239]

The central importance of *telos* in interpreting EU law may be explained not only by the difficulties related to the political process and the translated character of EU legislation which the Court interprets, but also by the Treaty system. Certainly, the Treaties do not so much establish mutual obligations between Member States as advance a project and create institutions entrusted to pursue that aim.[240] As Lord Denning famously observes:[241]

> The Treaty is quite unlike any of the enactments to which we have become accustomed. The draftsmen of our statutes have striven to express themselves with the utmost exactness. They have tried to foresee all possible circumstances that may arise and to provide for them [...] How different is this Treaty! It lays down general principles. It expresses aims and purposes. All in sentences of moderate length and commendable style. But it lacks precision. It uses words and phrases without defining what they mean [...] All the way through the Treaty there are gaps and lacunae. These have to be filled in by judges [...] It is the European way.

---

236 Maduro 2007: 11–13.

237 MacCormick 2005: 20. MacCormick observes that, quite possibly, 'the claim to an objective soundness of legal reasons is the grandest rhetorical turn of all'.

238 In this respect, the use of *telos* as a guiding method of interpretation refers to the aims and purposes of particular provisions as well as the legal system as understood by the Court at a specific point in time. Since law aims at organizing society in a specific way, adjudication also functions on the basis of a particular understanding of how the particular society should be organized. This understanding consequently influences judges' reasoning. See, in this respect, Van Hoecke 2002: 61, 126.

239 See similarly Ojanen 2003: especially 203. He notes that the Court's case law must be read and applied in national courts by keeping in mind present-day conditions so that applying case law involves considering the relevance of that case law at the time of application, thus not remaining a mechanical process of application. See similarly Maduro 2010: xvii–xviii.

240 Itzcovich 2009: 537, Rosas 2006: 488.

241 *Bulmer Ltd v Bollinger SA* [1974] Ch 401, 425.

This European way[242] emphasizes the role of the Court in the process of integration. While the gradual emergence of secondary legislation might have filled some of these lacunae or gaps and provided the Court with legally 'heavier' tools for its interpretive task, it remains a truism of EU law that not only the EU Treaties but also other legal instruments, in particular directives, contain broad principles, goals and values functional to a project of transformation and harmonization (uniformization?) of Member States' legal systems. With regard to the Treaties, Maduro observes that deploying such universals (principles) fulfils two main purposes in the EU context. Firstly, it facilitates agreement on delicate and controversial political questions by deferring its practical effects to a legal solution to be derived from a universally agreed principle. Secondly, it provides an instrument for adaptation of the EU legal system to the continuously evolving temporal context in which EU law is applied. 'Universal principles maintain the legal text updated. They are a function of the dynamic character of the process of integration recognised in the Treaty'.[243]

Given this framework, the Court's task has been that of solving remaining (political) disagreements and (linguistic) uncertainties in a legal context. In this respect, the structurally dynamic and constantly evolving nature of EU constitutionalism relies on the Court's understanding of those principles in the context of the cases brought before it.

In this respect, arguing that in EU law other criteria of interpretation are often overridden by teleological considerations, Itzcovic describes the EU as a structurally uncertain political community aiming at transforming national legal systems. Due to this underlying aim of integration, the EU may be functionally defined on the basis of its fundamental objective of integration.[244] This conception can be deduced from the Court's recourse to teleological interpretation; from its refusal to construct a static EU legal system.[245]

However, the particularities of ECJ reasoning must nonetheless be relativized. Indeed, when compared to domestic courts, differences in arguments employed at the EU level – particularly the use of teleological arguments – seem nonetheless to be of degree.[246] Indeed, it would be more surprising if this were not the case: the Court is composed of judges possessing a background in Member State legal systems. Most importantly, ECJ judgments are expected to be followed by national courts. Consequently, arguments given to support a particular interpretation must not only be considered legally sound but also acceptable to the legal community, and not as merely political or evocative.[247]

242 Ojanen 1998: especially 349–359.

243 See *e.g.* Maduro 2007: 11.

244 Itzcovich 2009: 559. See also Jacobs 2003: 547.

245 Bengoetxea *et al.* 2001: 48.

246 For comparison of the Finnish Supreme Court and the ECJ, Paso 2009. See also MacCormick and Summers 1991: 531–540, Sankari 2011: 68.

247 Itzcovich 2009: 559.

To conclude, adjudication is a forum in which controversies over the meaning of the law are resolved.[248] Judicial decision-making may be characterized as a process whereby texts are given meaning. Through interpretive decisions, one may catch a glimpse of the underlying normative theory or, in Dworkin's terms, the political theory of the community.[249] This is what Tuori calls a hidden social theory that guides adjudication.[250] Certainly, our cultural background and hermeneutical prejudices necessarily influence the way we conceptualize and interpret law, just as in the case of other social phenomena. From this perspective, one might in fact argue that teleological reasoning that explicates not only the purposes of a provision but also discusses the possible consequences of the supported interpretation provides a useful tool for tying individual interpretations to a broader systemic context because it exposes this theory to debate among the legal community.

Summing up

This chapter elucidates the challenges that the Court faces in interpreting multilingual EU law. It is argued that EU law-making is based on a political bargain that requires a degree of fuzziness: this is the price to pay for reaching agreement with regard to the text adopted. Translation forms an integral part of this law-making process. The omnipresence of translation creates further uncertainty with regard to the meaning of final texts adopted in over 20 languages. Given the policy of linguistic equality, these versions carry equal weight in judicial interpretation. In individual cases brought before it, the Court determines the meaning of the law across language versions which are the final products of this complex multilingual political process.

Due to the absence of pre-interpretive meaning, the Court must, by way of interpretation, reconcile equally authentic language versions. In doing this, it resorts to judicial reasoning based on three primary categories of argument: linguistic, systemic and dynamic arguments. In this regard, the chapter sheds light on significant difficulties that relate to the use of linguistic arguments, including linguistic comparison, in the context of multilingual law: it is doubtful whether we can discover any uniform 'legislative will' or, indeed, an 'ordinary meaning' that would carry across all official languages.

Importantly, in addition to linguistic uncertainties that occur in relation to any language taken separately, additional uncertainty concerning the meaning of a text may become relevant for interpretation when that meaning is considered across several languages. In this context of linguistic plurality, it is not uncommon for the same text to point towards different textual interpretations depending on which language version we are looking at. In the context of linguistic arguments, we

248 Tuori 2007: 171.
249 Dworkin 1986: 245.
250 Tuori 2007: 224.

also flesh out the shortcomings of the comparative method arguing that, at best, linguistic comparison can offer a tool for discovering the common denominator or for revealing underlying differences. Since these language versions all carry the same legal value, the Court must 'arbitrate' linguistic conflicts arising from multilingual legislation by using other interpretive criteria.

Due to difficulties related to determining the meaning of EU law texts by means of linguistic arguments, the use of systemic as well as dynamic (especially teleological) arguments is of particular significance in the context of judicial decision-making at the Court. The use of systemic and teleological arguments, in particular, constitutes visible elements of the underlying normative theory of EU law followed by the Court in its case law. These arguments provide an explication to the Court's audience of the social theory that guides ECJ decision-making.

An approach that does not attempt to hide behind the wording of EU law provisions but construes meaning by appropriate reference to the underlying objectives of the text and the legal system as a whole might be said to better ensure that the Court's task of guiding national courts in interpreting and applying EU law is realized. It also better promotes substantive acceptability of judicial decisions in the present context. Teleological reasoning, tied to appropriate systemic and contextual arguments, may be said to carry more information about the content of EU law and the Court's underlying normative understanding of EU law than textual interpretation. Indeed, interpretation of multilingual EU law 'cannot be a matter of trying to read the meaning of a set of words taken in isolation' since one should read all parts of the text, from words to sentences to paragraphs and so on, 'in the setting of the whole Treaty scheme. The part makes sense in the context of the whole, and the whole gets its sense out of a dynamic interaction of the parts'.[251]

251 Bengoetxea *et al.* 2001: 45.

Chapter 2
Legal certainty – form and substance

What is legal certainty?

This chapter explains the different ways in which legal certainty has been conceptualized in the context of EU law. In the first instance, it fleshes out the basic tenets of the principle of legal certainty and provides an account of its different manifestations and contexts in the Court's case law. In the second instance, the chapter addresses the more theoretical underpinnings of legal certainty keeping in mind the theoretical division between formal and substantive legal certainty.

Formal legal certainty implies that laws and adjudication in particular must be predictable: laws must satisfy imperatives of clarity, stability, intelligibility, and predictability so that those concerned can calculate with relative accuracy the legal consequences of their actions as well as the outcome of legal proceedings.[1] Substantive legal certainty, then, is related to rational acceptability of judicial decision-making. On this view, it is not sufficient that laws are predictable; they must also be accepted by the legal community in question. Legal certainty – encompassing both its formal and substantive elements – forms an important principle in current national legal systems. Less evident, however, is whether and to what extent legal certainty enjoys a similar status in the EU legal system. Indeed, notions used in connection with national legal systems will not transpose *ipso facto* to the EU legal system. This also holds true for the notion of legal certainty.

Extensively discussed in legal literature, the principle of legal certainty can be defined in many ways.[2] Generally, however, it is taken to express a fundamental principle according to which the addressees of laws must know the law in order to be able to plan their actions in accordance with it. Law requires a certain degree of predictability so that those concerned are able to know in advance what the legal consequences of their actions are.[3] Indeed, the principle of legal certainty

---

1 Tridimas 2006: 262.

2 For discussion in the Nordic countries, see *e.g.* Wilhemsson 1986, Aarnio 1987, Peczenik 1989, Peczenik 1995, Jareborg 1992, Wihelmsson 1999, Frändberg 2000–2001, Mäenpää 2001, Gustafsson 2002, Tuori 2003, Raitio 2003, Raitio 2008. In the context of EU law, see *e.g.* Usher 1998, Schermers and Waelbroek 2001, Raitio 2003, Rasmussen 2003, Arnull 2006, Tridimas 2006, Groussot 2006, Arnull *et al.* 2006, Hartley 2010, Raitio 2008, who ties the Nordic discussion to the EU context.

3 Tridimas 2006: 242.

comprises a wide concept that enjoys an axiomatic role in EU Member States.[4] Groussot describes legal certainty as reflecting 'the ultimate necessity of clarity, stability and intelligibility of the law'.[5] The underlying ratio of predictability can thus be summarized as the imperative of clarity and certainty.

Transparency and legitimacy are seen as driving forces behind multilingualism. They are also closely connected to legal certainty through legitimacy: not so much formal validity of the legal system as substantive acceptability intertwined with legitimacy. Legal certainty is thus closely related to Habermasian dimensions of legal validity. On the one hand, established law guarantees enforcement of legally expected behaviour, and further, the certainty of law. On the other hand, rational procedures for making and applying the law are a guarantee of legitimate expectations.[6]

Law stabilizes behavioural expectations in society in order to create legal certainty that enables law's addressees to calculate the legal consequences of their own behaviour and those of others.[7] Consequently, legal norms must assume a comprehensible, consistent and precise form: they must be public – that is, made known to all addressees; they may not claim retroactive validity; and they must govern the factual circumstances in general terms and connect the factual situation with legal consequences so that it is possible to apply the norm to all persons and to all comparable cases in the same way.[8]

Stability and flexibility

To accommodate these (opposing) imperatives, legal certainty is traditionally divided into two elements. This division stems from analytical jurisprudence and more specifically, from Aarnio's and Peczenik's view of legal certainty: on this view, legal certainty is both formal and material, predictability and acceptability.[9]

It is argued that the inherent rationality of adjudication promotes legal certainty. On this understanding, legal certainty is a compromise between predictability of legal decisions and their acceptability. Legal certainty thus implies a commitment

4 See *e.g.* Beyer 1990: 22 *et seq.*, Peczenik 1995: 89 for different conceptions of legal certainty.

5 Groussot 2006: 189.

6 Habermas 1998: 135, 198. For Habermas, in order for the law to reach full normativity, it requires not only legal form and moral content but most importantly a *procedure* of law-making that assures legitimacy.

7 Habermas 1998: 143.

8 Fuller 1969: especially 33–84. This is in fact the basis of Fuller's thesis about the morality of law. Similarly, see Habermas 1998: 143–144.

9 Aarnio 1997: 190–192, Peczenik 1989: 33. See also Wilhelmsson 1986: 32, who seems to tie the notion of substantive legal certainty to material justice. Cf. Tuori 2003: 360–362, who is critical about the possibility of using this twofold conception of legal certainty when discussing the principle of legal certainty in the context of adjudication, *i.e.* as a principle used for deciding cases.

to finding the best compromise between predictability and other principles and policies considered important in the particular legal system: it is a balancing exercise between stability and flexibility.[10]

Here, substantive legal certainty is of particular interest. It underlines the importance of substantive acceptability in judicial decision-making. The courts' interpretation must be in accordance with the law, and further, that interpretation must be rationally acceptable to the legal community in question. It follows that a decision must be the outcome of rational judicial reasoning that uses acceptable interpretive methods in adapting the law to moral and teleological arguments and the facts of the case.[11] This substantive aspect of legal certainty refers to the legal community's perception of the acceptability of the decision in question.

In a nutshell, when formal legal certainty increases, the possibility for law's addressees to predict how their cases are decided by legal authorities increases accordingly. Instead, when substantive legal certainty increases, the possibility for materially just decisions increases.[12]

In this respect, clear and unambiguous legal rules are for instance said to produce the legal certainty and predictability required for a well-functioning market.[13] Substantive legal certainty is sometimes regarded as opposed to predictability. However, keeping in mind the complexities inherent in the EU legislative process charted above, it appears that speaking of an unequivocal norm underlying all official language versions rests on a fallacy. Similarly, arguing that vague standards ensure predictability better than clear and unambiguous rules, Raban suggests that the preference for unambiguity and clarity in assuring legal certainty and predictability is misguided: this is because a difference exists between the predictability of applying a legal rule and the predictability that a rule generates for those governed by the rule.[14]

On this view, a certain and predictable regulative environment (including predictable economic as well as social spheres) is of particular importance, rather than clear and determinate rules generating formally certain and predictable outcomes. Indeed, even the clearest monolingual provisions can run contrary to people's predictions and expectations concerning their rights and obligations.[15]

As we will argue in the following, when substantive legal certainty increases, predictability also increases (when understood as reflecting predictions and expectations of those governed by law). This is because looking beyond the words of legislative text may help courts configure their decisions to people's

10 Peczenik 1989: 33, Peczenik 1995: 40.

11 Aarnio 1987: 3, Aarnio 1997: 191, Raitio 2003: 342.

12 Wilhelmsson 1986: 32.

13 See *e.g.* Schauer 1991: 138–140, Sunstein 1995: 1021–1022. Cf. Wilhelmsson 2004: 222.

14 Raban 2010: 179. See similarly Wilhelmsson 2004: 221–222.

15 Raban 2010: 179–186.

predictions.[16] In this sense, flexible judicial decision-making taking into account purposes and consequences may often better correspond to people's expectations; at least more so than the (multilingual) text alone. According to Hayek, 'judicial decisions may in fact be more predictable if the judge is also bound by generally held views of what is just, even when they are not supported by the letter of the law'.[17]

In addition to formal and substantive legal certainty, some scholars have added a third element to the notion of legal certainty. Factual legal certainty may be considered as intertwining with formal and substantive legal certainty. This element requires efficiency in law. In this respect, Raitio – whose understanding of legal certainty is based on three types of validity; that is, formal, substantive and factual validity – gives the use of an obsolete law (*desuetudo*) in judicial decision-making as an example of how factual legal certainty works.[18] Using an obsolete law to decide cases would constitute a breach of factual legal certainty, since such laws are not considered to be in force *de facto*. However, it is argued here that although obsolete, formally valid legal norms, if applied, cannot strictly speaking be considered to be in breach of formal predictability. Instead, applying such norms goes against what is considered acceptable in the light of the social and moral norms in a particular society. Understood broadly, substantive legal certainty thus includes the factual aspect of legal certainty.[19]

Relation to the rule of law

The concepts of legal certainty and the rule of law are closely connected. The notion of legal certainty is generally used in civil law systems: the closest equivalent in common law appears to be the rule of law.[20] Thus, in view of its immediate connection to the concept of legal certainty, it is necessary to briefly sketch the basic tenets of the rule of law, a principle governing the power of authorities and guaranteeing the Aristotelian 'government of laws not men'.

The essence of the rule of law is captured in the aim of delimiting the use and abuse of power. According to Craig, the concept 'addresses the manner in which the law is promulgated, its clarity and temporal dimension'.[21] This is the

16 Raban 2010: 186.

17 Hayek 1973: 116.

18 See Raitio 2003: 373 *et seq.* for an analysis of three-dimensional legal certainty consisting of formal, substantive and factual legal certainty. He notes that development of the principle of legitimate expectations could be an example of factual legal certainty, where expectations related to administrative practices are seen as legitimate.

19 In a similar vein, Raitio 2008: 60. See also Gustafsson 2002: 1 *et seq.*

20 See *e.g.* Peczenik 1989: 31. See Tuori 2007: 221–247 and Tuori 2011: 207–240 for an analysis of different conceptions of the rule of law. Cf. Frändberg 1996: 22–23.

21 Craig 2003: 96.

thin conception of the rule of law.[22] However, employing the rule of law in this way implies that no assessment is made about the content of law. Instead, the concept expresses an essentially political ideal. The reality of the legal system can correspond to the ideal to a lesser or a greater extent.[23] In this respect, Raz warns against confounding the rule of law with other important virtues that legal systems should possess: these include democracy, respect for fundamental rights, equality, and justice.[24] As a thicker or substantive concept, the rule of law can be described in broad terms as a notion incorporating a 'fully elaborated theory of social justice'.[25] Tuori displays doubts about drawing parallels with other value-laden concepts by observing that the danger in their usage lies in that they are pumped up with almost everything experienced as positive and, thus, turned into 'rhetorical balloons'.[26]

In normative terms, the rule of law refers to the characteristics of an ideal legal system. Alternatively, it may refer to a concept that defines the content of law in the sense of a directly applicable principle of law (decision principle) in judicial decision-making or an interpretive principle in adjudication guiding statutory construction.[27] However, irrespective of the legal system in which the rule of law is referred to, at least one point exists on which everyone agrees: the principle escapes any precise definition.[28]

While legal scholars have argued over the virtues of the rule of law, at least some agreement exists as to the requirements of the rule of law: laws must be public, clear, coherent, prospective (set in advance), general and stable.[29] Furthermore, legislation and executive power must be governed by such laws, and there should be courts ensuring the rule of law.[30] This narrow conception may be said to represent a common framework that is amenable to a broad range of legal systems.[31] These features overlap with those tied to legal certainty. Overall, the above characteristics illustrate the aim that law must be capable of guiding the

22 Tamanaha 2009: 3–4. See also Tamanaha 2004. Charlesworth 2010: 44, Williams 2012: 73. See generally Dicey 1952. See also Habermas 1998: 134–135.

23 Tuori 2011: 211.

24 Raz 1979: 211.

25 Allan 1999: 221. See for analysis Tamanaha 2004: 102–113.

26 Tuori 2011: 211.

27 See *e.g.* paras 25 *et seq.* AG Maduro's opinion in case C-273/04, *Poland v Council* [2007] ECR I-8925. Here the rule of law is deployed as an interpretive principle in adjudication.

28 Tuori 2007: 225–226. For an attempt to define the rule of law, see the Venice Commission report on the rule of law of 4 April 2011 (http://www.venice.coe.int/docs/2011/CDL-AD(2011)003rev-e.pdf).

29 Tamanaha 2009: 4.

30 Endicott 2000: 185. Allan 1999 for a nuanced account of factors that should inhabit the rule of law.

31 Tamanaha 2009: 4.

behaviour of its subjects and articulate the need for confining the use of power.[32] Given the overlap, it seems that the rule of law forms an umbrella principle under which legal certainty can be posited.[33]

An approach to reasoning that openly articulates purposes and does not confine its role to judicial fact finding on the basis of a presumed pre-interpretive meaning of the wording, as argued for in Chapter 1, may seem in contradiction with the rule of law: if connection between text and application is not always clear, as may be the case in the context of multilingual EU law, it appears difficult to speak about certainty in relation to legal outcomes in specific cases. And, if this is the case, what happens to legal certainty? Perhaps even more importantly, what becomes of the rule of law? How can law govern the use of power?

The imperatives associated with the rule of law and especially that of clarity (be it in relation to the rule of law or legal certainty) seem to require that indeterminacy such as vagueness and ambiguity are avoided, otherwise no control of government – or for that matter, judicial decision-making – can be guaranteed.[34] But this immediately raises the following question: how can this view be reconciled with the reality of EU law drafted in over 20 languages – or more accurately, translated into a large number of languages – carrying different views about the meaning of the law?

Here, Raz's description of the rule of law as an 'organising principle', which states that the law must be capable of guiding behaviour in a given society, is helpful. Arguably, the rule of law requires that the prospect of change in accordance with context (or indeterminacy) does not forbid the use of existing law as a guideline.[35] The discussion in Chapter 1 illustrated how statutory interpretation at the Court lies on a particularly elusive basis, that of multilingual EU legislation: the ECJ performs an important role in construing meaning to EU law and assuring that judicial decision-making is predictable and thus capable of guiding behaviour.

Pinning down the central problem with the rule of law, MacCormick refers to law as 'a locus of argumentation' where arguments are expressed in indeterminate natural languages.[36] When the rule of law is observed, reasonable certainty exists with regard to the rules and standards by which conduct in a given society is judged from a legal standpoint. By virtue of the rule of law, people can have

32 Raz 1979: 214. See also Finnis 1980: 270–271.

33 Tamanaha 2009: 7. Cf. Frändberg 1996: 22–23. Similarly Tuori 2007: 225.

34 Cf. Tuori 2007: 225. He notes that it is generally accepted that the rule of law aims at limiting arbitrary decision-making and guaranteeing individual rights. For a revised account of the rule of law that takes both vagueness and indeterminacy into consideration, see Endicott 2000. See also Tamanaha 2004: 86–90.

35 Endicott 2000: 192–193.

36 MacCormick 2005: 13. See also Raymond 2000: 1, who summarizes the argumentative character in law in the following question: how can lawyers derive opposite conclusions from the same set of facts and the same body of law? He argues convincingly that every assertion in law may be contested due to the hopelessly ambiguous language in which law is expressed.

reasonable security in their expectations of the conduct of others and particularly those holding official positions under the law. Furthermore, they can also challenge governmental actions that affect their interests. This is possible provided that a legal system comprises reasonably clearly enunciated rules in terms of general categories.[37] Put differently, we have law expressed in indeterminate natural language(s) as well as the rule of law based on the idea of clearly enunciated rules that do not leave a great margin to subjective considerations.[38] This is also a key component behind legal certainty understood in terms of predictability.

How does this work in a multilingual legal system? In the following chapters, it is argued that in fact it is through judicial reasoning and use of rhetoric that the equilibrium between the two counterparts can be found.[39] Accordingly, judicial reasoning must satisfy conditions of rationality and reasonableness. This means that assertions must be accompanied by reasons (the process of justifying a decision) and whatever is asserted may be challenged as long as reasons are offered to justify such a claim.[40]

The rule of law forms a building block of any legal system, including that of the EU. Indeed, this is expressed in Article 2 TEU, according to which 'the Union is founded on the values of respect for human dignity, freedom, democracy, equality, the rule of law and respect for human rights [...]'.[41] In essence, the rule of law builds on the idea that laws, pre-announced rules that govern behaviour in a given legal system, are determinate. But, at the same time the rule of law requires that people have the possibility to challenge cases laid against them. This essentially entails that law is viewed, somewhat paradoxically, as both determinate and arguable, stable and flexible: on this view, law necessarily remains determinate and indeterminate at the same time.[42]

Williams asserts that depending on the (legal) relationships examined, different conceptions of the rule of law inhabit the institutional ethos of the EU both inside and outside its external borders.[43] In this regard, the value of the rule of law suffers from ambivalence as it is unclear whether it is based on 'a coherent conception of justice', as Allan requires.[44] According to Williams, in relation to Member States the rule of law thus operates as a means of ensuring that the underlying objective of integration is achieved. This idea is crystallized in the principle of primacy. In

37 Cf. Allan 2001 on the importance of generality of rules in relation to the rule of law.

38 MacCormick 2005: 16.

39 MacCormick 2005: 17 *et seq.*

40 MacCormick notes that it is an empirical question whether and to what extent practising lawyers, advocates and judges in any particular case confine themselves to rational and reasonable arguments. MacCormick 2005: 17.

41 See *e.g.* Walker 2009: 119–138 for the rule of law in present-day EU law.

42 See *e.g.* Raban 2010.

43 Williams 2012: 77 *et seq.*

44 Allan 1999: 223.

this respect, 'the concept in this dimension is [...] limited, consigned to the end of the spectrum that focuses on legality and governmental enforcement'.[45]

As regards the institutional dimension (the relationship between EU institutions and individuals), Williams distinguishes more substantive nuances in the concept of the rule of law: in this sense, the rule of law articulates a need for restricting arbitrary government, setting limits on European governance and ensuring judicial remedies against decisions taken by EU institutions.[46] Indeed, even a brief perusal of the Court's narrative on judicial review under Article 263TFEU seems to confirm this claim.[47]

Again, this relates to multilingualism and legal certainty. If the organizing principle is accepted as the guideline for reconstructing the ideal of the rule of law, then multilingualism and differences between language versions do not – as such – entail that EU legislation would cease to guide behaviour. Importantly, as long as multilingual EU law is not *too vague* and not *too easily changeable*, then it does fulfil the minimum requirement of the rule of law: the capacity to guide behaviour. In essence, it remains *predictable enough*. Complementing this relativist view of certainty is the imperative that those subject to law must be capable of challenging acts that concern them.

In this respect, to make sense of both the rule of law as well as legal certainty in the context of EU law, defining the role of courts seems particularly important. As Endicott puts it, 'their role in securing the rule of law for a community is not just the role of forensic fact-finding and the watchdog role of ensuring compliance; it is also the creative role of resolving unresolved disputes about the requirements of the law'.[48] To be sure, scholars have asked whether the ECJ is running wild and its case law has repeatedly been described in terms of judicial activism.[49] The law-making of judges in general, and particularly that of the judges at the Court, has been, and continues to be, a question that not only provokes debate and

45 Williams 2012: 105.

46 Williams 2012: 106, Dicey 1952.

47 For example, see case C-402/05 P, *Kadi and Al Barakaat International Foundation v Council and Commission* [2008] ECR I-6351, para 81. Following the formula already expressed in *Les Verts* (294/83, *Parti écologiste 'les Verts' v Parliament* [1986] ECR 1339), the need for restricting arbitrary decision-making is articulated in the following manner: 'The European Community is based on the rule of law, inasmuch as neither its Member States nor its institutions can avoid review of the question whether their acts are in conformity with the basic constitutional charter, the EC Treaty, which established a complete system of legal remedies and procedures designed to enable the Court of Justice to review the legality of acts of the institutions'.

48 Endicott 2000: 198.

49 See *inter alia* Rasmussen 1993, Hartley 1996, Cappelletti 1987, Pollicino 2004, who look at sex equality cases from the point of view of ECJ judicial activism. In the context of fundamental rights, see *e.g.* Cartabia 2007: especially 6 *et seq*. Cf. Bengoetxea *et al.* 2001: 43 and 84, Sankari 2011: 276–277. In her analysis, she comes to the conclusion that this criticism can be relativized.

confrontation between different doctrinal opinions, but also acts as a battleground for opposing ideologies regarding the functions, powers and limits of the judiciary in contemporary societies.[50]

Naturally, it would be tempting to argue that in order to limit the powers of the judiciary, and more specifically set limits on the way judges can interpret legal provisions, wording and more specifically linguistic reasoning should be given centre stage in judicial reasoning.[51] Yet as we have seen, in addition to translation issues, the EU political process of law-making brings together different, sometimes even opposing normative assumptions. Different political agendas are incorporated in strong institutional positions, consequently making it particularly difficult to reach political consensus at the time when laws are drafted. Hence, EU legislation could be characterized as 'incompletely theorised agreements'; that is, agreements reached on the basis of differing normative assumptions.[52]

Consequently, if the law itself is a result of political bargaining whose precise content is unclear – especially when expressed in over 20 languages with equal value in judicial interpretation – it appears problematic to tie the rule of law to how well a text can restrict the power of courts, for example. Just as a linguistic community determines the rules of a given language system, in legal systems the relevant legal community also plays an important role in determining the accepted behaviour of others.

The evolution of ECJ case law serves as an example. In legal literature, the Court has often stood accused of judicial activism; it has been accused of overstepping the limits of its powers as defined in the Treaties.[53] Without express authorization or support from the Treaties, the Court has gradually 'alimented' the EU legal system with concepts that have, in turn, had a profound impact on the evolution of rights stemming from EU law.[54] However, despite varying degrees of resistance from national courts, foundational concepts of EU law such as direct effect and primacy have gradually taken root in the EU constitutional order and are now accepted as residing at the very nucleus of European constitutionalism.[55]

---

50 Pollicino 2004: 1.

51 Cf. Klatt 2008, Conway 2012.

52 Maduro 2007: 9 who borrows the idea of 'incompletely theorised agreements' from Sunstein 1999. Although problems of political bargaining are particularly important in the EU, where 28 Member States with very different national interests participate in the legislative process, the incompleteness of law-making is not as such an unknown phenomenon in the national setting either. Collective labour agreements are a case in point. They are often left intentionally vague so that the negotiating parties can reach agreement: the problem of defining the actual content of the agreement is left for the courts. See also Koskinen 2000: 86, Van Hoecke 2002: 61.

53 For a critical analysis of this criticism, Dougan 2012: 114–122.

54 Amtenbrink 2012: 36.

55 Bengoetxea 2012: 229–230 on the confusion in legal scholarship between primacy and supremacy.

Parallels may be drawn with how linguistic communities function. In both law and language, breaking a rule induces criticism and sanctions. With regard to linguistic communities, it may be argued that although linguistic rules reflect a continuously changing practice, they have enough short-term fixity (stability) in relation to long-term flexibility that the relevant linguistic community can usually understand at a given point in time who is following the rules and who is breaking them.[56]

As in a linguistic setting, the ECJ was first criticized and even sanctioned in the sense that national courts did not accept the doctrines of primacy and direct effect without reticence.[57] However, the legal community has gradually accepted these interpretations so that the rules of the community have also changed in this respect; in essence, a shift has occurred from the initial micro-level reaction favouring stability towards macro-level flexibility. To be sure, the Court's case law concerning direct effect and the doctrine of primacy are now commonly accepted features of the EU legal system, so that the rules of the legal community have changed in this respect: ECJ case law articulating these principles is no longer seen as breaking the rules of the community, thus illustrating gradual permeation of new constitutional elements in national settings.

To conclude, using law as a guide and to dictate an outcome in each and every case is a helpful distinction.[58] Indeed, as suggested in Chapter 1, multilingual law can only be taken as a point of orientation towards the direction in which a judicial community consisting of the ECJ and national courts develop EU law; it does not give precise answers to each question the Court addresses. This is also an important point with regard to the role often attributed to predictability in analyzing the principle of legal certainty. Next, we turn our attention to the principle of legal certainty in the context of adjudication.

Role in adjudication: different levels of certainty

Principles such as legal certainty are used in judicial reasoning to justify judicial decisions. Legal justification can be divided into two distinct categories of reasons. These include authority reasons and substantive reasons. The former category covers legal norms, precedents and legal doctrine. The latter, then, includes values and principles, which include both rightness and goal reasons.[59] Placing emphasis on the central role of policy reasons in ECJ reasoning displays the challenge of fitting the well-known Dworkinian distinction between principles and policies to the context of EU law.[60] According to the proposed dichotomy, principles and policies can be distinguished from each other, since a fundamental difference

56 Schauer 2008: 1121.

57 For an overview of different reactions, see Mattli and Slaughter 1996.

58 Endicott 2000: 203.

59 Summers 1978: 716.

60 Moral Soriano 2003: 308.

can be discerned between the two groups of reasons: principles confer rights on individuals and policies represent common goals of a given society. According to their inbuilt ranking order, principles are superior to policies in adjudication: if principles and policies point to different interpretations, in those situations principles override policies because of their connection with individual rights.[61]

The difference between principles and policies and their inbuilt hierarchy as reasons seems unclear in the EU context. Nor is it possible to operate a straightforward distinction between these categories: their borderline is often difficult to define.[62] Policies are undoubtedly of particular significance in EU law: they permeate the judicial process through dynamic considerations in judicial decision-making. Within the context of EU law, policies – the category in which the four freedoms fit – have traditionally overridden considerations related to principles, such as fundamental rights.[63] Especially free movement of goods but also freedom of establishment and freedom to provide services possess only a remote connection to fundamental rights conferring rights on individuals.[64]

However, it may tentatively be argued that this hierarchy on which the Court's case law has long resided is gradually taking a new form given the gradual increase in importance of fundamental rights in the EU context. At the same time, typical policy considerations are also occasionally dressed up as fundamental rights in ECJ terminology; free movement of goods is sometimes framed as a fundamental principle of the EU, sometimes as a fundamental right.[65] The distinction between policies and principles may sometimes be one of perspective: for example, it can be argued that free movement of persons (*e.g.* the right to employment in the case of workers) is closely tied to individual rights. The same can be said about environmental protection (*e.g.* the right to a clean environment). Nonetheless, the central role of policies may also be explained by the teleological method of interpretation where the aims and purposes of the legal system impact on the choice between different understandings.

Therefore it is argued that in EU law, principles and policies form an interlocking unit of reasons (indeed, policies are often expressed through principles). The claim is that policies function as signposts signalling the course of action to secure a particular state of affairs (goal) that is considered desirable in the EU legal system. Policy reasons may be used to justify the Court's interpretation as that which

61 Dworkin 1977: 90–94.

62 Avbelj 2004: 67–70.

63 See, for example, the Viking Line and Laval cases, case C-438/05, *International Transport Workers' Federation, Finnish Seamen's Union* [2007] ECR I-10779 and case C-341/05, *Laval un Partneri* [2007] ECR I-11767) in which freedom of establishment was given precedence over the right to take collective action. See also Ojanen 2009: 1118.

64 Von Bogdandy 2000: 1326. See also Avbelj 2004: 68–70.

65 See *e.g.* case 240/83, *ABDHU* [1985] ECR 531, para 9 (freedom of trade as a fundamental right) and case C-112/00, *Eugen Schmidberger* [2003] ECR I-5659, para 51. Cf. C-112/00, *Eugen Schmidberger* [2003] ECR I-5659, opinion of AG Jacobs, footnote 38.

realizes the desired goal.[66] In fact, according to Moral Soriano, the most important feature of policy reasons is that they give rise to discussion as to the desirability of the goal that they aim to secure: they are closely related to rights and values.[67] Thus, it is helpful to consider both principles and policies as arguments of rights and policy: indeed, it appears that the Court does not approach rights and policies as distinct and mutually opposed spheres but rather as interlocking arguments, because both can be connected to each other to construct coherent supportive structures for legal decisions.[68]

The above intimately ties to the desirability of teleological reasoning. Policy arguments even when articulated in the form of principles (substantive reasons) make explicit the underlying political theory of adjudication in a given society. Through those arguments, the Court's understanding of the purpose of the legal system is made explicit in its judicial reasoning and is made open to debate.

Legal certainty may be included in the category of substantive reasons in legal justification. In fact, a perusal of ECJ case law on legal certainty suggests that the principle often functions as an argument that aims at justifying interpretative choices. Indeed, legal certainty not only confers rights on individuals, but rather it operates as a policy argument. Such arguments may be described as falling into the category of meta-principles.[69]

Put differently, the principle of legal certainty might best be understood as a command to optimize in ECJ case law. The difference between legal rules and principles as well as policies is not a semantic one but is rather related to their different roles in judicial reasoning. The outcome of applying principles or policies as commands to optimize are priority orders between colliding reasons or interests (such as policies, rights). What is more, the priority order may also change over time so that the way different reasons or interests are balanced also depends on the point in time that the balancing exercise is conducted.[70] Thus, they function as criteria for balancing and weighing colliding goals in judicial decision-making.

Describing the role of legal certainty in adjudication in the EU context as a command to optimize appears justified by the fact that in ECJ case law, legal certainty is often balanced against other interests and principles such as that of legality or used as an argument to confirm the desirability of the Court's understanding of the law.[71] In fact, this balancing exercise forms the core element

66 MacCormick 1994: 261–263.

67 Moral Soriano 2003: 309.

68 Moral Soriano 2003: 322. Indeed, many policies may even be expressed in the form of principles of EU law. As an example, the ECJ continually refers to free movement rules as general principles of EU law. Nonetheless, it is possible to ask whether in reality these fall into the category of policies since they primarily aim at realizing common goals.

69 Lasser 2004: 211 *et seq.*

70 Ojanen 2003: 183–184, Moral Soriano 2003: 321.

71 For an interesting account of the requirements set by the principle of legal certainty in the context of competition law, case T-22/02, *Sumimoto Chemical v Commission* [2005]

in Tuori's criticism of the above-described twofold conception of legal certainty intertwining both formal and substantive legal certainty. In essence, he explains that in the context of adjudication, formal and substantive considerations often point in opposite directions so that including a substantive aspect to the principle of legal certainty would only increase the complexities inherent in balancing between different principles in concrete cases.[72]

However, legal principles may be understood in two different ways. On the one hand, it is possible to speak about legal principles as expressly and discursively formulated norms that may be applied by courts.[73] On the other hand, legal principles may also refer to principles that harmonize, clarify and generate norms on the law's surface. These so-called 'background principles' are not directly used in adjudication, but rather function on the deeper levels of the law.[74]

To reconcile formal and substantive legal certainty, different levels of law need to be identified. For Tuori, modern law consists of three distinct levels, which consist of the law's surface, the level of legal culture and the deep level of the law.[75] Here it is argued that the principle of legal certainty presents different manifestations on different levels. On this account, legal certainty on the law's surface (as a principle applied by the Court either as a decision principle or as an interpretive principle) and legal certainty as a systemic value on the deeper levels of the law (background principle) form two distinct entities. On the surface, legal certainty takes the form of formal legal certainty as, for instance, expressed in ECJ case law often setting conditions on the application of the law in concrete cases. In black-letter law, legal certainty may with reason be equated with predictability and can be described as a command to optimize guiding the Court's judicial decision-making. Although it does not give a definite answer to a particular legal question, it is a value that has to be balanced against other values, principles and policies in the decision-making process.

However, as a systemic value, legal certainty also includes a substantive element, that of acceptability. Employing the principle of legal certainty in judicial reasoning as a command to optimize (here consisting of predictability) is not as such sufficient for assuring legal certainty in this substantive sense. Instead, the

ECR II-4065, paras 80 *et seq*. See in more detail about finding a balance between legal certainty and legality, Groussot and Minssen 2007. See also case 7/57, *Algera and Others v Assemblée commune* [1957] ECR 81, case 14/61, *Hoogovens* [1962] ECR 253, case 14/81, *Alpha Steel v Commission* [1982] ECR 749, case 15/85, *Consorzio Cooperative d'Abruzzo v Commission* [1987] ECR 1005, case C-248/89, *Cargill v Commission* [1991] ECR I-2987, case T-186/00, *Conserve Italia* [2003] ECR II-719, case C-224/01, *Gerhard Köbler* [2003] ECR I-10139 and case C-453/00, *Kühne & Heitz* [2004] ECR I-10239.

72 Tuori 2003: 361–362. See similarly Raitio 2008: 61, who notes that the two-dimensional approach to legal certainty functions primarily as a theoretical model and is not, as such, based on judicial practice.

73 Dworkin 1977.

74 Tuori 2003: 348, who places background principles on the level of legal culture.

75 See Tuori 2002: 147–196 for an analysis of the different levels of the law.

core of the latter is construed on the basis of ECJ reasoning. In this systemic sense, legal certainty might best be described as an ideal instead of a principle guiding decision-making. Rather than guiding decision-making in individual cases, systemic legal certainty refers to an ideal characteristic of the EU legal system including both predictability as well as rational acceptability of adjudication which requires that the solution, or the outcome of the proceedings, is right in that it is rationally acceptable.[76]

Therefore, adhering to Tuori's three-level conception of modern law, this book proposes a solution to the problem that stems from the division of legal certainty into formal and substantive elements and calls for a balancing exercise between formal justice and material fairness in judicial decision-making. On the law's surface, legal certainty understood in the formal sense of predictability is balanced against other competing values such as effectiveness and the principle of legality.[77] On the deeper levels, legal certainty forms an ideal that does not require a balancing exercise. It is both procedure and substance.[78] We come back to this idea of legal certainty in Chapter 3 where it is developed further.

Following this level-based distinction, the normative concept of legal certainty could be divided into a) a principle that may be used in determining the content of law as either a directly applicable principle of law or an interpretive principle applied in adjudication and b) an ideal describing the characteristics of a particular legal system.[79]

In the following, legal certainty is approached in the former sense: that is, as a principle used to determine the content of law in individual cases in ECJ case law. In particular, use of legal certainty is considered both as a directly applicable principle used in judicial decision-making as well as an interpretive principle influencing decision-making at the Court.[80]

The Court's case law

The Court has employed the principle of legal certainty 'with creativity, invoking it in diverse contexts',[81] both as a procedural and a substantive principle. This section suggests that the principle of legal certainty – as deployed in the Court's reasoning – operates primarily as an argumentative tool to which the Court makes recourse to justify a particular outcome.[82] Indeed, the principle of legal certainty

76 Moral Soriano 2003: 320.

77 Cf. Tuori 2003: 261–262.

78 Moral Soriano 2003: 320.

79 Tuori 2007: 226 on a similar distinction concerning the rule of law.

80 Tuori 2011: 190–196.

81 Tridimas 2006: 243.

82 See Tuori 2003: 361, Tuori 2011: 190–196. See also Raitio 2003: 125–128. For a similar understanding of the use of the commonly expressed goal of uniformity, see

has been used in innumerable ECJ cases and in various contexts and ways.[83] The aim of this section is thus to map the basic tenets of the principle of legal certainty as expressed in ECJ case law.

Expressing the fundamental principle common to contemporary (European) legal systems, according to which those concerned must know the law in order to be able to plan their actions in accordance with it, resides at the very core of the general principles of EU law.[84] Without explicit reference to the principle in the Treaties, the Court has had a decisive impact on determining how the principle of legal certainty is interpreted and applied in the EU context: in this respect, the principle forms an integral part of unwritten EU law.[85]

Legal certainty made its first implicit appearance in ECJ case law in the *Algera*[86] case. The case concerned revocability of unlawful administrative acts. In this case, the Court undertook comparative analysis which led to the conclusion that this principle was common to all Member States. In subsequent case law, the principle was clearly linked to legal certainty.[87] The Court made its first explicit reference to the principle of legal certainty in *SNUPAT*.[88]

More recently, the Court has held that the principle of legal certainty requires first of all that legal rules are clear and precise. Secondly, legal certainty aims to ensure that situations and legal relationships governed by EU law remain predictable.[89] An umbrella principle, it comprises different corollaries. These include non-retroactivity, acquired rights, legitimate expectations and *res judicata*.[90] Indeed, attempting to draw a clear line between the different sub-principles is often

---

Komárek 2010: 95 *et seq*.

83 Raitio 2003: 187–266.

84 Cf. Maxeiner 2006–2007 and 2008–2009, who notes that American legal theorists have since long given up on the idea of legal certainty.

85 Groussot 2006: 190.

86 Case 7/57, *Algera and Others v Assemblée commune* [1957] ECR 81.

87 See *e.g.* case 7/57, *Algera and Others v Assemblée commune* [1957] ECR 81, at 55 and 56, case 14/81, *Alpha Steel v Commission* [1982] ECR 749, para 10, case 15/85, *Consorzio Cooperative d'Abruzzo v Commission* [1987] ECR 1005, para 12 and case C-508/03, *Commission v United Kingdom* [2006] ECR 3969, para 68.

88 Case 42/59, *SNUPAT v High Authority* [1961] ECR 53.

89 Case C-63/93, *Duff* [1996] ECR I-2925, para 20.

90 Groussot 2006: 190, 194, Groussot and Minssen 2007: 386–387. See also Temple Lang 2000: 163 who argues that legal certainty may be categorized not only as an administrative principle, but also as a fundamental right. Indeed, it is settled case law that legal certainty comes with a number of corollary principles. In this respect, see *e.g.* case C-63/93, *Duff* [1996] ECR I-569, para 20 and case C-107/97, *Max Rombi* [2000] ECR I-3367, para 66. It is possible to argue, as Groussot does, that the criminal law principle of *ne bis in idem* forms one of these corollaries as well. See, *inter alia*, case T-236/01, *Tokai Carbon v Commission* [2004] ECR II-1181, para 130 and case C-397/03 P, *Archer Midland* [2006] ECR I-4429, paras 46–54.

unhelpful since they are closely interrelated and often overlapping.[91] And, as with all general principles of EU law, legal certainty may be applied as both a rule of interpretation and as a substantive right.[92]

However, at the outset, it should be emphasized that a difference can be discerned between legal certainty and protection of legitimate expectations due to their diverging temporal manifestations. Whereas legal certainty imposes an obligation according to which rules that apply at a given time are clear and precise, protection of legitimate expectations places a requirement on public authorities to exercise their power over a certain period so that situations and relationships lawfully created under EU law are not affected in a way that could not have been foreseen.[93] This is why legal certainty may be described as possessing a static character, whereas protection of legitimate expectations concerns the future. Indeed, while legal certainty may also sometimes be a source of substantive rights, it is generally invoked as a tool of interpretation due to its general character.[94]

Accordingly, legal certainty has been invoked at the Court, *inter alia*, in judgments in connection with protection of legitimate expectations, non-retroactivity, legitimate expectations arising from legislation, legitimate expectations arising from the conduct of EU institutions, revocation of beneficial administrative acts, legitimate expectations related to national measures, recovery of unduly paid EU monies, and finally, recovery of unduly paid state aids.[95] The recurring elements of legal certainty that may be deduced from ECJ case law are charted in the following.[96]

Clarity and predictability

The imperatives of clarity and predictability undoubtedly form the nucleus of the Court's understanding of legal certainty. In this sense, Tridimas describes situations that might be held to be contrary to the principle of legal certainty in the following terms: where the provision in question is completely meaningless or clearly irreconcilable with other provisions of the same legislative instrument;

---

91 This is well illustrated by Xavier Groussot and Timo Minssen, Groussot and Minssen 2007. See also cases C-224/01, *Gerhard Köbler v Republik Österreich* [2003] ECR I-10239, case C-173/03, *Traghetti del Mediterraneo* [2006] ECR I-5177, case C-453/00, *Kühne & Heitz NV* [2004] ECR I-837, case C-234/04, *Kapferer* [2006] ECR I-2585.

92 Groussot 2006: 190–191.

93 See *e.g.* case C-63/93, *Duff* [1996] ECR I-2925, Opinion of AG Coulmas, para 582.

94 Tridimas 2006: 252.

95 See *e.g.* case C-234/89, *Delimitis v Henninger Bräu AG* [1991] ECR I-935, case C-39/94, *SFEI and Others* [1996] ECR I-3547, case C-453/00, *Kühne & Heitz NV* [2004] ECR I-837 and case 41/74, *Van Duyn v Home Office* [1974] ECR 1337. See also Tridimas 2006: 242 *et seq.*, Raitio 2003: 187–266.

96 The categorization of cases under different sub-headings is based on Tridimas 2006: 242 *et seq.*, Groussot 2006: 194 *et seq.*

where EU law governing the issue is so complex (including primary and secondary legislation as well as case law) that it is impossible for citizens to know what the law is; or where a provision is repealed or amended, or alternatively burdens are imposed on citizens by a provision included in a legislative instrument governing a different area of law.[97]

In *Stichting ROM-projecten*,[98] the Court held that the principle of legal certainty requires that individuals must be able to ascertain unequivocally what their rights and obligations are and take steps accordingly.[99] Accordingly, where the conditions for the grant of financial assistance by the EU to a Member State are set out in a grant decision that has neither been published nor made known to the ultimate beneficiary of the assistance, it is not contrary to EU law to apply the principle of legal certainty so as to preclude repayment by that beneficiary of amounts wrongly paid, provided that it is possible to establish the beneficiary's good faith.[100]

In *SIAT*,[101] the principle of legal certainty was applied in the context of Article 49 EC. At issue was whether a rule of Belgian law, which was found to restrict the freedom to provide services, was justified under overriding reasons relating to prevention of tax evasion and effectiveness of fiscal supervision. First, the Court found that the relevant national rules pursued these objectives and that their application was in principle justified. Second, employing the principle of legal certainty, the Court held that, given the absence of any objective criterion for their applicability, the rules at issue were not compatible with the principle of proportionality. More particularly, the Court observed that 'a rule framed in such terms does not make it possible, at the outset, to determine its scope with sufficient precision and its applicability remains a matter of uncertainty'. Second, it confirmed that 'such a rule does not, therefore, meet the requirements of the principle of legal certainty, in accordance with which rules of law must be clear, precise and predictable as regards their effects, in particular where they may have unfavourable consequences for individuals and undertakings'. In the context of free movement, the Court thirdly construed the foundational rule according to which 'a rule which does not meet the requirements of the principle of legal certainty cannot be considered to be proportionate to the objectives pursued'.[102]

---

97 Tridimas 2006: 245–246.

98 C-158/06, *Stichting ROM-projecten* [2007] ECR I-5103, para 34.

99 Para 34. For earlier cases, case C-143/93, *Van Es Douane Agenten* [1996] ECR I-431, para 27 and case C-248/04, *Koninklijke Coöperatie Cosun* [2006] ECR I-10211, para 79.

100 The same idea of clarity and predictability can be found in the following cases: case C-209/96, *United Kingdom v Commission* [1998] ECR -5655, para 35, case C-108/01, *Consorzio del Prosciutto di Parma and Salumificio S. Rita* [2003] ECR I-5121, para 89, and case C-255/02, *Halifax and Others* [2006] ECR I-1609, para 72.

101 Case C-318/10, *SIAT*, not yet reported.

102 Paras 57–59.

Irrespective of the field of law in question, time limits can also be posited at the kernel of the Court's perception of the principle of legal certainty. The underlying aim of these limits – based on national or EU law – is to guarantee stability in legal relations. In *EMS-Bulgaria Transport*,[103] the Court confirmed that predictability and stability of legal relations is a core element of the principle of legal certainty. It concluded, in relation to a question put to it by way of preliminary reference on the deductibility of VAT, that the possibility of exercising the right to deduct without any temporal limit would be contrary to the principle of legal certainty, which requires the tax position of the taxable person, having regard to his rights and obligations *vis-à-vis* the tax authority, not to be open to challenge indefinitely.[104] Or, as the Court has stated in more general terms, the need to set time limits and to time-bar applications and actions brought after the expiry of such limits 'is in particular based on the consideration that the periods within which applications must be lodged are intended to safeguard legal certainty by preventing Community measures which involve legal effects from being called in question indefinitely'.[105]

Hence, legal certainty can be taken to include a requirement of clarity and predictability with regard to measures imposed on EU citizens as well as economic actors. The rights and obligations following from EU legislation must therefore be clear and precise so that those concerned are aware of their legal situation. Nonetheless, what 'clear and precise' means in the context of legal certainty escapes any normative definition: the imperative takes its specific form in context, in connection with each case separately. This is so not least because of the contextuality of interpretation and the absence of pre-interpretive meaning.

Effectiveness and stability of legal relations

Legal certainty is also intimately bound up with the imperative of effective enforcement of EU law.[106] The principle has in fact been used to enforce the binding character of EU law. This is particularly so with regard to enforcement of directives. According to the Court's case law, national rules through which directives take root in national law should be formulated unequivocally so that the persons concerned can gain a clear and precise understanding of the rules

103 Case C-284/11, *EMS-Bulgaria Transport*, not yet reported.

104 Para 48. See also case C-472/08, *Alstom Power Hydro* [2010] ECR I-623, para 16, case C-95/07, *Ecotrade* [2008] ECR I-3457, para 44. See also Groussot 2006: 192.

105 Case C-188/92, *TWD* [1994] ECR I-833, para 16.

106 See *e.g.* case 143/83, *Commission v Denmark* [1985] ECR 427, and case 238/84, *Röser* [1986] ECR 795. Recently, cases concerning revocability of national administrative decisions as well as state liability may be seen as expressions of this principle. In this respect, see C-453/00, *Kühne & Heitz* [2004] ECR I-837, case C-224/01, *Gerhard Köbler v Republik Österreich* [2003] ECR I-10239, case C-173/03, *Traghetti del Mediterraneo* [2006] ECR I-5177 and case C-470/03, *A.G.M.-COS.MET* [2007] ECR I-2749.

governing their rights and obligations and national courts are able to ensure that these rights and obligations are observed.[107]

National law must thus guarantee the effectiveness of EU law by national authorities. Additionally, the content of EU law obligations should be clear and precise so that individuals are made fully aware of their rights and, if necessary, may be able to invoke them in national courts. In this respect, to achieve the requirements set by legal certainty, it is not sufficient that national courts have given an interpretation compatible with EU law of the provisions of national law at hand.[108]

In *Commission v Ireland*,[109] the Court found that Ireland was in breach of its obligations under EU law, since it had failed to provide a clear, precise and unequivocal legal framework as required by Directive 76/464[110] as regards its obligation to establish specific programmes aimed at reducing pollution caused by certain dangerous substances. The national legislation at issue did not, amongst other things, provide a list of prohibited pollutants. It also left broad discretion to local authorities contrary to the requirements of the Directive.

According to the Court, given that the effectiveness of the system rests to a large extent on notices given by local authorities, the absence of uniform statutory criteria could not adequately guarantee a homogenous, comprehensive and consistent application of the Directive in the national context. The Court concluded that Ireland had failed to provide an authorization system of the kind required by EU law, as the national provisions in question were not sufficiently clear in practice, preventing those concerned from knowing the precise scope of their obligations.[111] As the case suggests, the requirement of effective enforcement of EU law at national level is intimately linked with the imperative of predictability and clarity. Indeed, to ensure the realization of those objectives, EU law must also be adequately enforced in the Member States, the latter forming the logical corollary of the former.

Not surprisingly, the need to ensure effective enforcement of EU law at national level is intimately tied to the principle of effectiveness, one of the principles – together with the principle of equivalence – employed by the Court to ascertain whether national procedural law makes exercising rights conferred by the EU legal

107 Case C-50/09, *Commission v* Ireland, not yet reported, para 47 and case C-508/04, *Commission v Austria* [2007] ECR I-3787, para 79. See for earlier occurrences *e.g.* case C-119/92, *Commission v Italy* [1994] ECR I-393 and C-208/90, *Emmott* [1991] ECR I-4269.

108 See, *inter alia*, case C-236/95, *Commission v Greece* [1996] ECR I-4459, para 13, and case C-144/99, *Commission v Netherlands* [2001] ECR I-3541, para 21.

109 Case C-282/02, *Commission v Ireland* [2005] ECR I-4653.

110 Council Directive 76/464/EEC of 4 May 1976 on pollution caused by certain dangerous substances discharged into the aquatic environment of the Community (OJ 1976 L 129, p. 23).

111 Paras 81–82. See also case C-119/92, *Commission v Italy* [1994] ECR I-393, para 17.

system impossible or excessively difficult. In this respect, the Court consistently refers to the following standard formula in the case law:

> In the absence of relevant European Union rules, it is, under the principle of procedural autonomy of the Member States, for the domestic legal system of each Member State to regulate the legal procedures designed to ensure the protection of the rights which individuals acquire under European Union law [...] provided, however, that they are not less favourable than those governing similar domestic situations (principle of equivalence) and that they do not render impossible in practice or excessively difficult the exercise of rights conferred by the European Union legal order (principle of effectiveness) [...].[112]

Indeed, the twin requirements of equivalence and effectiveness which bite in the delicate area of Member State procedural autonomy aim to ensure full effectiveness of EU law. Additionally, Groussot interprets these requirements as a means of ensuring that Member States cannot take advantage of their own failure to comply with EU law.[113] In this context, the Court has nonetheless repeatedly held that laying down reasonable time limits for bringing proceedings is in accordance with EU law in the interests of legal certainty in view of protecting both the individual and the authorities concerned.[114] The underlying ratio is that such time limits – as long as they remain reasonable – are not liable to make it in practice impossible or excessively difficult to exercise rights conferred by EU law.[115] Again, we can see how considerations of legal certainty relate to the foundational need of stabilizing expectations and legal relations.

Although full enforcement of EU law and the principle of legal certainty are in certain circumstances placed on the same side of the scale in interpretation,

112 Case C-249/11, *Byankov*, not yet reported, para 69. See also case 33/76, *Rewe* [1976] ECR 1989, para 5, case 45/76, *Comet* [1976] ECR 2043, paras 13 and 16, case C-231/96, *Edis* [1998] ECR I-4951, paras 19 and 34, case C-343/96, *Dilexport* [1999] ECR I-579, para 25, case C-78/98, *Preston and Others* [2000] ECR I-3201, para 31, case C-201/02, *Wells* [2004] ECR I-723, para 67, case C-446/04, *Test Claimants* [2006] ECR I-11753, para 203, case C-392/04, *i-21 Germany* [2006] ECR I-8859, para 57 and case C-168/05, *Mostaza Claro* [2006] ECR 10421, para 24.

113 Groussot 2006: 192. See, *inter alia*, case 80/86, *Kolpinghuis Nijmegen* [1987] ECR 3969, case C-168/95, *Arcaro* [1996] ECR I-4705 and case C-60/02, *X* [2004] ECR I-651.

114 Case C-246/09, *Bulicke*, not yet reported, para 36, and case C-272/10 *Berkizi-Nikolakaki*, para 49.

115 See *e.g.* case 33/76, *Rewe* [1976] ECR 1989, para 5, case 45/76 *Comet* [1976] ECR 2043, paras 17–18; case 61/79, *Denkavit Italiana* [1980] ECR 1205, para 23, case C-90/94, *Haahr Petroleum* [1997] ECR I-4085, para 48, case C-261/95, *Palmisani* [1997] ECR I-4025, para 28, case C-231/96, *Edis* [1998] ECR I-4951, para 35, case C-228/96, *Aprile* [1998] ECR I-7141, para 19, case C-445/06, *Danske Slagterier* [2009] ECR I-02119, para 32 and case C-542/08, *Barth* [2010] ECR I-03189, para 28.

they also frequently constitute opposing forces in the Court's reasoning. This paradoxical relationship is illustrated in the Court's case law concerning *res judicata* of final administrative and judicial decisions.

As the Court has recently confirmed in *Byankov*,[116] the finality of an administrative decision contributes to legal certainty. Consequently, EU law does not require that an administrative body be under an obligation to reopen an administrative decision which has become final.[117] By the same token, however, the Court observed that particular circumstances may be capable of requiring a national administrative body, by virtue of the principle of sincere cooperation arising now from Article 4(3) TEU, to review an administrative decision that has become final. Accordingly, such a body may be under an obligation to take account of the interpretation of a relevant provision of European law which the Court has subsequently given. As the Court itself framed the essentially relativist character of legal certainty arising from its case law, 'the Court has taken account of the particular features of the situations and interests at issue in order to strike a balance between the requirement for legal certainty and the requirement for legality under European Union law'.[118]

In this regard, Groussot and Minssen distinguish between *res judicata* in relation to administrative acts and judicial decisions: as regards the latter, basing their conclusions on a reading of *Kapferer*[119] in conjunction with *Kühne & Heitz*,[120] they argue that given its foundational role in stabilizing expectations and ensuring the independence of the judiciciary, *res judicata* can only in very exceptional circumstances give way to considerations of effectiveness, even when balanced against the need to guarantee effective judicial protection for individuals.[121]

Accordingly, it appears that when final administrative decisions are involved, the threshold for the need to review such decisions is set at a lower level than for judicial decisions. These two lines of case law which relate to *res judicata* in two intimately related but nonetheless separate fields thus illustrate how the Court evaluates the appropriate balance between the imperatives of legal certainty (*res judicata*) and the requirement of legality and effective judicial protection of individuals in cases where EU law has been infringed. It seems feasible to conclude that whenever the Court considers final and conclusive judicial decisions

116 Case C-249/11, *Byankov*, not yet reported.

117 Para 76. See also Case C-2/06, *Kempter* [2008] ECR I-411, para 37.

118 Para 77. For the criteria that must be satisfied to justify reopening an administrative decision, case C-453/00, *Kühne & Heitz* [2004] ECR I-837, case C-2/06, *Kempter* [2008] ECR I-411 and case C-392/04, *i-21 Germany* [2006] ECR I-8859, paras 51 and 52. In the context of state aids, a similar approach has been adopted. See, notably, case C-119/05, *Lucchini* [2007], para 63.

119 Case C-234/04, *Kapferer* [2006] ECR I-2585.

120 Case C-453/00, *Kühne & Heitz* [2004] ECR I-837.

121 Similar conclusions can be drawn in the context of state liability, see case C-224/01, *Gerhard Köbler v Republik Österreich* [2003] ECR I-10239 and case C-173/03, *Traghetti del Mediterraneo* [2006] ECR I-5177.

(as opposed to administrative decisions), it confers more significance on the values of independence of the judiciary and legal certainty when balancing them with the requirement of effective judicial protection.

Of equal constitutional relevance is the linkage between the principle of legal certainty and the need to guarantee the unity and coherence of the EU legal system. Recently, in *Air Transport Association of America*[122] the Court confirmed, with reference to settled case law, that to safeguard the integrity of the EU legal system, national courts cannot declare acts of EU institutions invalid.

Indeed, from the standpoint of ensuring uniform effectiveness of EU law and uniform application of EU law at national level, divergences between national courts in declaring EU acts invalid would result in an undesirable situation where different rules would apply in Member States. According to the Court, this would pose a threat to legal certainty, particularly with regard to uniformity.[123] Further, it held that the imperative of uniformity is particularly significant when the validity of an EU act is in question: 'divergences between courts in the Member States as to the validity of EU acts would be liable to jeopardise the very unity of the EU legal system and detract from the fundamental requirement of legal certainty'.[124]

Here, the Court's understanding of legal certainty seems to be intimately linked with its concern about the need to maintain the *status quo* of centralized judicial review of EU acts. This relates to a more prospective aspect of this type of reasoning: it suggests that the Court also employs uniformity and coherence as 'a device for uniformly developing a system of laws'.[125] Although the question of what, exactly, are the fundamental requirements of legal certainty in this context remains unanswered, it appears well founded to argue that, in the final analysis, the Court is once again concerned about the (procedural) stability of legal relations, and not so much about predictability understood as clarity and precision of legal rules that would require that those subject to the law can unequivocally determine their rights and obligations.

Indeed, the Court's case law offers fruitful material for discussion about the nature of the principle of legal certainty as it manifests itself on the law's

122 Case C-366/10, *Air Transport Association of America and Others,* not yet reported.

123 See also Komárek 2010: 95 *et seq.* He argues that the recurrent use of the notion of uniformity in the Court's rhetoric serves, in reality, as justification for its involvement in cases of minor importance that could without difficulty be resolved on the national level. The Court's concern about the uniformity of EU law is an illustration of the evolving character of the EU legal system and its relative systemic immaturity.

124 Para 47. See for similar expressions of the Court's aim to centralize judicial review, case 314/85, *Foto-Frost* [1987] ECR 4199, para 15, see case C-143/88, Zuckerfabrik Süderdithmarschen and Zuckerfabrik Soest [1991] ECR I-415, para 17, case C-6/99, *Greenpeace France and Others* [2000] ECR I-1651, para 54, C-344/04, *IATA and ELFAA* [2006] ECR I-403 para 27, and case C-188/10, *Melki and Abdeli* [2010] ECR I-5667, para 54.

125 Bertea 2005a: 169.

surface. Inevitably, precision and clarity required by the Court are not absolute: more particularly, this ultimate demand for clarity functions as a criterion eliminating application of rules that are completely meaningless, unlimited in time, or arbitrary. To be sure, this seems a feasible standpoint not least in view of multilingualism and problems related to EU language policy as charted in Chapter 1. In fact, predictability appears to operate first and foremost as an underlying value requiring that legal relations remain stable. More particularly, similar to other general principles of law, legal certainty is relative so that the imperatives of predictability and stability can and will give way to other considerations such as that of legality or effectiveness if circumstances in individual cases so require.

In this sense, the position occupied by time limits and *res judicata* in the Court's perception of legal certainty indicates that predictability can also be approached from a procedural perspective. In this respect, while realistically multilingualism should set constraints on the Court's reliance on arguments on legal certainty in terms of 'substantive' predictability (requirement of clarity), it appears that predictability functions as a useful tool in judicial interpretation when employed on the procedural plane: it sets limits on decision-making and requires that procedural guarantees are given due consideration. This very strict understanding of the principle of legal certainty mirrors the expectation of legal protection without any substantive claim.[126]

In sum, ECJ case law offers a profusion of examples where the principle of legal certainty has been employed for the purposes of justification. The cases discussed in this section allow us to conclude that legal certainty constitutes a complex umbrella principle covering many sub-principles and in practice stretching its influence over every imaginable aspect of EU law.[127] Because of the reach and elusiveness of legal certainty as a principle, difficulty seems to arise in drawing borders between its different components whose application is intertwined. Although occasionally a direct source of rights, legal certainty generally forms an interpretive argument employed by the Court to justify its understanding of the law. Thus, legal certainty constitutes a tool or conceptual aid in interpreting EU law.[128] The following sections shed more light on this particular aspect of the principle of legal certainty.

Legal certainty as an interpretive tool

The view that legal certainty is employed by the Court as a meta-principle, as a means of promoting its understanding of the underlying values of the EU legal

126 Aarnio 1987: 3.

127 Groussot 2006: 190.

128 Tridimas 2006: 372–376. See also Groussot and Minssen 2007, who analyze the interrelationship between *res judicata*, the effectiveness of EU law and legal certainty.

system and its objectives, is most prominently associated with Lasser.[129] As a meta-principle, legal certainty thus occupies the role of an argument justifying interpretive choices in a given situation.[130]

In fact, viewed in these terms, legal certainty can be used to support contradictory results. The principle is thus understood as a means of supporting a particular outcome or a specific reading of the law, not as a substantive principle conferring rights on individuals. In this respect, even though legal certainty can sometimes also refer to a substantive right, it rarely dictates a specific outcome in itself. Rather, as Tridimas observes, it is used as a conceptual aid that must not be viewed in isolation but rather in the context of judicial reasoning taken as whole.[131]

To that end, the Court has itself noted that the principle of legal certainty is not absolute, since the principle of legality must be observed in its application.[132] It has held that the prevalence of one interest over another depends on the circumstances of the case: often, it is a question of comparing private interests – such as the good faith of a beneficiary – to a specific public interest.[133] In this sense, the principle of legal certainty appears to require that a balance is struck between, on the one hand, the individual interest of certainty and the public interest of legality on the other.[134]

Predictability as a meta-principle

The idea that legal certainty rarely dictates a specific outcome in ECJ case law follows Tuori's description of legal principles that are used as interpretive tools in judicial decision-making.[135] Indeed, despite the general requirements considered above that can be associated with the principle of legal certainty and irrespective of the way they are categorized, the Court also deploys legal certainty in its reasoning on a high abstract level, often in connection with other so-called 'meta-principles' such as uniformity, effectiveness and legal protection. In essence, these meta-principles are not always directly connected to the case at hand and indeed

129 Lasser 2004.

130 Lasser 2004: 211 *et seq.*

131 Tridimas 2006: 243.

132 See *e.g.* case 7/56, 7/57, *Algera and Others v Assemblée commune* [1957] ECR 81, case 14/61, *Hoogovens v High authority* [1962] ECR 253, para 5, case 14/81, *Alpha Steel v Commission* [1982] ECR 749, paras 10–12, case 15/85, *Consorzio Cooperative d'Abruzzo v Commission* [1987] ECR 1005, paras 12–17, case C-248/89, *Cargill v Commission* [1991] ECR I-2987, para 20 and case T-118/00, *Conserve Italia* [2003] ECR II-719, para 77.

133 42/59, *SNUPAT v High Authority* [1961] ECR 53. See also Groussot and Minssen 2007: 389–390, who note that the principle of legal certainty is relative.

134 Groussot 2006: 194–214. In this sense, it seems realistic to say that balancing different interests relates to the principle of legitimate expectations and other sub-principles of legal certainty such as acquired rights and non-retroactivity whereby legality and certainty are weighed against each other on a case-to-case basis. Cf. case 238/84, *Röser* [1986] ECR 795, para 15.

135 Tuori 2007: 226.

operate on a high level of abstraction: reasons for invoking them in the context of a specific case are often left unexplained. As we have seen, the principle of legal certainty sometimes occupies the position of a supporting argument for the need to ensure, for example, the coherence and unity of the legal system or for the Court's choice to demonstrate restraint in applying the principle of effectiveness.

Clearly, when referring to legal certainty, the Court is essentially referring to formal legal certainty in the sense that it clearly associates legal certainty with predictability: the test appears to be to ask whether the outcome can be argued to be predictable for at least one of the parties in the case, or whether the solution contributes to stability of legal relations. However, the Court does not generally flesh out what kind of legal certainty and to whose legal certainty it is referring, although the context of the decision often helps elucidate this point to the Court's audience.

For example, in infringement proceedings, legal certainty may function as an argument supporting the conclusion that a Member State has failed to fulfil its obligations. According to the Court, 'it is particularly important, in order to satisfy the requirement of legal certainty, that individuals should have the benefit of clear and precise legal situations enabling them to ascertain the full extent of their rights and duties and, where appropriate, to rely on them before national courts'.[136] Or, 'the provisions of directives must be implemented with unquestionable binding force, and specificity, precision and clarity is necessary to satisfy the requirements of legal certainty'.[137]

In other words, legal certainty might be argued to function as an argument used in connection with justifying policy choices and to support or confirm the Court's understanding of the law. In the *Mayr*[138] case, the ECJ was asked to rule on the meaning of 'pregnant worker' for the purposes of Directive 92/85/EEC.[139]

Ms Mayr, who worked in Austria, was undergoing in-vitro fertilization ('IVF') treatment when she was given notice of dismissal. At the time, the embryo had not yet been implanted. Ms Mayr brought a claim under Austrian legislation protecting pregnant workers against dismissal, arguing that she was pregnant at the time of dismissal. Against this background the referring Court asked the ECJ to clarify whether a worker who undergoes IVF is a 'pregnant worker' within the meaning of the Directive from the moment 'in-vitro' fertilization occurs.

The Court held that the health and safety objective of the prohibition against dismissal means that the earliest point of pregnancy has to be chosen to determine when protection against dismissal begins. However, on the basis of considerations

136 C-49/00, *Commission v Italy* [2001] ECR I-8575, para 22.

137 C-159/99, *Commission v Italy* [2001] ECR I-4007, para 32.

138 C-506/06, *Mayr* [2008] ECR I-1017.

139 Council Directive 92/85/EEC of 19 October 1992 on the introduction of measures to encourage improvements in the safety and health at work of pregnant workers and workers who have recently given birth or are breastfeeding (tenth individual Directive within the meaning of Article 16 (1) of Directive 89/391/EEC) (OJ 1992 L 348, p. 1).

related to legal certainty, the Court ruled that protection cannot be granted before an embryo has been *de facto* implanted.[140] In this respect, the Court concluded – after extensive discussion of the objectives of the Directive – that 'it cannot be accepted, for reasons connected with the principle of legal certainty, that the protection established' would extend to the period prior to transfer of the fertilized ova into the worker's uterus.[141]

However, the Court did not clarify the content of the 'reasons connected with the principle of legal certainty'. Nor did it specify the perspective: for whom should the outcome of the case be predictable?[142] To be sure, as the Court noted, 'artificial fertilisation and viable cells treatment is a very sensitive social issue in many Member States, marked by their multiple traditions and value systems'. Deploying the sensitivity of the issue at hand in its judgment to justify its partial silence, the Court held that it was not called on to 'broach questions of a medical or ethical nature, but must restrict itself to a legal interpretation of the relevant provisions of Directive 92/85 taking account of the wording, the broad logic and the objectives of that directive'.[143]

While not explicitly fleshed out, it appears that – once again – legal certainty closely connects with the need to stabilize legal relations, with the need to guarantee a predictable socio-legal environment while at the same time assuring pregnant workers protection against discrimination in accordance with the objectives of the directive. In short, it is about balancing: legal certainty relates to a balancing exercise between the objective of protecting pregnant workers against discrimination, on the one hand, and that of guaranteeing a stable environment for undertakings in the EU. Both considerations are linked with the purposes of the Treaty system. Additionally, the outcome of the case may be said to remain sensitive to different views on the delicate issue at hand, marked by multiple traditions and value systems in different Member States, thus leaving appropriate discretion to national courts in other similar cases.[144]

Predictability and multilingualism

What about multilingualism? According to the Court, legal certainty entails a requirement of clarity and precision so that those concerned know their rights and obligations. Looking at predictability from the viewpoint of multilingualism is helpful in understanding the difficulties related to convincingly conceptualizing legal certainty in terms of 'substantive' predictability (clarity or unequivocality)

140 Para 41. See also C-63/08, *Virginie Pontin* [2009] ECR I-10467, paras 60–62.

141 Para 41.

142 See similarly Raitio 2008: 62, who notes that it may well be that both parties in a case rely on the principle of legal certainty (here, predictability). In that situation, it is for the ECJ to decide whose viewpoint should prevail.

143 Para 38.

144 See Sarmiento 2012 for different types of silence. See Sunstein 1996.

in the multilingual EU legal system. Briefly put, the underlying problem relates to the unreliability of language versions in guiding action. Following the requirements expressed in *CILFIT* case law, comparing language versions may orient interpretation even today, with over 20 official language versions. However, while the *CILFIT* guidelines concern courts, the requirement of comparison can also impact private actors.

More particularly, if language versions are not compared, a private actor runs the risk of relying on a misleading text. In this respect, it is often argued that the obligation to compare official versions runs contrary to (formal) legal certainty and protection of legitimate expectations, as one cannot rely on each of the language versions separately.[145] While certainly true with regard to identifying translation errors or syntactical ambiguity on the surface of the text, comparison will not reveal subtle differences in meaning that stem from systemic or cultural aspects of compared languages. As we have seen, the translated nature of EU legislation implies that although officially equal, language versions cannot be assumed to be equal in meaning, they cannot 'signify *identically*'.[146] In fact, one could say that multilingualism highlights the relative character of predictability: since adjudication can in no circumstances reach absolute predictability, how much predictability is enough?

The Court answered this question in *Skoma-Lux*.[147] Czech customs authorities had levied penalties on Skoma-Lux, a Czech company, as it had infringed EU customs regulations after the accession of the Czech Republic to the EU but before these provisions were officially published in the Czech edition of the EU Official Journal.[148] The Court was asked to rule on whether a regulation can be applied against an individual if it has not at the relevant time been published in the EU Official Journal in the official language of the Member State in question. The Court based its decision on considerations reflecting its view on legal certainty. Those affected by EU law must have the possibility to acquaint themselves with provisions that may confer rights or impose obligations on them. This can be guaranteed by publishing EU legislation in the official language of those concerned.[149]

---

145 For a recent example, see Case C-261/08, *Zurita García and Choque Cabrera* [2009] ECR I-10143. See also Schermers and Waelbroeck 2001: 13 and Schübel-Pfister 2005: 333.

146 Glanert 2008: 164.

147 Case C-161/06, *Skoma-Lux* [2007] ECR I-10841.

148 See for detailed analysis of this case *e.g.* Lasiński-sulecki and Morawski 2008. See also Bobek 2006–2007 discussing problems related to unpublished legislation in new Member States.

149 Case C-161/06, *Skoma-Lux* [2007] ECR I-10841, para 38. See for earlier case law *e.g.* case 98/78 *Racke v Hauptzollamt Mainz* [1979] ECR 69, para 15. The ECJ has repeated this view, *inter alia,* in case C-370/96, *Covita* [1998] ECR I-7711, para 27, case C-228/99, *Silos* [2001] ECR I-8401, para 15 and case C-108/01, *Consorzio del Prosciutto di Parma and Salumificio S. Rita* [2003] ECR I-5121, para 95.

In the present multilingual landscape, the minimum requirement of predictability seems thus to be that the legislation in question is published in the relevant language version. While one of the aims of the unwritten principles of EU law is protecting the rights of individuals, principles rarely dictate a specific outcome: in different cases, legal certainty is used to protect different interests. In *Skoma-Lux*, a balance had to be struck between legal certainty (clarity and precision of obligations and rights in EU legislation), the necessity of applying EU customs provisions uniformly, and the principle of effectiveness of EU law. Instead of turning on a question of interpretation (on how a specific provision should be interpreted, all language versions considered), at issue was the relevance of the absence of a Czech version of the regulation at issue (although it was available on the Internet).

To be sure, if the relevant language version is not available, then no need to consult other versions exists. When a language version does exist, a person subject to EU law may need to check (*i.e.* by comparing different language versions) that their interpretation of the relevant text is in accordance with other language versions. In view of multilingualism, predictability can take us only as far as to ensure that EU legislation is officially available in all languages irrespective of any qualitative requirements. Nor does it protect from an interpretation that might – although this occurs only in extremely rare cases – be said to be contrary to or outside the confines of what might be accepted as within the wording in a specific language version. Indeed, legal certainty offers an interpretive tool for the ECJ to promote its normative understanding of the EU legal system and the teleological reading given to EU law in its judgments.

More recently, the Court was faced with a similar issue in *Pimix*[150] where it framed legal certainty as a fundamental principle of the EU legal order which 'requires that a measure adopted by the public authorities cannot be enforced against individuals before they have the opportunity to make themselves acquainted with it through its proper publication in the Official Journal'.[151] Indeed, a different reading allowing an act that has not been properly published to be enforceable against individuals by virtue of the principle of effectiveness would, according to Court, 'result in individuals in the Member State concerned bearing the adverse effects of a failure by the EU administration to comply with its obligation to make available to those individuals, on the date of accession, the entire *acquis communautaire* in all the official languages of the Union'.[152]

To conclude, legal certainty can be used as an argument to orient, support or confirm an interpretation reached by other means. Indeed, legal certainty in the form of predictability is an argument that adapts not only to the particularities of each case but also to the Court's interpretive solutions in different contexts. Applying Maduro's conception of meta-teleology and its virtues in the EU context

150 C-146/11, *Pimix*, not yet reported.

151 Para 33.

152 Para 44.

to the present discussion on legal certainty, it could be argued that legal certainty in fact forms a normatively strong argument for promoting the Court's systemic understanding of the EU legal system and its underlying values.[153] Next, we turn our attention to acceptability; to the substantive element of legal certainty.

Legal certainty and judicial reasoning

The formal aspect of legal certainty is only one of the two aspects of legal certainty discussed in this book. On deeper levels of the law, considerations of clarity and stability are substituted by substantive legal certainty in the form of acceptability: whereas formal legal certainty sets the requirement that rights and obligations resulting from EU law are precise and clear, substantive legal certainty emphasizes the acceptability of judicial decision-making. In this section, the substantive element of legal certainty is considered as a systemic value of the EU legal system. The aim is to explain how it may be constructed on the basis of ECJ judicial reasoning.

As noted above, multilingualism has an impact on the relevance of the wording of a provision in interpretation: the importance of multilingualism in judicial reasoning is reduced due to possible discrepancies between official language versions that may point towards different understandings of the law.[154] The fact that language versions can differ from each other might be said to be problematic from the viewpoint of assuring predictable judicial decisions. While predictability as clarity and stability is generally understood as referring to predictability of the actual outcome of legal proceedings, it can also refer to judicial reasoning, to justification. On this understanding, even if the outcome of a specific case can be difficult to predict, the requirement of certainty can be achieved on a higher level if judicial reasoning fulfils certain criteria of transparency, consistency and coherence.[155]

Predictable reasoning

Predictable reasoning may be said to constitute an important building block for substantive legal certainty whereby the outcome of the procedure should be 'right' and acceptable.[156]According to Wilhelmsson, predictable reasoning is intimately bound up with the transparency of stated arguments: arguments that have in fact influenced the outcome of the case in question should be stated explicitly in reasoning.[157]

153 Maduro 2007: 5.
154 Bengoetxea 1993: 235, Urban 2000: 55.
155 Wilhelmsson 2004: 220.
156 Aarnio 1987: 3–5.
157 Wilhelmsson 2004: 220.

Certainly, it is a truism that the imperative of transparency is intimately linked not only to the particularities of EU law, but also to the dynamism of present-day societies in which law is applied. Indeed, predictability of judicial decisions – in the sense of predictable outcomes based on clear, unequivocal rules – may be reduced not only as a result of the constraints set by multilingualism but also as a result of the temporality and contextuality of each interpretive exercise in which courts engage.

Firstly, therefore, although not identical to transparency, predictable reasoning is necessarily intertwined with the normative requirement of transparent and open argumentation. Frequently, simple recourse to wording cannot fulfil that imperative: on the contrary, due to the weak justificatory force of linguistic arguments in the present context, avoiding opacity may require openly distinguishing previous case law or discussing consequences of different interpretations, taking the purpose of the provision and the legal system as a starting point for that analysis. Predictability of judicial reasoning can transpire from such transparency. However, it should be noted that this does not imply a claim of transparency that would require, for example, overly elaborate judgments: in these cases, the message – no matter how transparently and discursively expressed – might be less accessible for those concerned. The argument here is thus qualitative, not quantitative.[158]

Apart from transparency, predictable reasoning also requires a certain degree of consistency in reasoning in order to contribute to substantive acceptability. This enables those partaking in proceedings to predict and look for relevant arguments for deciding the case. In addition to openly stating the reasons for a given solution in each individual case (be they related to purposes, policies, or principles within the context of the EU legal system), predictable reasoning requires that in similar cases, articulated reasons are taken into account and analyzed in a similar way.[159] Although systemic arguments necessarily carry benefits in this regard because of their inbuilt capability in tying an individual case to a longer line of cases and articulating its systemic relevance, it should be emphasized that purely systemic considerations can be problematic from the standpoint of predictable reasoning: establishing apparent coherence to contradictory legal material by recourse to systemic arguments can in fact contribute to opacity in reasoning. As Wilhelmsson observes, parties to proceedings are unable to predict which arguments are relevant when the abstract system is applied to their case.[160] Thus, openly articulated *telos* would seem to support transparency as it mirrors values and goals taken into consideration in the decision-making process and enables external feedback from the legal community on ECJ judicial decision-making.

Secondly, predictable reasoning may also be said to exist if the decision is construed so that it follows patterns of judicial reasoning accepted in the relevant

158 For quality standards that could be applied in the context of judicial adjudication, Bengoetxea 2007.

159 Wilhelmsson 2004: 220.

160 Wilhelmsson 2004: 221. See also Aarnio 1987: 6.

legal community. Although transparent, substantive arguments are necessary in order to contribute to certainty in judicial reasoning; the form in which these reasons are presented must follow certain predetermined criteria.[161] As we have seen, ECJ judicial reasoning involves considering not only the wording but also the wider context of the provision, as well as the objectives of the rules of which the provision forms part. Justifying decisions in the context of hard cases in accordance with accepted criteria of interpretation establishes a (relatively) stable framework in which judicial adjudication aims to reconcile conflicting legal materials one case at a time.

Clearly, both of the above elements of predictable reasoning (transparency, use of accepted criteria of interpretation) may contribute to stabilizing procedural expectations in the context of judicial decision-making. In this respect, predictable reasoning does not require absolute certainty in law; rather, it may be seen as a stabilizing framework for behaviour in the judicial context.[162] While it could be said that such reasoning does not make the argumentative character of law disappear, it may be said to set constraints on the Court's decision-making process.

Arguing that a method of interpretation that pays due attention to teleological and meta-teleological considerations is appropriate in the context of the EU legal system, Maduro notes that this approach is an increased necessity in the context of a pluralistic legal system: this is so since (both legal and linguistic) pluralism increases textual ambiguity of legal provisions and enhances potential for conflicting legal norms.[163] In the EU legal system, this is a cumulative consequence of its plurality of languages and of the different legal traditions inherent in these languages. Arguably, in such a context, linguistic reasoning seldom offers sufficient transparency to assure substantive acceptability of judicial decision-making in hard cases.

However, in this respect it should be noted that teleological reasoning can take different forms. On the one hand, teleological considerations expressed in ECJ case law may concern the aims and purposes of individual Treaty provisions or other EU legislation. On the other hand, the Court often refers to the purposes of the legal system, therefore engaging in systemic debate by anchoring purposive arguments to a very high level of abstraction, to macro-level purposes.[164]

Clearly, meta-teleological reasoning lies at the very core of ECJ judicial reasoning.[165] While teleological argumentation carries great importance in a multilingual legal system – especially from the standpoint of legal certainty – this purpose-oriented approach also involves problems. More specifically, when purposes given to justify a specific interpretation are directly connected to the relevant provisions in the case at hand, the teleological approach may enhance

161 Cf. Habermas 1998: 225.
162 Van Hoecke 2002: 66.
163 Maduro 2007: 8. For his account of constitutional pluralism, Maduro 2011.
164 Lasser 2004: 229–238.
165 Bengoetxea *et al.* 2001: 45.

predictable argumentation and the substantive form of legal certainty in that it openly expresses the aims and objectives on the basis of which a certain text has been interpreted in a specific way. However, if no linkage is provided between the stated purposes and actual provisions under consideration, a risk exists that the reasoning becomes complex and confusing.[166]

Admittedly, when meta purposes dominate judicial reasoning, transparency may be difficult to maintain. This is because the purposes on which the decision is based become in themselves instruments deployed for promoting other more 'fundamental' values. As purposes are no longer directly connected to the legal issue involved in the individual case, they may be more likely to induce confusion than transparency. The internal coherence of judgments is intimately bound up with the imperative of predictability in judicial reasoning. This aspect of justification is discussed in the following.

Notions of coherence

Coherence is often left undefined. Certainly, the idea of coherence is deeply rooted in contemporary legal systems and is often understood as including elements such as consistency, comprehensiveness and completeness as well as cross-connection and mutual justification between the parts of a whole. In legal theory, these aspects of coherence are often used to describe global or local coherence of a legal system.[167]

More particularly, as Bertea observes, coherence is held to be something more than mere logical consistency of propositions. Importantly, while legal scholarship generally accepts that coherence may be characterized in the negative as a lack of inconsistencies, the question of how coherence might be defined in positive terms remains without a definitive answer.[168] In this respect, it remains unclear what exactly coherence amounts to. Indeed, coherence is often defined in figurative

166 For an example of this kind of reasoning in an AG's opinion, Lasser 2004: 210. See also Conway 2008: 805. Conway analyzes the level of generality in ECJ judicial reasoning and concludes that a need exists to control the level of generality in ECJ judicial reasoning for reasons of objectivity and certainty in law. He is particularly concerned about the meta-teleological approach whereby a result is reached by means of very broadly stated goals of effectiveness and integration.

167 Levenbook 1984: 367–374. She discusses global and local coherence with special focus on problems related to global, systemic coherence. See also Bertea 2005a, Alexy and Pezcenik 1990.

168 Bertea 2005a: 156–157. Neil MacCormick's work on judicial reasoning has paved the way for analysis of coherence in legal theory. It is seen as an important element of law and as a regulative criterion of legal argumentation. See in this respect MacCormick 1994: especially 152–194.

language as the equivalent of 'hanging together', 'making sense as a whole', 'cohesion', 'consonance', and 'speaking with one voice'.[169]

Although generally referred to as the ideal or actual features of a legal system, of particular significance for present purposes is that coherence can also be employed, as Moral Soriano does, in the context of judicial reasoning to evaluate the internal coherence of judgments; that is, arguments put forward in justifying judicial decisions. The notion of internal coherence is helpful in assessing whether each of the arguments adduced in support of a specific decision is coherent with the others or whether a given judgment is in line with the fundamental principles of a legal system. In this respect, a judicial decision may be argued to be 'correct' if the arguments on which it is based are well connected with one another. Focusing on coherence in judicial reasoning helps make sense of the contradictory materials on which law is construed.[170]

Dworkin's argument about law as integrity is a prominent example of a theory concerning coherence in a legal system (global coherence): it focuses on fitting decisions into the legal system, and on fitting together all elements of the particular legal system.[171] At the same time, theories that focus on judicial reasoning are interested in arguments that are used to justify decisions, and in whether those arguments are connected so as to form a coherent whole. Because coherence of judicial reasoning precedes any attempt at construing systemic coherence, Moral Soriano contends that we should not begin by asking whether a rule or a norm construed in a given decision coheres with the legal system. Instead, one should ask whether the reasoning in that individual case coheres.[172] The relation between micro-level coherence (internal coherence of judgments) and systemic coherence can be framed in the following terms: coherence in judicial reasoning (arguments given to justify a decision creating a coherent justification) are signposts that help us make sense of the path (the legal system).[173] Gradually, coherence in judicial reasoning may even enhance coherence in the systemic (global or local) sense.

Judicial reasoning is based on giving arguments or reasons that cumulate, form chains, or form nets of cumulative arguments.[174] To ensure that reasoning is rationally acceptable, a degree of coherence in judicial reasoning is required. Here, in the EU context, discussing coherence in judicial reasoning – instead of systemic coherence – entails that instead of trying to fit all the components of the legal system under a set of values or principles organized in a specific hierarchical order, the pluralistic nature of the EU legal system is accepted as a starting point.

---

169 MacCormick 1984: 235, MacCormick 1994, Zaccaria 1990: 269, Villa 1990: 433, Dworkin 1986: 165. See also Bertea 2005b for an analysis of arguments of coherence in judicial reasoning.

170 Moral Soriano 2003: 302.

171 Dworkin 1986: 228–255.

172 Moral Soriano 2003: 297.

173 Moral Soriano 2003: 308.

174 Bengoetxea 1993: 225.

Because of the interplay of constantly interacting languages, cultures and legal systems, this approach to coherence appears well founded: it recognizes the existence of diverging and incommensurable values that form part of the same legal system.[175] The imperative of internal coherence of judgments admits that a legal system interlocks even conflicting values. A choice is made between those values in legal adjudication.

Naturally, coherence of the legal system as a whole and coherence in judicial reasoning in individual cases are intimately linked. This relationship is twofold. Firstly, by bringing together and explicating the interrelationship between several foundational elements of the legal system in a judgment (for example, by striking a balance between conflicting values), the Court makes a new connection between different elements of the same system. Secondly, judicial adjudication also connects the legal system with political, moral and constitutional theories. Indeed, because judgments necessarily carry systemically external elements which are employed to justify and support the chosen interpretation in a particular case, they also offer justification for the legal system.[176]

Coherence in judicial reasoning

The 'modest' notion of coherence developed by Moral Soriano asks: 'Does the argumentation which supports the ruling R cohere?'[177] It offers a 'bottom-up' approach to coherence: coherence is built up from individual cases. This viewpoint shifts our attention from coherence of the legal system (global) or parts of it (local) to the process of justifying decisions. While global and local coherence provides a strategy with which to reconstruct a legal system (or a branch of it) without internal dissonance, the case-specific notion of coherence employed here accepts the dissonance and internal disagreement present in the EU legal system.

Unlike the above-mentioned notions of coherence which take as a starting point the legal system and focus on the test of fit in the Dworkinian sense of the term – that is, on exploring how well specific rulings cohere with the underlying values of the legal system – the notion of coherence proposed by Moral Soriano explains ECJ judicial reasoning. This approach to coherence takes pluralism seriously: it looks at elements that make the legal system intelligible without denying its multifaceted character. Thus, coherence does not mean ignoring law's complexity or supporting an unrealistic ideal of a tension-free legal system. In this regard, accepting coherence as a central value in the legal system does not prevent us recognizing that EU law is a result of both linguistic and political compromises

175 Moral Soriano 2003: 297.

176 Moral Soriano 2003: 300.

177 Moral Soriano 2003: 305.

reflecting different and often competing ideologies and interests of perpetually changing political forces that govern the EU.[178]

In fact, the 'modest notion of coherence' referring to the coherence of arguments is based on correctness of legal adjudication; that is, on correctness of reasoning which may be seen as an element gradually enhancing the legitimacy – or even coherence – of the system as a whole.[179] Belonging to the world of rhetoric, judicial reasoning is not a matter of proving the truth or falseness of a given decision: rather, it is a question of claiming that the reasoning and the arguments are correct.

This claim of correctness is interrelated with a claim of justifiability. On the one hand, judicial reasoning is a rational activity that aims at giving reasons to support the *legal correctness* of a given decision. Thus, the decision must be justified according to valid law, valid legal arguments. However, this is not sufficient. On the other hand, legal decisions must be perceived as correct; that is, they must be in accordance with what is perceived as rational – but also fair (and substantially right) – in the legal community in question.[180] This reveals the link between internal coherence of judgments and substantive legal certainty: to justify and convince the legal community in question of the correctness of an outcome in a particular case, the given arguments must form a coherent unit. Put differently, judicial decisions are coherent if arguments provided in the judgment to justify the chosen interpretation form a coherent unit. Coherence in judicial reasoning does not, therefore, depend on whether a particular ruling fits into the legal system taken as a whole.[181]

Two aspects of correctness in legal adjudication can be identified. Firstly, a judicial decision is correct if it is justified in accordance with valid law (legal quality of arguments). Secondly, and perhaps most importantly from the viewpoint of substantive legal certainty, a judicial decision is correct if it fulfils the requirement of rationality or fairness.[182] Hence, judicial reasoning amounts in fact to giving reasons to support the correctness of a given ruling. The connection between the correctness of a decision and coherence is clear: arguments given to support the decision must form a coherent chain or net of reasons. This bottom-up understanding of coherence, focusing on whether the reasoning offers coherent supportive structures of arguments and establishes nets or cumulative chains of reasons, explains why the quality of judicial reasoning should be taken seriously for ensuring substantive acceptability.

Clearly, this notion of coherence is closely linked to case-by-case judicial decision-making: it does not provide a definitive answer as to the weight of

178 Bertea 2005a: 158–159. See also Raz 1994: 298 for criticism of the idealizing use of coherence in the context of law that separates law from politics.

179 Moral Soriano 2003: 306.

180 Aarnio 1987: 4.

181 Moral Soriano 2003: 307.

182 Cf. Peczenik 1995: 94.

colliding reasons (that is, norms, values, rights and policies), because evaluation is closely related to the particularities of a given case.[183] It adapts to a pluralistic and multilingual legal system that is constantly evolving. Additionally, it does not undermine value pluralism, a central feature of the EU's pluralistic legal system.[184] A case exists that in applying this internal approach to coherence that takes as its starting point coherence of reasoning in individual cases, it is possible to reconcile value pluralism and coherence: the balancing of different values and goals is done on a case-by-case basis.

However, the modest notion of coherence does require that a priority order between reasons is articulated in individual cases.[185] This, in turn, is related to the systemic understanding by the ECJ of its decision. Arguably, this understanding shapes the Court's reasoning. Through articulation of value choices and a priority order between reasons given for a specific interpretive solution, the ECJ may be argued to provide a constitutional interpretation of the Treaties and of the EU legal system.[186]

Policy arguments are of particular importance, as the teleological method of interpretation used by the Court suggests.[187] Indeed, precisely because of the importance of purposes in the Court's reasoning, it has often been accused (and found guilty) of inappropriate (negative) judicial activism.[188] Forming a justification that satisfies the imperatives of coherent judicial reasoning requires that the ECJ give a comprehensive account of the reasons on which the decision has been based. If coherence is analyzed in terms of reasoning, it displays the uneasy foundation on which criticism concerning judicial activism is based: policy arguments must be taken into account and connected to other arguments from rights and values. Hence, what is important is not the kind of reasons used to justify a decision – either authority or substantive – but rather evaluating whether they are coherently connected.[189]

183 Cf. Dworkin 1977: 90–94.

184 Moral Soriano 2003: 307, 321.

185 Moral Soriano 2003: 315.

186 Maduro 2007, Itzcovich 2009.

187 C-376/11, *Pie Optiek*, not yet reported, paras 33–37. See also case 327/82, *Ekro* [1984] ECR 107, case C-287/98, *Linster* [2000] ECR I-6917, and case C-190/10, *Génesis*, not yet reported. See also Campana 2000: 38 *et seq*.

188 See *e.g.* Rasmussen 1986, Phelan 1997. See also Cartabia 2007: 6 *et seq*. Cf. Sankari 2011, Craig 2012: for synthesis 11–12. In short, Craig argues that the ECJ is only one among several factors that have contributed to the expansion over time of EU powers – a worry for many who criticize the ECJ for judicial activism. The reality of EU competence has resulted from symbiotic interaction between four different elements: Member State choice as to the scope of EU competence; Member State acceptance – and since the SEA, EP acceptance – of legislation developed on the basis of Treaty articles; the jurisprudence of Community courts; and finally, decisions taken by the institutions as to how to interpret, deploy and prioritize the power accorded to the EU.

189 Moral Soriano 2003: 308–309. See also Bengoetxea *et al.* 2001: 82–83.

Certainly, continuous conflicts of reasons occur in judicial adjudication at the Court, not only between legal norms and rights but also between community values and goals: although sometimes incommensurable – such as environmental protection and free movement of goods – they need to be balanced in a rational way in judicial decision-making.[190] Indeed, both can be posited at the very core of EU constitutionalism.[191] The existence of conflicting and in principle non-hierarchical values results in a balancing exercise in adjudication. Because the Court does not apply an 'all-or-nothing' approach to rights, these have to be balanced against other rights and goals related to a given case in order to determine their weight in the case at hand. To be sure, taking account of the elusive value-basis on which the Treaty system is built, it would be difficult to determine any absolute order between conflicting values, principles and policies. Therefore, the modest notion of coherence cannot be employed to determine a systematic order among values and goals as it does not impose a hierarchical order among them, but rather is used as a tool for measuring the internal coherence among reasons which are given to justify the decision that has been made.[192]

Reasons: comprehensiveness

In her account of coherence in the realm of judicial reasoning, Moral Soriano observes that ideally, in order to reach coherence of arguments and to persuade the Court's audience, the supportive structure of reasons should contain a cumulative net – or chain – of reasons which give strong support to the decision. Further, where more than one reason (*e.g.* principles or policies) applies to the case, a priority order between those reasons must be established.[193] This means that in judicial reasoning, emphasis should be placed on including as many justifying elements as possible in the judgment: a comprehensive account of reasons (at the same time bearing in mind that justification must eventually stop somewhere). In fact, from the viewpoint of coherence in judicial reasoning, the quality of these reasons – be they primarily authority or substantive reasons – is irrelevant as long as they are coherently connected.[194] More often than not, coherence in judicial reasoning requires both authority and substantive reasons.

EU environmental law offers a fruitful example of a field of law where contradictions among different values occupy a central position. More particularly, contradictory objectives and values are constantly brought to the fore in cases before the Court which require balancing between free movement of goods and environmental protection. While the latter has only gradually infiltrated the core of the EU legal system, the former has traditionally benefited from preferential treatment as one of the foundational principles of EU integration.

190 Bengoetxea *et al.* 2001: 65.

191 Case C-28/09, *Commission v Austria*, not yet reported.

192 Bengoetxea *et al.* 2001: 79.

193 Moral Soriano 2003: 311–317. Cf. Peczenik 1989: 163 *et seq.*

194 Moral Soriano 2003: 309.

In *ABDHU*,[195] the question put to the Court was whether a system of permits for shipment of waste oils established in accordance with Directive 75/439/EEC,[196] concerning disposal of waste oils, was compatible with the principles of free movement of goods, free trade and free competition. Although environmental protection was not at the time mentioned in the Treaties and it was unclear whether the environment belonged to Community competence, the Court held that the restrictions caused to the free movement of goods were justified on the grounds of environmental protection.[197]

Viewed objectively, the ECJ had two options. It could apply interests recognized in the system of the Treaties; that is, essentially economic rights. Alternatively, it could balance these with other values that were not legally recognized, at least from the point of view of EU law.[198] The fact that the Court opted for the latter posed a further problem. Namely, the structure of its reasoning:

> 12. In the first place it should be observed that the principle of freedom of trade is not to be viewed in absolute terms but is subject to certain limits justified by the objectives of general interest pursued by the Community provided that the rights in question are not substantively impaired.
>
> 13. There is no reason to conclude that the directive has exceeded those limits. The directive must be seen in the perspective of environmental protection, which is one of the Community's essential objectives. [...]

Although the first premise (relative character of the principle of freedom of trade) supports the second premise (environmental protection as one of the Community's essential objectives), we can detect a problem from the standpoint of deduction because the latter does not follow from the former. As Moral Soriano observes, the connection between premises and their mutual support could have been reinforced by fleshing out other premises 'supporting either the desirability of environmental protection as a goal or by its desirability as a means'.[199]

The primary reasons referred to in justifying the decision can be categorized as policy arguments. Here, principles and policies are employed as interlocking reasons with no predetermined order of importance.[200] Both are particularly useful because of their capacity to open up decisions for discussion as to the desirability of the chosen interpretation. In this respect, they mirror rights and values. When using policy arguments as well as arguments from principles, connections have

195 Case 240/83, *ABDHU* [1985] ECR 531.

196 Council Directive 75/439/EEC of 16 June 1975 on the disposal of waste oils (OJ 1975 L 194, p. 23).

197 Case 240/83, *ABDHU* [1985] ECR 531, especially paras 12–13. See *e.g.* Ojanen 2003: 195–196 for a brief overview of environmental protection in the EU.

198 Moral Soriano 2003: 309.

199 Moral Soriano 2003: 312.

200 MacCormick 1994: 261.

to be elaborated between them in order to create the necessary support and justification for the decision.

In *ABDHU*, it is difficult to distinguish between rights and policies. Both environmental protection and free movement of goods can be categorized as policies, especially at the time of the decision.[201] As in other cases where the Court has been asked to balance environmental protection and free movement, a number of reasons must be taken into account in the process of justification: sustainable development, the right to a healthy environment, the principles of legality and legal certainty, and the rights of economic actors. In order to assure coherence in judicial reasoning, policy arguments are of particular importance, since they combine authority and substantive reasons. Expressed in the form of teleological reasoning, they are of particular significance in explicating the Court's normative understanding of the foundations of the EU legal system.

In this context, Moral Soriano suggests that when the ECJ is confronted with conflicting reasons, authority reasons as well as substantive reasons are necessary. However, to assure coherence in judicial reasoning, it is not sufficient to give a comprehensive account of reasons to justify a particular decision if they do not constitute a supportive structure for the outcome. But at the same time, it must be underlined that this does not entail never-ending reasoning: it needs to remain in the realm of the legal, *i.e.* use of arguments that are *legally* relevant, not every possible argument that might justify the decision. Indeed, even providing separate chains of (legal) reasons may be problematic and weaken the justification. As Moral Soriano observes, judicial 'justification is a matter of connecting reasons. Two chains of reasons mirror a more coherent legal justification only if the given chains are connected. Otherwise, one of the chains is superfluous and part of the justification redundant'.[202]

In essence, the claim is that although policy arguments related to the desirability of environmental protection were given in the decision and these were weighed against the fundamental freedoms of the EU legal system, the Court gave no indication as to why environmental considerations belonged to Community competence in the first place or as to the reasons for including environmental protection in Community competence.

Therefore, in connection with the *ABDHU* case, it appears realistic to say that taking different reasons comprehensively into account is not sufficient to enhance coherence in judicial reasoning. In addition, a supportive structure must exist in order to tie these arguments together and to the surrounding legal system. This supportive structure is based on a coherent chain of arguments, thus supporting the interpretive solution that strikes a balance between conflicting values and goals, rights and policies.

201 For recent case law, see case C-28/09, *Commission v Austria*, not yet reported.

202 Moral Soriano 2003: 314.

Reasons: support

A supportive structure requires the existence of connections between the reasons deployed for the purposes of justification. However, it is not sufficient to establish a connection between reasons and the final outcome. From the standpoint of coherence, the way these arguments are connected together is also important. To demonstrate, the well-known *Walloon waste*[203] case – also connected to the delicate area of balancing between fundamental freedoms and environmental protection – can be taken as an example of a decision justified by strong support of arguments. In that case, the Court followed its established case law in the field of free movement of goods, holding that mandatory requirements based on the Court's *Cassis*[204] case law such as environmental protection – as opposed to justification grounds governed by now Article 36 TFEU – can justify derogations from free movement of goods as long as the measure in question is non-discriminatory. Interestingly, however, the measure at issue was clearly discriminatory (prohibition of importing waste oils to the Walloon Region). Despite the discriminatory nature of the national measure, the Court held that the measure in question was justifiable under the mandatory requirement of environmental protection. The following extract demonstrates:

> 32. It follows that the argument that the contested measures were justified by imperative requirements of environmental protection must be considered to be well founded.
>
> 33. The Commission argues, however, that those imperative requirements cannot be relied upon in the present case, given that the measures in question discriminate against waste originating in other Member States, which is no more harmful than waste produced in Wallonia.
>
> 34. Imperative requirements can indeed be taken into account only in the case of measures which apply without distinction to both domestic and imported products […]. However, in assessing whether or not the barrier in question is discriminatory, account must be taken of the particular nature of waste. The principle that environmental damage should as a matter of priority be remedied at source, laid down by Article 130r (2) of the Treaty as a basis for action by the Community relating to the environment, entails that it is for each region, municipality or other local authority to take appropriate steps to ensure that its own waste is collected, treated and disposed of; it must accordingly be disposed of as close as possible to the place where it is produced, in order to limit as far as possible the transport of waste.
>
> […]
>
> 36. It follows that having regard to the differences between waste produced in different places and to the connection of the waste with its place of production, the contested measures cannot be regarded as discriminatory.

203 C-2/90, *Commission v Belgium* [1990] ECR I-4431.

204 Case 120/78, *Rewe-Zentral AG* [1979] ECR 649.

In connection to this case, Moral Soriano maintains that despite a logical 'jump' in the Court's reasoning ('discriminatory limitations of shipment of waste comply with EC legislation' does not follow logically from the premise 'environmental protection may justify limitations of free movement of goods, provided that the measure is proportional and non-discriminatory'),[205] the ECJ managed to create strong support for its decision through elaboration of sets of premises from which the reasoning follows logically.[206]

However, elaborating supportive premises to create a supportive structure for the decision seems neither sufficient nor predictable (which arguments are considered relevant) when examined in the light of its systemic context. Indeed, even when analyzing the internal coherence of a judgment, we never quite manage to escape from the constraints of the system. Although objectively the discriminatory nature of the measure is difficult to deny, the Court held that notwithstanding appearances, this was not the case and allowed justification under the mandatory requirement of environmental protection. Certainly, to compensate for the lack of consistency in its deductive reasoning, the Court referred to a set of other legally strong and value-laden premises. These were the nature of waste as goods, the environmental aim of the measure and the principle according to which environmental damage should be remedied at source which is consistent with the principles of self-sufficiency and proximity enshrined in international law. These arguments form strong support for the outcome so that it partly remedies the breach. Nevertheless, this does not make the systemically significant logical inconsistency disappear.

More particularly, the inconsistency is intimately bound up with a systemic aspect of the decision. That is, the unclarity relates to the juxtaposition between distinct justification grounds expressly mentioned in now Article 36 TFEU and those developed in the Court's case law (the *Cassis* justification grounds that do not enjoy express support from the Treaties). Confusion is induced by the Court's silence with regard to the reason for deviating from established case law concerning the scope of application of mandatory requirements capable of justifying restrictions on free movement of goods, environmental protection being one of those requirements.[207]

More particularly, the fallacy relates to the absence of an enunciated nexus between the nature of waste, environmental principles and the potentially discriminatory character of a measure. If one endeavours to maintain the distinction between different grounds of justification, AG Jacobs' analysis appears more accurate:

205 Moral Soriano 2003: 312.

206 Moral Soriano 2003: 312–313.

207 Cf. para 24 of AG Jacobs' Opinion of 19 September 1991.

> 24. Applying those principles, it seems to me that at least some restrictions on the transfer of waste could be justified on environmental grounds. Since environmental protection is a mandatory requirement not mentioned in Article 36, any such measure would however have to be indistinctly applicable to domestic and foreign waste. [That] condition may not be satisfied by a measure which simply restricts the use of the waste disposal facilities of a particular region or locality to waste produced in that locality or region. A provision of that type clearly favours domestically produced waste, especially where [...] exceptions may be made in the case of waste coming from other regions of the same Member State. Hence, in the circumstances of the present case, the measures in issue cannot be justified on grounds of environmental protection. In contrast, a provision applying throughout a region of a Member State, requiring waste to be disposed of within its locality of generation, might be said to be indistinctly applicable. Such a provision would prevent the exportation of locally produced waste to another locality or another Member State in exactly the same way that it prevented the disposal of waste coming from another State or locality. Such a measure might moreover be justified in terms of the need to reduce the amount of waste in transit and to limit the areas used for waste disposal. Whether or not the measure was in fact proportionate to those objectives could of course only be decided in the light of all the relevant circumstances.

Certainly, the Court's subsequent case law denotes willingness to allow environmental protection to be pleaded without close inquiry into the diverging rationales of Article 36 TFEU and the *Cassis* grounds.[208] Indeed, in cases such as *Aher-Waggon*,[209] *PreussenElektra*,[210] and most recently *Brenner Heavy Lorries*,[211] a similar approach has been employed by the Court; it has applied the *Cassis* ground of environmental protection to measures whose discriminatory nature cannot at the outset be excluded. In fact, as early as in *PreussenElektra*, AG Jacobs criticized the Court's approach in *Walloon waste*, observing that from a logical standpoint, determining the discriminatory nature of a measure is a preliminary and neutral step deployed to determine the applicable justification ground and not to assess the appropriateness of the measure at issue.[212]

Although the contours of these grounds are now far from clear-cut, a contextually and systemically reasoned prescription for understanding the role of environmental protection as a justification for measures obstructing trade between Member States would be that the overriding requirement of environmental protection must be read in conjunction with environmental principles expressed

---

208 Case C-463/01, *Commission v Germany* [2004] ECR I-11705, para 75, Case C-320/03, *Commission v Austria* [2005] ECR I-9871, para 119.

209 Case C-389/96, *Aher-Waggon* [1998] ECR I-4473.

210 Case C-379/98, *PreussenElektra* [2001] ECR I-2099.

211 Case C-28/09, *Commission v Austria*, not yet reported.

212 Paras 225 and 233 of AG Jacobs' opinion.

in now Article 191 TFEU. As in *Walloon waste*, they form a recurrent element in the Court's reasoning in the field.[213] However, from the perspective of internal coherence, the fact that EU environmental principles lie at the core of European constitutionalism as enshrined in the Treaties is unhelpful insofar as the nexus between those principles and the chosen interpretive standpoint is not explicated. To enhance internal coherence of the justification further, it might have been useful to draw arguments from the growing importance of environmental protection as an EU policy (goal) and to expressly discuss the requirements that should govern the use of different justification grounds and, essentially, answer the question: does discrimination matter?

More particularly, the *Walloon waste* case also illustrates the central role of principles in ECJ judicial reasoning. As Bengoetxea, Moral Soriano and MacCormick observe, principles as commands to optimize offer 'directions to perform an optimal weighing and balancing of colliding principles and policies rather than criteria that provide a clear and ultimate solution'.[214] It might in fact be argued that employing principles as commands to optimize (depending on the circumstances, principles of proportionality, equality, legal certainty and effectiveness may be used in this manner as well) in judicial reasoning contributes to its internal coherence: they act 'as balancing criteria, [...] criteria which rationalize the process of evaluating the weight of reasons in particular cases without imposing or determining the outcome'.[215]

In this respect, referring to principles (and policies) in justifying decisions raises a crucial question of time, of historicity and temporality of interpretation.[216] Put simply, it is possible that at a given point in time the priority order established by the Court between reasons differs from the priority order achieved at a different point in time. In other words, time influences both the perception of the universal – that is, rules and principles – and that of the particular, the features of the case.[217]

In this respect, the imperative of coherence in judicial reasoning takes account of time as an important aspect in a legal system. Consequently, a judicial decision may be coherent at one time whereas at a different point in time it may be considered incoherent because new rules and principles have become part of the legal system. However, not only normative changes, but also new factual circumstances come into play when we analyze the relevance of certain policies and principles: if a particular feature of a case was irrelevant at a previous point in time, the same feature may become relevant later on when the factual situation has changed.[218]

213 Raitio 2010: 385. See also para 233 of AG Jacobs's opinion in case C-379/98, *PreussenElektra* [2001] ECR I-2099.

214 Bengoetxea *et al.* 2001: 81.

215 Moral Soriano 2003: 316. See also Bengoetxea *et al.* 2001: 67.

216 Cf. Tontti 2004: 101 *et seq*. See also Ojanen 2003 on changing times in case law.

217 Moral Soriano 2003: 321.

218 Moral Soriano 2003: 321. See also Bengoetxea *et al.* 2001: 45.

A justification that does not consider environmental protection in the 1970s does not appear incoherent in relation to what is known about the political and socio-legal situation in that particular period.[219] But when the *Walloon waste* case was decided, both the legal and the political and social environment had changed, so that not giving environmental protection (permeation of environmental principles in all areas of EU law as codified by the Treaties) considerable weight in reasoning would have been incoherent with regard to the evolutionary narrative of the EU legal system.

Limiting the reach of coherence to judicial reasoning accepts that value choices are continuously made in adjudication. More importantly, it makes evaluating those choices rationally possible. Free movement might be given preference over fundamental rights at one point in time. The interrelationship between these values and whether they are considered relevant at one point in time rather than another are choices that are closely connected to values underlying the legal system at a particular point in time.[220] Choosing a particular priority order among those values must be justified by reasons that connect to the values of the legal community in question. In this respect, the development of environmental protection in the EU serves as an interesting example because it highlights the existence of a connection between a system of beliefs and law.[221]

Here, two factors are required in reasoning: the system of values and beliefs must be arranged coherently and reasons must be given to support the choices made. This view comes close to Aarnio's thesis on rational argumentation in law. On this understanding, the interpretive choice must be justified both by legal interpretive criteria and more general, rational arguments.[222] Depicting a holistic view of judicial reasoning, Aarnio's thesis claims that the justificatory force of reasons can only be examined as a whole, not separately.[223] The justificatory force of reasons and their coherence is thus also case-dependent.[224]

Reasons: telos *and system*

As noted above, the modest notion of coherence is particularly useful for present purposes because it adapts to value pluralism without requiring commitment to a limited set of values. As a rapidly evolving legal system that flexibly adapts to the needs of society, EU law is construed on diverging, sometimes even colliding values, principles and policies between which the ECJ must strike a balance.

219 See Ojanen 2003: 183–184 on changes in law and the surrounding socio-political environment that have an impact on case law.

220 Moral Soriano 2003: 320.

221 Paunio 2012: 199–202.

222 Aarnio 1987: 198–201.

223 Nuotio 2003: 158.

224 See Paso 2009 for an analysis of ECJ reasoning from the standpoint of rhetorical analysis. Essentially, Paso argues that ECJ argumentation is too often based on authority reasons that do not guarantee rational acceptability of decisions.

As briefly suggested above, the internal coherence of a given judgment (coherence of proposed justification) cannot be fully separated from the external coherence of that ruling. External coherence refers to (a coherent) connection between a specific case and its wider systemic context. Judicial decisions are read in context: the Court's audience situates ECJ judgments in the context of the EU legal system, since understanding is – as Gadamer's description of prejudice[225] suggests – always based on subjective preconceptions and previous experiences.

Thus, evaluating the internal coherence of a judgment is necessarily bound up with the way it is connected to the legal system surrounding it. In this respect, internal coherence is also closely tied to predictable reasoning: not only must the arguments used to justify a specific decision be transparent, they must also be predictable from the viewpoint of the legal system in which the judgment is given. That is, the arguments given to support the decision must be acceptable and, in the context of that particular legal system, in accordance with the accepted method of judicial interpretation. This is why decisions in which the ECJ departs from earlier case law are of particular interest: substantive acceptability requires that such interpretive choices are justified in a way that makes the decision fit into their systemic context. Arguments satisfying these requirements are those that overtly express the underlying normative assumptions and objectives that have affected the outcome in the case.

For Dworkin, the idea of coherence is related to the metaphor of judicial decision-making as a chain novel. Coherence in the systemic (global) sense requires that judicial decisions are justified by reasons that include the pragmatic property of constituting a rationally motivated agreement among participants in argumentation. This agreement may be reached by substantive arguments.[226] Further, drawing from Dworkin's understanding of judicial decision-making based on a rational reconstruction of the legal system and its underlying principles, one might suggest that reasoning which articulates guiding principles and policies (as interlocking reasons) may in fact also enhance coherence in the systemic sense.[227] Coherence does not exist *ex ante* as a result of the political process of law-making. Rather, it can be established *ex post* in the Court's case law.

Coherent and predictable reasoning may partly attenuate impairment caused to predictability (clarity and stability) by the reflexivity that is necessary in the dynamic and multilingual EU legal system.[228] While ECJ judicial reasoning in a given case can be regarded as coherent in the 'modest' sense of the term, legal certainty – substantive acceptability – cannot be ensured without some degree of coherence between different parts of the whole (field of law or the whole legal system).

225 Gadamer 2006: 277 *et seq.*
226 See Habermas 1998: 211 *et seq.*
227 Bengoetxea *et al.* 2001: 65.
228 Moral Soriano 2003: 308.

This is why the Court's teleological narrative, which openly considers the goals and purposes guiding the decision-making process, can be argued to be of particular significance. In fact, through (meta-)teleological reasoning that makes explicit the systemic consequences and articulates the constraints that the relevant purposes set on the Court's understanding of the law, individual cases are bound to the wider context of the legal system, to the 'entire constitutional enterprise'.[229] Put differently, meta-teleological reasoning ties the Court to its view of the legal system and limits the interpretive possibilities available to it in particular cases. That is, not only should the reasoning in a given case cohere and be rational, it should also be consistent with previous case law as to balancing of given interests. If this is not the case, more supportive arguments (principles and policies which cumulate and form nets) for the chosen interpretive direction are called for.

In relation to the importance of searching for coherence in EU law, Bertea asserts that coherence should in fact be considered a fundamental, albeit not absolute, value in every legal system, for it relates to the idea that the system has to make sense as a whole. This quest is particularly relevant in the EU context where Raz's description of law as a 'higgledypiggledy assemblage of the remains of contradictory past political ambitions and beliefs' rings true.[230] It is 'a hodgepodge of norms derived from the conflicting ideologies and the pragmatic necessities which prevailed from time to time over the many years of evolution'.[231] Seen from this perspective, the Court's reasoning reveals an attempt to impose order on EU law provisions and transform different threads of this legal system into a coherent whole that stays together and, in Dworkin's terms, speaks with one voice.[232]

Although an attempt to define the EU legal system in accordance with three principles, such as those used by Dworkin in his theory of integrity (justice, fairness and procedural due process)[233] seems a futile exercise, the imperative of internal coherence endeavours to ensure that value choices and a priority order among reasons are articulated in ECJ reasoning. In order for argumentation to be coherent, it must follow the established constitutional reading by the ECJ of the relevant provisions.[234] Or, equally, when the Court's systemic understanding changes with regard to priority order among reasons, this change must be accordingly stated. This is intimately bound up with the imperative of transparency.

229 Bengoetxea *et al.* 2001: 45.

230 Raz 1994: 280.

231 Raz 1994: 281. Similarly Jääskinen 2008: 148, who refers to Hayek 1973: 11–13, 40–41.

232 Bertea 2005a: 170, Bengoetxea *et al.* 2001: 48 and 82–85, on the connection between coherence and integration.

233 Dworkin 1986: 225 *et seq.*

234 Maduro 2007: especially 8. For some, the driving value in the Court's case law is integration. See, in this respect, Bengoetxea *et al.* 2001: 82–85 and Bertea 2005a: 170.

A case exists that coherence of judicial reasoning promotes legal certainty in its substantive form. However, it constitutes a 'criterialess criterion'[235] that does not definitively resolve the tension between competing interpretations. Nor does it answer the question of how different principles, policies, interests and values should be balanced in legal adjudication at a given point in time: looking at coherence in judicial reasoning in individual cases accepts that a great number of values and goals which are incommensurable exist in the legal system so that conflicts between them form an inescapable aspect of judicial decision-making.[236] It does not hide the possibility of colliding interpretations which can be reached on the basis of principles deployed as balancing criteria to weigh colliding goals.

In this respect, legal certainty is 'both law and valuation, or rational and reasonable'.[237] Importantly, while coherence in judicial reasoning undoubtedly does little if anything for legal certainty as formal predictability in that it does not resolve the argumentative character of law (it remains open to argument on the basis of principles and policies), it appears realistic to say that coherence forms a prerequisite for substantive legal certainty since it not only ensures that procedural rules that regulate the decision-making process must be followed and that formal legal sources are taken into account, it also expresses values in judicial decision-making. In other words, while procedural rules cannot determine the types of argument employed, the imperative of internal coherence ensures that value choices are balanced and articulated in justification.[238] In this sense, internal coherence requires 'both procedure and substance'.[239]

Summing up

This chapter explored different meanings attributed to the concept of legal certainty in the context of EU law. The principle encompasses different, even opposing notions: stability and flexibility. These notions are intimately bound up with two central elements of legal certainty: predictability and acceptability.

First, reconstruction of the Court's case law suggests that the principle of legal certainty primarily functions as a command to optimize, as a criterion for determining the mutual weight of colliding reasons in cases brought before the Court. Although also employed as a directly applicable principle, legal certainty generally inhabits the realm of interpretive principles that guide the Court in its

235 Moral Soriano 2003: 320.

236 Moral Soriano 2003: 305.

237 Moral Soriano 2003: 320. For Aulis Aarnio, the outcome of the procedure must be 'right', Aarnio 1997: 191. For Alexander Peczenik, the result must be 'morally acceptable', Peczenik 1989: 257. See also Habermas 1998: 198, who highlights the importance of rational acceptability of judicial decision-making.

238 Bengoetxea *et al.* 2001: 50.

239 Moral Soriano 2003: 320.

interpretive task. The Court's perception of legal certainty is a relativist one: considerations of legal certainty may give way to other considerations such as that of legality or effectiveness. A brief perusal of the Court's case law illustrates that the principle of legal certainty is intimately bound up with the need to guarantee predictability and stability; with the foundational need to stabilize expectations and legal relations.

In that context, the principle not only relates to the imperative that individuals must be able to ascertain unequivocally what their rights and obligations are and take steps accordingly; it also possesses an important procedural facet which emerges in cases concerning the significance of time limits and *res judicata* for the purposes of stabilizing legal relations. Indeed, although multilingualism may realistically be argued to undermine predictability (clarity) so that its relative nature is highlighted, it appears that predictability is of particular significance on the procedural plane: it sets limits on decision-making and requires that procedural guarantees are given due consideration.

Viewed in a different light, legal certainty – predictability – may be argued to operate as a meta-principle, as a principle with which the Court justifies interpretive choices in a given case. Essentially, this implies that legal certainty may be employed to support contradictory outcomes. On this view, legal certainty is understood as a means of justifying a certain outcome or interpretive choice, not as a substantive principle; indeed, it rarely dictates a specific outcome in itself. Rather, it forms a conceptual aid in the context of judicial reasoning taken as whole. From this viewpoint, legal certainty might in fact be said to represent a tool with which the ECJ justifies its normative understanding of the underlying values of the EU legal system.

Secondly, legal certainty may also be analyzed from the perspective of judicial reasoning. Legal certainty is thus no longer approached as a principle applied in judicial decision-making, but as a background principle that resides on the law's sub-levels. Here, considerations related to substantive legal certainty, to acceptability, come into play. While formal legal certainty may be said to require that rights and obligations resulting from EU law are precise and clear, substantive legal certainty emphasizes the soundness, the acceptability of the judicial decision in question.

A precondition for substantive acceptability is the requirement of predictable reasoning. Taking account of the relativist nature of predictability (clarity and stability), certainty can be achieved on a higher level if judicial reasoning fulfils certain criteria of transparency, consistency and coherence. Predictable reasoning thus requires transparency of arguments and a degree of consistency as to use of pre-established interpretive criteria accepted by the legal community in question. To that extent, predictable reasoning also contributes to stabilizing procedural expectations in the context of judicial adjudication.

Although conceptually independent, the imperative of predictability in judicial reasoning possesses a close linkage with the internal coherence of reasoning. Instead of trying to fit colliding legal materials under a set of values or principles, the 'modest' notion of coherence explains what internal coherence of the justification offered by the Court for its ruling requires. Internal coherence requires both establishing a comprehensive account of reasons (use of principles and policies as interlocking reasons) and elaborating supportive premises to create a supportive structure for the ruling.

In this sense, the perspective of individual decisions highlights the virtues of teleological reasoning. Although internal coherence does not resolve the problem of competing interpretations, it forms a prerequisite for substantive legal certainty. This is because it not only ensures that procedural rules that govern the decision-making process are followed and that formal legal sources are taken into account, it also emphasizes the importance of articulating value choices in Judicial reasoning.

Chapter 3
Discourse and legal certainty

Communicative underpinnings of legal certainty

This chapter fleshes out the pronounced status of judicial reasoning in conceptualizing legal certainty as a systemic principle in the present multilingual context. In essence, it asserts that substantive acceptability can only be achieved through discursive communication, through judicial reasoning.

Communication denotes 'intentional transmission of information by means of some established signalling system'.[1] It belongs to the realm of 'interaction that is symbolically structured on the basis of conventionally determined rules of meaning'.[2] It forms a practice for 'producing meanings' and provides 'ways in which systems of meaning are negotiated by participants in a culture'.[3]

Here, in the context of judicial decision-making, the specific form of communication expressed in discourse on legal meaning among legal actors is of particular significance. It refers to considering different points of view and to a dialectical exchange of ideas and viewpoints. A rational dialogue among legal actors offers a tool for ensuring acceptable interpretations and adjudication in the context of law.[4] For present purposes, the dialectic relationship between national courts and the ECJ in the context of the preliminary ruling procedure is of particular relevance.

Taking this discursive turn necessarily implies that language becomes a focal part of the analysis. Language is discourse, a broader communicative practice of a specific social group, not limited to a stable system of symbols.[5] More particularly, discourse depends on and affects the social contexts in which it is used: what is and can be said is determined by the social embedding of discourse.[6] However, this social context does not remain stable: discourse itself contributes to redefining and changing the context. Importantly, therefore, language use impacts

1 Lyons 1977: 32.

2 Habermas 1987.

3 Shirato and Yell 2000: 1.

4 Van Hoecke 2002: 7–8.

5 See *e.g.* Fairclough 1992: 4. Fairclough defines discourse in terms of 'discursive events'. These events are, in different terms, instances of discourse, which simultaneously embody a piece of text, an instance of discursive practice and a manifestation of social practice.

6 Fairclough and Wodak 1997: 258.

on the knowledge base of those participating in discourse, on their concepts and conceptions about the world.[7]

Judicial adjudication is a product of legal discourse that occurs through a process whereby written legal texts are interpreted and applied by legal actors as part of legal practices in which they take part (such as adjudication).[8] In the legal sphere, where the legal system in question forms the context in which discourse takes place, legal discourse both mirrors the features of the legal system and contributes to revising them. In this respect, legal discourse both reproduces and transforms legal systems.[9]

According to this view, judicial reasoning shapes the legal system by contributing to changing the way words and concepts are employed within a specific legal community, within a legal system. Importantly, therefore, as was noted in Chapter 1 in relation to interpretative techniques employed by the Court, words, expressions and broader textual units used in legal texts do not exist on their own, independent of the context in which they are *employed.* Their meaning depends on the way legal actors interpret and apply these texts and on the discourses in which they are used.[10] Legal actors participating in EU legal discourse have their background in different legal systems and speak different languages. However, these national languages and legal systems do not remain fixed and unchangeable: on the contrary, both are constantly reinterpreted and remoulded in *EU legal discourse.*[11] It is argued that this occurs, in particular, through the Court's influence on meaning construction on a pan-European scale.

Since language forms a context-sensitive means of communication, the role of actors in communication is highlighted: to shed light on how this transformation process functions, emphasis in the following is placed on discourse among legal actors and, most importantly, on discourse among the ECJ and national courts that daily apply EU legislation. The ECJ and national courts engage in 'judicial dialogue'.[12] This dialogue turns on the question of correct meaning of EU law provisions and consequently on the acceptability of adjudication, on substantive legal certainty. From a discursive standpoint, the meaning of multilingual EU law, which emerges in judicial decision-making, is the result of a complex interplay between texts, context and discourse. Through this interplay, EU judicial dialogue contributes to moulding and reshaping the EU legal system.

---

7 Kjær 2004: 391.

8 Weigand 2008: 236.

9 Kjær 2004: 393.

10 Kjær 2008a: 257.

11 Kjær 2008a: 262.

12 Rosas 2007a: 4. See also Chalmers 2004: 34–35, Davies 2012a: 78 *et seq*., Sarmiento 2012: 286.

Discursiveness of law and legal certainty

This underlying idea of communication may be traced back to Habermas' theory of communicative action.[13] Functioning as the basis for his understanding of law, this theory is based on the idea that actors in a particular society seek to reach a common understanding and to coordinate actions by reasoned argument, consensus and cooperation rather than strategic action that strictly aims at realizing the participants' own goals.[14] Based on a distinction between two concepts of rationality that shape knowledge and guide action, the concept 'communicative action' is deployed to demonstrate that inter-subjective agreement may be reached with regard to norms and values. However, because no such thing as objective truth can be discerned, the key to this consensus lies in discourse.[15]

Of particular interest here is what is framed as communicative rationality. It underlies action that, unlike strategic or instrumental action, is aimed at mutual understanding, and is conceived as a process of reaching agreement among language users to harmonize their interpretations of the surrounding world; it is discourse oriented towards understanding.[16] Rationality is, therefore, something that does not exist independently, but must be negotiated by communicating with others.[17]

However, although the search for agreement is emphasized here, agreement does not form the necessary outcome of all communicative processes. As Williams observes, disagreement does not necessarily need to be overcome: it may remain an important and constitutive feature of interpersonal relationships.[18] Indeed, the search for agreement does not as such exclude the possibility of dissent as the result of distorted or unresolved communication.[19] It is only through language, and further, under conditions of rational argumentation, that social actors can coordinate their actions in order to reach mutual understanding.[20]

Law is legitimated on the basis of the discourse principle in justification discourse by voluntary, inter-subjective agreement among all those affected. The law can then be impartially applied in application discourse through the principle of appropriateness.[21] Here, the principle of discourse ethics is of particular significance as it requires that for norms to be valid, they should be capable of

13 Habermas 1984.

14 Habermas 1984: 22 *et seq.*

15 Habermas 1998: 166–167.

16 Habermas 1998: 3–4.

17 Van Hoecke 2002: 9.

18 Williams 1985: 133.

19 Sunstein 1996: 58. Cf. Stone Sweet 2004.

20 Habermas 1984: 319–328. For an introduction to the theory of communicative action Deflem 1996.

21 Habermas 1998: 222–236.

meeting 'with the approval of all affected in their capacity as participants in a practical discourse'.[22]

Whereas a rationally motivated consensus – the starting point for Habermas – rests on reasons that convince parties in the same way, a compromise is reached when different parties accept a decision for different reasons.[23] Indeed, this universal consensus also forms the foundation for Habermas' account of the 'correctness' of norms.[24] Arguably, the EU law-making process is based on the above-described implicit 'agreement not to agree'.[25] This form of bargaining resulting in compromise, not consensus, appears to form a typical element of the EU law-making process. The result is legislation based on different normative assumptions: political bargaining facilitates compromise in this deliberative process where issues of political importance are left undecided.[26] As a result of these shortcomings in the political process of law-making, emphasis necessarily shifts to adjudication, to the role of the ECJ in justifying general legal rules by way of individual judgments. Consequently, it may be argued that the role of the Court in giving justification for EU law is highlighted.[27]

In Habermas' analysis, legal certainty requires that decisions are consistent with the framework of the existing legal system. On the other hand, the claim to legitimacy demands decisions that are not only consistent in relation to the surrounding legal system, but that also should be rationally justified so that all participants can accept them as rational decisions. Importantly, the rationality problem that Habermas discusses is the following: how can contingently emerging law be applied in a way that assures the requirements of both certainty and soundness?[28] Alternatively, the key question is how can the appropriateness of selective decisions be justified so that all participants perceive them as acceptable?[29]

Because of the significance placed on the existence of a paradigm of law, a degree of affinity can be discerned between Habermas' thinking and Dworkin's constructivist understanding of judicial decision-making. Constructivism highlights the importance of a particular paradigm of law which forms the implicit social theory of a legal system that guides the process of interpretation.[30]

22 Habermas 1990: 66. Cf. Aarnio 1987: 225.

23 Habermas 1998: 166. See in a similar vein Perelman and Olbrechts-Tyteca 1971: 65–66. Cf. Rawls 1995: 133 *et seq.* In Rawlsian theory of 'overlapping consensus', agreement is not required with regard to reasons supporting a particular conclusion. Rather, it allows for agreement on diverging premises.

24 See in more detail Torres Pérez 2009: 105.

25 Stone Sweet 2004: 24. See also Sunstein 1996, Habermas 2003.

26 Maduro 2007: 9.

27 Cf. Günther 1989 for a distinction between justification and application discourses, Wasserfallen 2010: especially 1132 *et seq.* on the role of the Court in the political process of law-making.

28 Habermas 1998: 198–199.

29 Habermas 1998: 202.

30 Habermas 1998: 194–195.

Constructivism makes the rationality of the interpretive process explicit by reference to a specific purpose. On this reading, constructive interpretation is in fact a matter of imposing purpose on an object or practice in order to make the interpretation the best possible example of the form or genre to which it is taken to belong: interpretation forms a constant search for the best possible answer. In this respect, an interpretation is an instance of an assumed enterprise so that interpretation takes different forms depending on the context.[31]

In accordance with the juxtaposition of justification and application discourses identified by Günther, the choice as to the relevant facts and their description is made within application discourses.[32] Put differently, courts decide which of the facts are significant for interpreting the situation in the case at hand and further, they must determine which of the *prima facie* valid norms (determined in justification discourses) are appropriate for deciding the case. An essentially hermeneutical process, adjudication offers a platform that weaves together norm application and a description of the circumstances plus a concretization of generally valid norms: interpretive issues are finally decided by making explicit a meaning equivalence between the description of the facts in the case at hand and the descriptive component of norms, *i.e.* their application conditions.[33]

In fact, the distinction between justification and application discourses problematizes the role of certainty in law, since – viewed even from this perspective – legal norms do not contain any predetermined application procedures: their applicability is decided in the context of the interpretive situation. Hence, a legal system cannot guarantee that court decisions contain the degree of predictability required by the principle of legal certainty. Indeed, as we have seen, according to this formal view of legal certainty based on the idea of predictability, 'legal certainty' expresses a principle that must itself be weighed and balanced against other interests and principles in the case at hand. As illustrated in the previous chapter, in the Court's case law, considerations of legal certainty (*i.e.* predictability) are often weighed against other principles such as that of effectiveness and legality. Although other interests sometimes override that of predictability, certainty of law may be assured on a different level.

---

31 Dworkin 1986: 52 *et seq.*

32 Günther 1989: 157, Habermas 1998: 218. Because legal rules expressed in statutes are only *prima facie* candidates for application, courts must engage in application discourse to test whether they apply to a specific case or whether they have to give way to another norm in the context of application. The validity of a norm prior to application only tells us that it has been impartially justified; a valid decision in a particular case requires that it has also been impartially applied. Understood this way, application discourses in judicial decision-making concern a norm's appropriate reference to a situation, not its formal validity.

33 Habermas 1998: 218.

Procedural certainty and rational acceptability

To resolve the paradoxical relationship between certainty and acceptability, procedural guarantees enter the stage. Instead of guaranteeing certainty of outcomes in individual cases, procedural certainty ensures 'a discursive clarification of the pertinent facts and legal questions'.[34] In this respect, what is important is not the predictability of the outcome itself but rather the certainty that those concerned may have their legal situation affirmed in a court procedure according to a predetermined set of procedural rules.[35]

More particularly, once we accept the unavoidable uncertainty of content (as a result of multilingualism, for example), emphasis shifts to procedural rights. To a certain extent, procedural rules are intended to compensate for the 'fallibility and decisional uncertainty resulting from the fact that the demanding communicative presuppositions of rational discourses can only be approximately fulfilled'.[36] This is particularly true in the EU context, as illustrated in Chapter 1. As Davies notes with regard to the wording of the Treaties, the Member States 'made an imprecise deal for reasons of political and legal expedience, and are faced with imprecise legal consequences'.[37]

It is certainly a truism that in the context of adjudication, procedural safeguards standardize neither admissible arguments nor the course of judicial reasoning.[38] Nor do they affect the discovery phase in judicial decision-making. However, procedural safeguards may be said to secure a stable space for legal discourse: different views expressed by the parties to a process contribute to a discourse aiming at an impartial decision.[39] While the picture sketched by Habermas appears mainly to concern parties to the process, no reasons exist that would preclude a similar analysis with regard to discourse among courts, such as the preliminary ruling procedure where procedural rules also define the systemic framework for rational discourse among EU courts.

In this procedure, a rational discourse concerning the content of rules may take place. Due to the arguably flexible and 'liquid' nature of EU law expressed in a multiplicity of languages, the EU legal system remains in constant movement so that priority relations among arguments, values and principles change over time.

---

34 Habermas 1998: 220.

35 In fact, it is possible to discern a close affinity of procedural certainty with the individual's expectation of legal certainty referred to in analytical jurisprudence, which in the final analysis boils down to the legitimate expectation of individuals that their rights may be determined before impartial courts in a rational and acceptable way. See Raitio 2003: 340. Also Aarnio 1987: 3, 23, Aarnio 1997: 189–190, Peczenik 1989: 29–31.

36 Habermas 1998: 234.

37 Davies 2012a: 80.

38 Cf. Tuori 2002: 111, who points out the problems related to speaking of individual judicial processes in these terms due to the role of the judge as a non-party to the dispute.

39 Habermas 1998: 234–235.

Environmental protection discussed above illustrates the issue: the emergence of environmental considerations in the Court's reasoning coincided with general political developments in the Member States.[40]

What orients judicial decision-making, then, is the paradigmatic legal understanding of the legal community prevailing at a specific point in time. In other words, although no guarantee exists as to predictability of the outcome in individual cases, inter-subjectivity of judicial decision-making nonetheless restricts the possibilities of the courts.[41] For Dworkin, this inter-subjectivity is expressed by the political morality of the community in question that directs judicial decision-making.[42]

However, equating predictable judicial decision-making with a specific legal paradigm reveals its weakness: the outcome of a procedure is predictable for the parties only insofar as the relevant paradigm determines a background understanding that both legal experts and citizens share. It follows that coherent interpretations within a fixed legal paradigm in fact remain indeterminate when they compete with equally coherent interpretations of the same case within an alternative paradigm.[43]

Indeed, as no such pre-interpretive norm expressed unequivocally in over 20 language versions exists that could be said to ensure formal predictability in ECJ decision-making, the role of procedural guarantees combined with judicial reasoning expressing the paradigm followed by the Court gains key significance. The question, then, is how the Court may facilitate communication that would lead to agreement as to the legal paradigm to be followed in interpreting EU law.

Although procedural safeguards admittedly function as a stabilizing framework (creating procedural predictability) for pinning down the meaning of the law, an impartial procedure appears insufficient to guarantee acceptability of judicial decision-making. To remedy this breach, we need judicial reasoning that satisfies the requirement of rational acceptability. In the present context of multilingual EU law, it is possible to argue that legal certainty is in fact a combination of procedural safeguards and judicial reasoning. In this respect, the Court's role may be argued to consist of giving reasons in support of its decisions that convince the legal community of the acceptability of the decision.[44]

The question we are thus faced with is how the legal community can agree on a specific legal paradigm so that the problem of indeterminacy in judicial decision-making can be resolved. Following the path of communicative action, agreement among the legal community with regard to the interpretation of legal texts in a specific case would appear to require that in judicial reasoning, the rights of all participants are recognized. In fact, the paradigmatic pre-understanding of law

40 See *e.g.* Jans 2000: 3–10, Krämer 2003: 3–5.

41 Tamanaha 2004: 89.

42 Dworkin 1986: 239, 256.

43 Habermas 1998: 221.

44 See *e.g.* Wilhelmsson 2004: 220 on predictable argumentation.

can limit the indeterminacy of judicial decision-making and guarantee a sufficient degree of legal certainty insofar as the paradigm is shared by all citizens and expresses the self-understanding of the entire legal community.[45]

While we must admit the purely theoretical and idealistic underpinnings of this theory, Habermasian discourse theory may offer a helpful point of reference when treated as 'a critical standard' with which to test actual agreement.[46] Indeed, even if we limit the sphere of actors relevant for the analysis of acceptance, this theory highlights the need for communication, for a constant dialectic intended as a means of searching for a shared pre-understanding of the paradigm that governs judicial decision-making.

More particularly for present purposes, since the procedural understanding of law is closely connected to the idea of 'discursively regulated competition among different paradigms', this implies a connection between legal certainty and judicial dialogue among European courts. That is, the ECJ is in constant interaction with national courts as well as the European Court of Human Rights (ECHR). Most importantly, it is here argued that the Court's reasoning must first and foremost be accepted by national courts – and more broadly other authorities – which apply EU law.[47] Arguably, therefore, the way ECJ decisions are justified is particularly important because of the normative instability resulting from multilingual legislation.

In this respect, it is worth noting that communication between the above courts is not built on the same normative basis. While communication between the ECJ and national courts functions on the basis of Article 267 TFEU requiring national courts to request a preliminary ruling in cases related to interpretation and validity of EU law, 'discourse' between the ECJ and the Strasbourg court is – at least as long as the EU is not a signatory to the ECHR – built on a more voluntary basis, although the Convention unquestionably forms a minimum standard for assessing rights protected under both instruments.[48]

In the preliminary ruling procedure, while national courts are required to follow ECJ case law, when a question is referred, ECJ interpretations are often of a general character, in practice leaving to national courts the application of rules stated in ECJ case law.[49] For Davies, the reason is twofold. Firstly, open norms

---

45 Habermas 1998: 222–223. Habermas attempts to develop Dworkin's One Single Right Answer thesis beyond the monological, judge-centred view that appears to be at the centre of Dworkin's theory. Indeed, Dworkin does not address the issue of different legal paradigms that can be simultaneously observed in a given community.

46 Torres Pérez 2009: 105.

47 On transnational judicial dialogue, see Littlepage 2008.

48 See Rosas 2003: 97–98, Morijn 2006: 18. See also C-238/99 P, *Limburgse Vinyl Maatschappij NV (LVM)* [2002] ECR I-8375, paras 273–274 and case C-94/00, *Roquette Frères* [2002] ECR I-9011. See also the explanations relating to the EU Charter (OJ 2007 C 303, p. 17).

49 See Sarmiento 2012 for a reconstruction of different types of silence that can be found in the Court's judgments.

govern fields of EU law possessing both social and legal significance. Secondly, fact finding and application belong, as a matter of principle, to the authority of national courts referring questions to the ECJ.[50] In line with Davies, who argues forcefully that the systemic features of the preliminary ruling procedure allow for restraint and discretion on both sides of this dialectical relationship, it is argued that when national courts do refer questions, the relevant actors engage in dialogue where the meaning of EU law is negotiated under premises allowing for mutual understanding and acceptance. This is explained by the division of labour of these courts, the Court being the final authority on interpretation and national courts on concrete application of that interpretation in the concrete cases before them.[51]

Indeed, even when the Court trespasses on the domain of application by framing its answer in a nuanced manner and thus venturing into making its own findings on compliance, 'it is more plausible to explain this in terms of assistance and co-operation with the national court [...] than as an attempt to dominate or control them'.[52] In that context, a shared paradigm of law can be negotiated. This is intimately bound up with the question of what counts as a 'good reason' in the context of ECJ judicial reasoning.[53] The ECJ needs to give arguments to justify its decisions that are accepted by the multilingual legal community. Arguments are the reasons that are used in this discourse to justify a validity claim raised by speech acts. Certainly, as stated in Chapter 1, the justificatory force of linguistic arguments – as opposed to teleological arguments explicating the Court's underlying normative understanding of the legal system – remains particularly weak in the multilingual EU setting, where uncertainty as to the meaning of legislation expressed in over 20 official languages is increasing and where meaning is primarily constructed in judicial decision-making. Framing this in Habermasian language, the underlying idea is therefore to rationally motivate those taking part in discourse to accept the corresponding descriptive or normative statement as valid.[54] In other words, the ECJ puts forward arguments in its decisions to convince the EU legal community of the soundness of its decisions so that their validity is enhanced.

In the legal sphere, validity can be divided into systemic, factual and axiomatic levels of validity.[55] Systemic validity implies that the norm has been enacted in

50 Davies 2012a: 79 *et seq*. The Court frequently reiterates the foundational rule which governs this division of labour. Accordingly, the Court has no competence to rule on either facts or the conformity of national measures since this application procedure belongs to the authority of referring courts. See for a recent example case C-246/09, *Bulicke* [2010] ECR I-7003, para 28.

51 Davies 2012a: 83 *et seq*.

52 Davies 2012a: 85.

53 Ultimately, in a legal context, what counts as a good reason is decided by systemic factors.

54 Habermas 1984: 22–42.

55 Wróblewski 1992: 76. Wróblewski sees the systemic form of validity as generally applicable in legal contexts whereas factual and axiological validity can be applied to law only in exceptional cases.

accordance with the rules of that system. Factual validity refers to 'law in action' *i.e.* law as actually followed and applied; whereas axiological validity requires that law is acceptable in the light of a particular community's values.[56]

Somewhat differently, MacCormick contends that validity forms a conceptual tool for distinguishing between what is operative within the system and what is not.[57] In fact, this pragmatic property of the concept of validity explains why validity is not a quality inherent to a norm *per se*. It can 'only be revealed, ascertained and confirmed through an act of interpretation occurring within a linguistic game, and this is to say that both law and procedure, theory of games and linguistic use are also in a position to afford relevant aspects'.[58]

Concretely, before the Court gives pragmatic meaning to EU legislation, it is only formally valid. In the EU context, this view of validity is again related to ECJ case law: applying EU legislation in individual cases makes EU law operative. Indeed, tying this view together with the idea that axiomatic validity is necessary for law to be fully valid implies that validity closely relates to reasoning and arguments as expressed by the Court to justify its decisions.

'Good reasons' for convincing relevant actors to accept a statement as valid may only be identified in the light of the reasoning taken as a whole, *i.e.* by assessing the contribution it makes in accordance with the rules of that game for deciding the interpretive question with regard to a contested claim in the case at hand.[59] Essentially, the soundness of judicial decisions is ultimately weighed against how well judicial reasoning satisfies the communicative conditions of reasoning that form a prerequisite for impartial decision-making.[60] On this understanding, no objective 'right answer' exists; rather, the soundness of a specific decision is weighed against the prevailing understanding of the values in a legal system in a particular legal community. In this context, procedural rules compensate for uncertainty in judicial decision-making resulting from the fact that the imperatives of rational discourse can only be approximately fulfilled.[61]

In essence, the acceptability of ECJ decisions depends on the reactions of other EU courts because of the dialogical relationship between national courts and the ECJ, as mentioned earlier in this section. More particularly, the acceptability of the Court's reasoning is tested in the context of national proceedings and tried against the paradigm adopted by the national court, reflecting national policy considerations. As Davies observes, the Court is aware of this: especially when the Court gives an abstract answer based on general principles, thus 'providing

56 Raitio 2003: 343, Aarnio 1997: 33–46.

57 MacCormick 1998: 500–501.

58 Varga 2000: 164.

59 Habermas 1998: 227.

60 Habermas 1998: 230.

61 Habermas 1998: 233–234.

rules of wide application', it accepts that its answer is only capable of guiding the national court, but possesses no control over outcomes.[62]

Stressing the plurality of international, European and national norm-givers and norm-appliers, Rosas underlines the importance of European values and principles. Values and principles articulated in judicial reasoning contribute to tying together the pluralistic whole, thus affording predictability and stability to the legal system. The role of courts, and more specifically that of the ECJ in the European context, is increasing with regard to articulating and interpreting these values and principles.[63] Therefore, what counts is that the Court indicates 'what types of arguments, interests and values may be considered and how they are to be balanced and weighed'.[64]

Because of the intersection of values and principles employed in judicial reasoning between the pragmatic, the ethical, and the moral, reasons offer a tool for revealing the rationale behind judicial decision-making, but more generally can provide justification for law whose context remains uncertain until its meaning is reconstructed in concrete cases before the Court. In this sense, because these reasons reveal the underlying paradigm guiding decision-making, they function as useful parameters not merely for the referring court but also for other judges confronted with similar issues. Reasons also constitute a medium for the Court's audience to evaluate the Court's judgments. From a deliberative vantage point, these values and principles emerge and evolve in a process where courts interact in search of acceptability.[65] Essentially, although the communicative interaction between the ECJ and national courts allows national courts a degree of leeway (issues such as deciding on the need to refer and applying the interpretive guidelines issued by the Court remain largely in the hands of national courts), finding a common understanding rests on the Court's ability to communicate underlying values and principles in its decisions to the scrutiny of the legal community.

In the following, we build on this theoretical discussion to illustrate how the Court may enhance legal certainty (rational acceptability of judicial decision-making) through judicial reasoning.

62 Davies 2012a: 83. Davies makes an interesting additional point by observing that when the Court engages in the specificities of the case before it by providing, for example, a concrete answer on justification or proportionality, by the same token it makes it easier for other national courts to distinguish the case. Thus, concrete answers which may tie the hands of the referring court may result in less generally applicable rules, leaving more discretion to other courts faced with similar issues.

63 Rosas 2007a: 1.

64 Davies 2012a: 79.

65 Rosas 2007a: 15.

Constructing meaning through judicial reasoning

Adjudication is based on and implemented by means of constant communication among legal actors.[66] Within the context of this book, what is interesting is the way the ECJ communicates its decisions to the legal community; how it guides decision-making in national courts which daily interpret and apply multilingual EU law. This communication is based on judicial reasoning.

Here, precisely because of the uncertainty related to the meaning of multilingual EU legislation, the role of the Court in constructing meaning on the basis of different language versions takes centre stage. In doing so, the Court must communicate its choice to its particular ideal audience: the EU legal community. In this respect, while the legislative raw material – on the basis of which the Court works – is multilingual, the reasoning of the Court itself remains primarily monolingual.[67] So, the ECJ communicates its interpretive choices to its audience by monolingual means.

Before exploring the question of how new meaning – valid across official languages – can be established in the EU context, it is necessary to briefly shed light on different ways in which understanding generally occurs. The following distinctions are based on a so-called Connectionist model of meaning construction.[68] In abstract terms, understanding signifies creating a meaningful combination of connections between different words and concepts. Mapping different aspects of understanding, we can identify three forms of understanding: routine (frequent use), new constructions (combination of textual elements and previous knowledge) or modification of routine (*e.g.* guided change).[69] Here, the last form of understanding is of particular significance because understanding textual elements can change as a result of, *inter alia*, convincing and authoritative external input such as judicial reasoning.

As explained by Engberg, in the field of statutory interpretation and judicial decision-making in the EU, the meaning of legal texts generally changes as a result of the Court's input: through judicial reasoning, the ECJ can modify the meaning of words, expressions or other textual elements routinely understood in a particular way in Member State legal systems on the basis of the Court's authority in this linguistic community.[70] Further, modification of routine clearly exposes the connection between subjectivity in judicial interpretation and its connection to the surrounding legal system and previous case law; that is, its inter-subjectivity.

---

66 See *e.g.* Salmi-Tolonen 2005: 59–60.

67 Bengoetxea 2011a: 11.

68 Herrmann *et al.* 1996: 120 *et seq*. The Connectionist model claims that meaning is constructed by activating relations between different groups of knowledge in the brain; that is, meaning is given on the basis of relations existing between words and concepts, and among concepts.

69 Engberg 2004: 1146.

70 Engberg 2004: 1147.

Change in legal meaning therefore occurs through change in the surrounding systemic framework: change in meaning on a higher institutional level (at the Court) modifies the way national courts interpret statutes when they agree on the acceptability of the proposed interpretation. In this respect, even subjective evaluations that are necessarily present in judicial interpretation are conditioned by other legal actors in the legal system in question. As such, change occurs through discourse, in communication with others.

In fact, as briefly suggested at the beginning of this chapter, from the viewpoint of discourse, moulding the legal system and its language occurs through a process whereby written legal texts are interpreted and applied by legal actors as part of legal practices in which they take part (such as adjudication).[71] In the realm of law, legal discourse functions as both a reflection of the features of the legal system and as a force that changes them.[72]

With regard to creating meaning through modifying routine understanding, the following sections consider the role of the ECJ in changing national courts' routine interpretations. The virtue of the Connectionist model resides in its ability to explain certain regularities in the way people react to new ways of using words. This is particularly important with regard to understanding how a multilingual legal system can function and how it may be possible to gradually develop EU law that is interpreted in a relatively uniform manner throughout the EU although expressed in over 20 different languages.[73]

Language in context

Discourse may involve modifying the way legal actors routinely understand words. As stated in Chapter 1, teleological reasoning is open to criticism because, unlike linguistic or purely systemic reasoning, it acknowledges the existence of uncertainty in adjudication and exposes the necessarily subjective character of interpretation.[74] However, this criticism corresponds to a narrow conception of the role of courts in a legal system: instead of interpreting and construing law, courts should confine themselves to simply applying it.[75]

This view is, moreover, based on the assumption that statutory texts carry autonomous and pre-interpretive meaning: they are supposed to be normative in

71 Kjær 2004: 391.

72 Kjær 2008a: 257.

73 Engberg 2004.

74 Cf. Wasserfallen 2010: 1132, who observes that systemic features and general principles 'equip the Court with an almost unrestricted potential to advance integration'.

75 Cf. Rosas 2007a: 2, Rosas 2007b: 33–63, Maduro 2007: 7. In this respect, it is interesting to note that this conception of the role of courts may be traced back to the classic idea of separation of powers. At the same time, however, the particularities inherent in the EU law-making process described above might be argued to speak in favour of a somewhat differentiated understanding of the role of courts in the EU legal system.

their own right. This would in fact mean that courts are devoid of any normative preferences or value choices: judicial decisions would be exempt from value judgments and deprived of discretion. This view is based on a static concept of language on 'the strong language theory'.[76]

However, it is here argued that legal texts remain subject to the same constraints as any human communication (*e.g.* contextuality, pragmatic fuzziness, vagueness). In the EU context, to these we still need to add problems of translation so that the limitations of this idea of language are clearly exposed. In order for the text to gain meaning, it must be interpreted in context: this involves evaluative considerations.[77]

In the legal sphere, the normative meaning of legal texts develops and is moulded in judicial decision-making. This 'weaker language theory' makes clear that in order to interpret a legal text, the interpreter (or, more specifically, the judge) has recourse to the individual knowledge base. It is based on a dynamic conception of language that recognizes language as a constantly changing and developing phenomenon that does not exist in a vacuum: texts gain meaning in a complex interplay of text, writer and reader (or text, sender and addressee) and their knowledge of the world.[78]

Therefore, as noted in Chapter 1, reference to 'ordinary meaning' does not make judicial reasoning more transparent or objective, or indeed more predictable, since determining something as 'ordinary', for example, necessarily contains a subjective appreciation. The definition given to a word by lawmakers does not represent the final stage of interpretation but rather the starting point. Importantly, therefore, the meaning of words – both in legal and non-legal contexts – changes over time. It follows that the normative context of application (judicial decision-making) is the most important factor in defining the 'correct' legal meaning of a textual element.[79] In essence, the 'correct' legal meaning of a specific word, sentence, provision or a broader legal text cannot be definitely determined in advance. The meaning of a legal text may, therefore, only be defined through the act of interpretation and application whereby the text is given a specific meaning in the context of an individual case.[80]

Applying the above to the EU context, it appears realistic to say that instead of finding existing meanings, the ECJ (or any other court) in fact decides on meaning in the context of the case it decides; this process continuously moulds and develops existing legal experience. By way of judgment, the Court ends the meaning conflict between the parties in a specific case, or at least the part that concerns EU law: in essence, the normative meaning of a specific text is constructed by using the text as 'raw material' for creating meaning in a specific

76 Engberg 2004: 1140 *et seq.* See also Kjær 2004: especially 379–381.
77 Endicott 2001: 380 *et seq.*
78 Kjær 2004: 383.
79 Van Hoecke 2002: 98–100.
80 Tontti 2004: 126.

context.[81] Put differently, emphasis on context urges judicial interpretation to look beyond the wording to the legal, social and political implications of the decision by employing teleological reasoning to express these considerations.

In this regard, the ECJ makes a choice among numerous interpretations of the provision in question with regard to the legal framework of which the text in question forms part. This is why linguistic arguments offer insufficient support for convincing the players in the game of law of the chosen interpretation: their own view of the most suitable interpretation might be different.[82] Reference to language, especially in cases where incongruity exists between language versions – a difference detected in comparing language versions – seldom functions as an argument that convinces the legal community of the interpretation, as no way exists to definitely pin down the meaning of words in general, or in the EU in particular. This is especially the case when language versions, taken separately, do not seem unambiguous or vague but rather appear to give a clear answer to the dispute at issue.

This weaker language theory highlights the subjectivity and fuzziness present in all human communication. Thus, placing emphasis on subjectivity might at first sight appear at odds with traditional legal thinking focusing on predictability – which, as we have seen, is also an important element of the principle of legal certainty – of judicial decision-making. Indeed, predictability would appear to call for clear boundaries as to the meaning of words and structures. However, looking at the question more closely reveals that subjectivity cannot be avoided: rather, it is an inherent element of judicial interpretation. While judicial interpretation can be compared to normal human understanding, important differences also exist.[83]

While in everyday communication, the interpretive process is often unconscious, judicial interpretation is based on a conscious process in which the interpreter tries to establish a consistent interpretation of the text in question – at least *ex post*, after arriving at a conclusion perhaps unconsciously.[84] Judicial interpretation also involves sources, which do not normally enter into the interpretive process of a text. These sources include written sources such as precedents, other statutes and doctrine. However, despite the influence of these sources, the text must nevertheless be interpreted *in context* in order for it to gain meaning.[85] In a legal system where pragmatic meaning is construed on the basis of legal materials that are multilingual and to a certain extent contradictory, the need for transparent reasoning is highlighted. Instead of hiding behind language, exposing the rationale of the rules and reconstructing their purpose in reasoning

81 Engberg 2002: 380.

82 Cf. Conway 2012: 130–131.

83 Engberg 2004: 1139 and 1147, Lindroos-Hovinheimo 2012.

84 Cf. Ojanen 1998: 23.

85 Cf. Conway 2012: 130, who opines, omitting the significance of context in interpretation, that 'the legislative use of specific words [is] deliberate and designed to convey a precise idea to the audience'.

opens up the decision-making process based on judges' individual knowledge base to debate and (democratic) control.

For instance, Klatt asserts that the possibility to determine limits for wording of norms from a semantic vantage point is a key condition for the idea that law, and legal rulings, can be objective.[86] However, viewed in a different light, one could say that the question is not why language is generally understood and why certain ways of understanding words are preferred over others. Instead of trying to conceptualize judicial decision-making as objective, it seems more fruitful to look at whether speakers of a given (legal) language can develop a common referential basis to reality, and further, whether such a common basis for understanding can develop among speakers of different languages. Legal languages are expressions of different legal systems so that they do not necessarily share identical systems of reference. This naturally begs the question how a common referential basis may be developed for EU law encompassing over 20 national legal systems and thus a corresponding number of arenas of application.

Modifying meaning

Here, the idea of Connectionism fleshed out above comes in useful for present purposes. Understanding a word in a specific way means that a meaningful combination of connections is established in the brain.[87] Meaning attributed to textual elements may change if, for instance, reasoned argument convinces the interpreter of a more suitable meaning in the particular situational conditions at hand. Here we approach the essence of our argument. The reasoning the Court offers in support of its reading of EU law functions as its sole armoury in its attempt to modify how its multilingual audience constructs the content of EU law.

In this respect, one could argue that a degree of agreement among the legal community is essential for meaning formation. According to Klatt, the so-called scorekeeping model shows that implicit normative structures arise from participation in a language game. The idea is that participants keep score of attitudes, commitments and entitlements in a specific communicative situation. By such scorekeeping, it is possible to deduce what the community in question considers to be correct or incorrect with regard to speech acts such as judicial decisions.[88]

The idea of scorekeeping is also interesting from the standpoint of EU law. One could depict the EU judicial process in these terms: as the abundance of doctrinal work on the Court's case law illustrates, the EU legal community – the Court's audience – also keeps score of arguments employed by the Court in deciding cases. This may be argued to contribute to formation of an implicit normative

86 Klatt 2008: 278 *et seq.*

87 Herrmann *et al.* 1996: 120.

88 Klatt 2008: 131.

structure that limits the possibilities of the interpreter, *i.e.* the ECJ. This relates closely to what was said about predictable reasoning in Chapter 2.

In this respect, it appears plausible to argue that it is possible to reach agreement understood in terms of a common referential basis regarding meaning, even in situations involving several languages. It is possible to argue, as *inter alia* Jääskinen does, that on the level of legal culture, EU Member States share certain basic ideas about law: these include a particular set of sources of law and principles. In turn, their application to specific situations reflects a view about law as a consistent field of normative meaning.[89] On this view, at least the possibility exists of shared understanding about law, something that could be argued to form a prerequisite for building a common referential basis for those involved in the process of interpreting and applying EU law. This is because one never interprets input from the outside world in a *tabula rasa* situation; rather, input is interpreted by comparing it to the interpreter's existing perception of the situation.[90]

Here, the most interesting type of constructing meaning is modification of routine: if convincing arguments are given to support a new meaning for a word already in use, this will modify the way knowledge chunks are connected and the way words are understood. This is also connected to what Schauer observes in relation to the tension between short-term fixity of linguistic rules (at a given time, rules can be established and language users identify the way words have been used previously – this sets the 'outer limits' of what can be accepted) and their long-term flexibility.[91] Language is subject to continuous change. One way of influencing change of routine understanding is using linguistic authority, or more generally, convincing reasoning, to modify the process of routine understanding in which certain words are automatically connected to a given meaning.[92]

Linking the threads made up by Connectionism and discourse among legal actors for conceptualizing legal certainty in substantive terms, we can observe how the focus turns to communication between specialists influencing meaning construction in the EU legal system. On this view, whether national courts follow ECJ case law depends, then, on the Court's ability to change routine meaning construction by national courts. The key here is judicial reasoning. Change may occur by convincing reasoning so that the linguistic community in question changes the way it routinely understands given words.

Taking account of the Court's task in reconciling language versions, it must give arguments to justify a decision that might in some cases support a reading which may appear *prima facie* counter-intuitive, without proper analysis of the provision's systemic context and its corresponding purpose. More particularly, problems arise from systemically conditioned meaning in domestic settings.[93]

89 Jääskinen 2008: 217, also van Hoecke 2002: 31, Kjær 2004: 395.

90 Engberg 2004: 1145.

91 Schauer 2008: 1121.

92 Engberg 2004: 1146, 1166.

93 See Pozzo 2006: 6–12 on different demarcation functions of legal concepts.

Whether the Court succeeds in modifying the routine understanding of the legal community depends on its ability to communicate the reasons for the result in the particular case.

Importantly, therefore, whether or not language or law is objective is beside the point. Rather, what is important is that those belonging to the relevant legal community can agree on the meaning attributed by the Court to words, provisions or broader textual elements. Without this inter-subjective understanding with regard to meaning, interpretive choices will only with difficulty be accepted *substantively*. In this respect, meaning construction is essentially dependent on the reactions of other members of the legal community. If the inherently subjective character of language and judicial interpretation is accepted, tools are needed to *control* subjectivity. And controlling subjectivity in adjudication requires judicial reasoning that opens the interpretive process to the relevant legal community so that they have the tools to decide on the acceptability of the decision from a substantive point of view.[94] Illustrating the role of communication in conceptualizing objectivity, Posner notes that the fact that 'persons of diverse backgrounds, values, and so forth can be brought to agree on a matter is the practical meaning of "objective"'.[95]

Additionally, from a linguistic standpoint, the idea that objective meaning exists independently without connection to human agents appears unlikely. In this respect, it appears difficult to justify the view that a meaning (of a text) exists separately from communication: this is so because meanings only exist as constructions in the minds of individuals built on the basis of perceived underspecified textual signs and existing mental models. Importantly, all meanings are potentially dynamic and may be influenced by communication; they may also be subject to constraints of communicative norms.[96]

Lastly, it can be said that subjectivity cannot be avoided in judicial interpretation. It follows that judicial decision-making can never be fully predictable. In a dynamic, multilingual and continuously changing society where different players influence the content of law, substantive legal certainty that is based on context-sensitivity and substantive acceptability of legal decisions is highlighted. The test is not objectivity but whether the answer given to a specific legal question is 'correct' in the view of the political morality of that community.[97] The result of the interpretive process is perceived as correct insofar as the reasons given to justify the decision are convincing. Consequently, contextuality of law must be accepted so that it is no longer necessary to hide behind the text and the notion of objectivity in adjudication. This, then, requires that judicial reasoning opens the interpretive process to the relevant legal community by means of substantive, not

94 Paunio and Lindroos-Hovinheimo 2010: 415.

95 Posner 2008: 82–83.

96 Engberg 2004: 1142.

97 Dworkin 1986: 255.

formal, arguments. We now move on to illustrate the argument with the help of examples from ECJ case law.

Harmonizing EU law meaning at the Court

As illustrated above, the ECJ works on the basis of translated originals. Due to its role as the 'guardian' of uniform interpretation and application of EU law, the ECJ has a special interest in harmonizing legal meaning.[98] On the basis of official versions, the Court determines one meaning valid for all language versions. From a linguistic viewpoint, the ECJ may encounter the following problems in this process. When it detects that different language versions diverge in meaning, a choice must be made between different meanings in language versions. This implies that the ECJ needs to create a new meaning for one or more languages involved. Essentially, this meaning construction entails that the ECJ is required to create new meaning which, *prima facie*, may appear contradictory to the meaning found in one or more language versions.

While understanding due to routine may be possible in legal systems in which mutual understanding among specialists already exists as to the legal meaning of specific words, in the EU change in meaning guided by decisions of the Court is needed to change the way specific words are understood in the EU context. In other words, before the multilingual legal community of the EU can routinely connect certain words with concepts, changes must happen as to the meaning connected to specific words in purely national contexts.[99] The ECJ enjoys a pronounced status in this respect.

From the standpoint of Luhmannian systems theory, legal concepts take shape in communicative processes within a particular legal system. On this view, legal concepts develop in judicial reasoning: they assume their form gradually by being applied repeatedly in similar cases. They do not remain stable; rather, they are constantly regenerated and moulded in judicial reasoning.[100] However, although concepts are continuously subject to this kind of refinement in judicial practice, they nonetheless relate to a particular legal system, expressing legal thought in that system. As such, the interrelationship between a particular legal system and legal concepts strongly suggests that this connection makes legal communication across legal systems problematic.[101]

While this illustrates how language functions in establishing, maintaining and reconstructing concepts, concept formation described in systems theory remains in

98 Engberg 2004: 1157.
99 Engberg 2004: 1145–1146.
100 Luhmann 2004: 341 on how concepts store legal experience.
101 Kjær 2004: 389.

the confines of a single legal system.[102] The question, then, is how communication and understanding occurs across legal systems and legal cultures. As we have seen, change in legal concepts occurs through judicial reasoning – or as one could also say, through legal discourse among legal actors.[103] The meaning of national legal concepts may only change when legal communication is no longer isolated in national settings; when legal actors take part in EU legal discourse.[104]

To generate a new 'EU meaning', and change the way in which the multilingual legal community perceives given words or expressions, the Court has to convince the legal community of the correctness of its interpretation through judicial reasoning that can be said to mould not only legal concepts but the conceptions that those participating in discourse possess about law. Referring to linguistic arguments is not particularly helpful in this respect, because these arguments do not present the arguments which have influenced the interpretive process: they do not present the argumentative process behind the subjective process. In the words of Engberg, 'subjectivity is a potential problem, but one that we cannot get rid of by going back to the words and their literal meanings'.[105]

Since the same rule may be open to rather different textual interpretations depending on the language version, and since all language versions in principle possess equal value, the ECJ has to decide these linguistic disputes using systemic and teleological reasoning to resolve linguistic indeterminacy, not only in the case in question but also on a more general level. Through teleological reasoning, the ECJ can guide national courts when they are interpreting EU law. In this way, the ECJ not only provides a discursive clarification of the immediate legal question, it also offers a broader normative frame of reference to which national courts can refer in future cases.[106]

This would not be possible through linguistic reasoning, due to linguistic uncertainty. However, the fact that the Court creates new meaning in a judgment does not automatically result in acceptance of that interpretation by the legal community of various Member States, since the judgment does not in itself guarantee that the legal community would adhere to that interpretation, irrespective of the language used. The Court's importance as an institution harmonizing meaning in the EU depends on how convincing its reasoning is. However, this does not preclude the established division of functions between national courts and the ECJ: national courts possess an 'applicatory monopoly' on the Court's interpretation, allowing for a degree of differentiation between Member States.[107]

---

102 Luhmann 1993. Indeed, as the title of Luhmann's book suggests, system theory relates to functioning of systems as autonomous entities.

103 Kjær 2004: 389.

104 Cf. Kjær 2004: 393–394.

105 Engberg 2004: 1163.

106 Maduro 2007: 9; see also Davies 2012a: 79 *et seq.*

107 In this respect, most notably Davies 2012a: 79. Davies gives an interesting example of a case before the English Court of Appeal which found that the national court

Ideally, to harmonize meaning, the reading attributed to a specific text must be accepted, on the one hand, by lawyers in a linguistic community and on the other hand, through acceptance by lawyers, by other members of the linguistic community in question. The process by which acceptance of the interpretation is widened can be performed only by means of communication and reasoning.

Boats and locomotives: what counts as a vehicle?

H.L.A Hart's classic example concerning the concept of 'vehicles' offers us a telling example of how linguistic and legal indeterminacies may be detected in judicial interpretation: what does 'vehicle' mean if the legal rule forbids taking vehicles to the park?[108] According to Hart, the notion of 'vehicle' in this hypothetical question can refer to a number of things, such as cars, ambulances or even skates. In the cases analyzed in the following, the Court was asked to determine what the notion of 'vehicle' meant, not only with regard to English, as in Hart's example, but with regard to over 20 official language versions.[109]

The *Fonden Marselisborg Lystbådehavn*[110] case involved determining the scope of VAT exemptions under the Sixth Directive. The list of exemptions contained in the Directive aims at ensuring that the Communities' own resources can be collected in a uniform manner in all Member States. Article 13B (b) of the Sixth Directive provides that leasing or letting immovable property is exempt from VAT. According to that provision, the exemption does not include the letting of premises and sites for parking vehicles. Fonden Marselisborg Lystbådehavn – a Danish company letting a site for boats – argued that this activity was not covered by the word 'vehicles' within the meaning of the Sixth Directive.

Asked to rule on whether the word 'vehicles' in Article 13B (b) (2) of the Sixth Directive includes boats, the Court noted that different language versions of the Directive were not equivalent. Analyzing a number of versions (*e.g.* the French, English, Italian, Spanish, Portuguese, German and Finnish versions), it held that the chosen expression encompasses means of transport in general so that it admits aircraft and boats. By contrast, according to the Court, the Danish, Swedish and Dutch versions had opted for a more precise term with a more limited meaning serving to designate 'land-based means of transport', thus excluding boats. The Danish word 'kjøretøjer' offered a clear exposition of this difference since it was understood as referring only to land-based transport on wheels.[111]

---

can ignore a particular point of the Court's answer if it finds that that evidential issue is not correctly portrayed in the ECJ's judgments.

108 Hart 2012: 126.

109 Cf. Kjær 2008a: 252 on the problematic notion of a common European legal language based on 23 interacting national legal languages.

110 Case C-428/02, *Fonden Marselisborg Lystbådehavn* [2005] ECR I-1527. See also Paunio and Lindroos-Hovinheimo 2010: 412 *et seq.*

111 Case C-428/02, *Fonden Marselisborg Lystbådehavn* [2005] ECR I-1527, para 41.

Despite this observation, the Court held on the basis of the purpose and aims of the Sixth Directive that the provision in question must be interpreted as covering boats, even though it acknowledged that the Danish version could, taken separately, be understood differently.[112] To reconcile this divergence, the Court reiterated its well-established position on the criteria to be applied in case of divergence and emphasized the need to interpret the provision at issue by looking at its purpose and giving due consideration to the general scheme of the rules of which it forms part.[113]

Similar to the *Fonden Marselisborg Lystbådehavn* case, in *Lietuvos geležinkeliai*,[114] the Court was asked to determine the meaning of 'motorized vehicle' for the purposes of determining the scope of exemptions from import duties and VAT. The question arose in a preliminary reference put to the Court by a Lithuanian tax tribunal. The core issue in the national proceedings was whether, under relevant provisions of EU law, exemptions from import duties and VAT concerning fuel contained in the standard tanks of 'commercial motor vehicles' (in Lithuanian, '*motorinės transporto priemonės*') should be understood as applying to fuel carried in locomotives. The Court compared all language versions and held:

> 31. The notion of 'commercial motor vehicle' is defined in [the provisions at issue] as 'any motorised road vehicle' satisfying certain specific conditions, which could in principle be fulfilled just as well by locomotives as by other land vehicles.
>
> 32. In that regard [...] there are divergences between the different language versions of the provisions at issue here. In the Bulgarian, Spanish, Czech, German, Estonian, Greek, English, French, Italian, Latvian, Lithuanian, Hungarian, Maltese, Polish, Portuguese, Romanian, Slovak, Slovene and Finnish versions, the vehicle in question is expressly described as being a 'road' vehicle, whilst the Danish and Dutch versions contain no such specification; they refer simply to the notion of 'motorised vehicle'.
>
> 33. In the Romanian and Swedish versions, there is a difference on this point in the drafting of the relevant regulations and directives. In the Romanian version, whereas the definition in Regulations Nos 918/83 and 1186/2009 refers to the notion of 'motorised road vehicle', the one found in Directives 83/181 and 2009/132 refers to the notion of 'motorised vehicle'. In the Swedish version, on the other hand, the definition in Regulations Nos 918/83 and 1186/2009 refers

112 See Kjær 2010: 307–309 for an analysis of the terminology used in the Danish version. See also the opinion of AG Jääskinen in case C-56/11, *Raiffeisen-Waren-Zentrale*, not yet reported.

113 Case C-428/02, *Fonden Marselisborg Lystbådehavn* [2005] ECR I-1527, paras 41–45. See similarly case C-372/88, *Cricket St Thomas* [1990] ECR I-1345, para 19 and C-384/98 *D* [2000] ECR I-6795, para 16.

114 C-250/11, *Lietuvos geležinkeliai*, not yet reported.

to 'motorised vehicle' and Directives 83/181 and 2009/132 refer to 'motorised road vehicle'.

Unable to draw any definitive conclusions or legal consequence from the observed divergence, the Court considered, due to the overriding requirement of uniform interpretation of EU law, that the provisions in question must be interpreted by reference to their purpose and general scheme of the rules of which they form part.[115] Despite the doubts entertained by the national court as to the appropriateness of applying different fiscal schemes to different categories of vehicle, the Court considered, on the basis of the objectives of the provisions at issue, that the application of import duty relief and the VAT exemption as provided for by those provisions to locomotives did not meet the objective that the EU legislature wished to pursue in adopting those provisions; namely that of, on the one hand, making it easier for individuals to cross EU external borders and, on the other, lightening the customs and tax checks to be conducted by the competent authorities. It thus concluded that the exemptions do not apply to locomotives.[116]

The cases illustrate how, in the context of multilingualism, the Court deploys language versions as raw material from which it construes a meaning that takes not only the legal but also the political and social context into account. In linguistic terms, the ECJ in fact resolved a meaning conflict – within the limited context of its 'linguistic jurisdiction' – between the parties and 'overruled' the existing differences in meaning found in the language versions.[117] In both cases, the meaning conflict is related to inter-lingual uncertainty in that, taken separately, one could say that no apparent linguistic uncertainty in one language exists, but once it is compared with other languages, linguistic uncertainty emerges.[118]

Indeed, if one of the versions of the texts in question was interpreted separately, linguistic (semantic) uncertainty would be primarily caused by vagueness, since no definite way exists for determining the notion of 'vehicle' and its boundaries, as Hart's example illustrates. In this context, Hart speaks about the core and the penumbra of meaning.[119] While 'car' may be argued to constitute the core of the meaning of the notion of 'vehicle', 'boat' and 'locomotive' are located in the penumbra, in the borderline area of the notion of 'vehicle' in the particular context of the cases examined.

In fact, a similar distinction as regards members of categories has been made in Cognitive Science.[120] According to the prototype theory, every concept

115 C-250/11, *Lietuvos geležinkeliai*, not yet reported, para 34. See also case C-341/01, *Plato Plastik Robert Frank* [2004] ECR I-4883, para 64.

116 C-250/11, *Lietuvos geležinkeliai*, not yet reported, especially paras 35–38.

117 Engberg 2004: 1159–1166.

118 Cao 2007b: 74.

119 Hart 2012: 124 *et seq.*

120 See *e.g.* Rosch 1973: 328–350.

possesses features that are more central than others.[121] Applying this theory to the concept 'vehicle' provides us with the following observation: when asked to give an example of the concept 'vehicle', 'car' is more likely to be mentioned than 'locomotive'. When more languages are involved, the initial uncertainty about meaning does not disappear but, rather, a new element of uncertainty is added, namely that of inconsistency of meaning between terms used in language versions.

In connection with the Hartian 'no vehicles in the park' example, Solan notes that in principle one can argue about whether this rule is applicable to a child riding a tricycle, but it would not be possible to argue that this same rule sets a minimum age for buying tobacco products, or regulates the dumping of toxins in the sea. While often not constraining the range of possible interpretations to one, comparison in discerning the meaning of EU legislation may reveal that the provision at issue does not allow for any number of interpretations.[122]

But what about the meaning of *parking*, *premises* or *site* in the context of the expression at issue in the *Fonden Marselisborg Lystbådehavn* case? Does looking at the expression as a whole tell us something more as to what the meaning of the provision here should be?

The Court is called on to decide on the meaning of the word 'vehicle' in the relevant case. Importantly, it is not about explicating the semantic meaning of the expression in different languages, but rather deciding on what it means in this particular legal context. Because of the contextuality of any instance of interpretation, the Court's preferred analytical framework, taking its cue from both the provision's systemic context as well as its purpose, is required to reveal what counts as '*premises and sites for parking of vehicles*' in the particular context of the Sixth Directive or as '*fuel contained in the standard tanks of commercial motor vehicles*' in the particular context of relief from customs duties and exemptions from VAT. In this respect, we are looking for and determining (pragmatic) meaning for the expression in question.

Certainly, especially in language, but also in law, a continuous tension exists between agreement, dissent and authority.[123] If someone started using 'cat' to mean 'dog', this would be labelled as incorrect usage in dictionaries and by 'linguistic authorities'. However, if enough participants in discourse followed this usage, it might become accepted and standard.[124] In this respect, it seems that the most important difference between clear and hard cases is the degree of agreement among relevant legal actors (lawyers participating in the communicative game of judicial decision-making) as to the correct interpretation. However, no way exists to exactly pin down the point at which clear cases become hard cases and the point

121 For example, when asked to give an example of the concept of 'furniture', chair is more frequently stated than bookshelf. See Solan 2009a: 47–48.

122 Solan 2009b: 10. See also matrix proposed by Hartley 1996: 96.

123 Bix 1993: 65. Perju 2009 for analysis of authority in ECJ judgments.

124 See Schauer 2008: 1121. Cf. Lindroos-Hovinheimo 2006: 57 on the condition of speaking of standard meaning.

at which the number of dissenters becomes relevant to the categorization of clear and hard cases.[125] This is why it is of pronounced significance that the relevant legal community accepts the proposed interpretation, irrespective of possible disagreements as to whether the case could have been decided in some other way.

In law there is a recurrent tendency to make claims about the objective correctness of certain interpretations. This occurs especially in 'clear cases': in these cases, no great disagreement exists as to the correct interpretation. Indeed, it could in fact be argued that the correctness of an interpretation is not determined by objectivity but rather by (inter-subjective) agreement. That is, correctness of meaning is defined either by agreement as to the correct interpretation, agreement as to which authority to defer to, or by agreement about the correct decision-making procedure. 'Objectivity' in the legal context as something neutral and independent might be said to consist of (or be a particular function of) the 'subjective'; that is, of individual and perspective considerations.[126]

In a monolingual legal system, agreement as to correct interpretation may be argued to be easier to attain in that the relevant actors are not only more limited in number but also speak the same language. In essence, such a consensus is not based on language in that it matters little, if anything, that certain propositions are indeterminate or not, but rather on the 'ground rules of the legal enterprise', as Dworkin describes the purpose of the provision in question in the context of the surrounding legal system.[127]

Here, it appears plausible to argue that in interpreting multilingual EU law, the number of hard cases – or in other words, cases that are not automatically categorized as routine cases – is greater than in the national legal context. Similarly, from a hermeneutical perspective, a case appears as 'clear' to the judge when it is seen as a reflection of the stereotypical images stemming from the cultural, social, political and legal tradition in which the interpreter lives and of which he or she is part.[128]

Gadamer's concept of *prejudice* lies at the very heart of judicial decision-making. The challenge that the ECJ essentially faces in a multicultural and pluralistic legal system is the following: how can it, essentially by way of reasoning, influence the way law-applying courts and authorities in national contexts interpret and apply EU law? Essentially, the difficulty lies in differentiating between interpreting national legislation and interpreting EU law: the same word or expression may or may not possess a different meaning in these different interpretive contexts. In other words, how can the *stereotypical narratives* associated with specific texts be changed?[129]

125 Bix 1993: 64.

126 Bix 1993: 65. See also Dworkin 1985: 168–162.

127 Dworkin 1985: 135.

128 Tontti 2004: 177–178, also Jackson 1995: 152–154, Jackson 1996: 241–245.

129 Jackson 1995: 152–154, Jackson 1996: 241–245.

Discussing problems related to legal transplants, Teubner notes that a transplant 'will be reconstructed in the different language of the social system involved, reformulated in its codes and programmes, which in turn leads to a new series of events'.[130] The same applies to the interaction between national and EU law. Due to differences between these systems, the context in which a particular rule, for instance, is applied quite naturally affects the outcome of the case.

Clearly, in the context of multilingual EU law, linguistic uncertainty may become relevant for judicial reasoning even in cases where no apparent linguistic uncertainty exists – when language versions are examined separately. Consequently, within that relevant linguistic community, agreement exists as to the legal meaning of the relevant text. In *Fonden Marselisborg Lystbådehavn* and *Lietuvos geležinkeliai*, the expressions 'kjøretøjer' and 'motorinės transporto priemonės' and their equivalents in other official languages do not possess identical semantic fields. In fact, in the first part of its reasoning, the Court looked at the wording of the provision in different languages in order to establish whether reference to linguistic arguments – also described as 'the default principle'[131] of statutory interpretation – is sufficient to resolve the meaning conflict. Due to insufficient overlap between the semantic fields in different language versions, the Court created a new (pragmatic) meaning by reference to the purpose and the general scheme of the provisions in question.[132]

Works on dykes: what counts as canalization and flood-relief works?

The *Kraaijeveld*[133] case concerned correct construction of the expression 'canalization and flood-relief works' in Directive 85/337/EEC.[134] The referring Court asked whether that expression, contained in point 10(e) of Annex II to the Directive, is to be interpreted as including certain types of work on a dyke running alongside waterways. In view of the wording of the English version of the directive, the national court considered that projects falling under that heading of Annex II involve activities likely to have significant effects on the environment, so that the expression could encompass certain works relating to a dyke.[135]

According to the Court, examination of the various language versions of the provision at issue revealed that they fall into two distinct categories depending on whether the terms employed denote the idea of flooding. The English ('canalization and flood-relief works') and Finnish ('kanavointi- ja tulvasuojeluhankkeet')

130 Teubner 1998: 28.

131 Engberg 2004: 1158. See also MacCormick and Summers 1991: 516–517.

132 See generally on the role of relevance in constructing pragmatic meaning, Sperber and Wilson 1995.

133 C-72/95, *Kraaijeveld* [1996] ECR I-5403.

134 Council Directive of 27 June 1985 on assessment of the effects of certain public and private projects on the environment (OJ 1985 L 175, p. 40).

135 C-72/95, *Kraaijeveld* [1996] ECR I-5403, paras 21–22.

versions are similar, whereas the German, Greek, Spanish, French, Italian, Dutch and Portuguese versions refer to canalization and regulation of watercourses, the Greek version including in addition the French term 'canalization' in brackets after the Greek term. However, the Court went on to note that unlike the other versions, the Danish and Swedish versions contain only a single expression reflecting the idea of regulating watercourses ('anlaeg til regulering af vandloeb', 'anlägggningar för reglering av vattenflöden').[136]

Just as in the *Fonden Marselisborg Lystbådehavn* and *Lietuvos geležinkeliai* cases above, the Court was asked to determine an 'EU law meaning' for an expression that might, at the outset, appear unambiguous in one language version, but when interpreted together with other language versions, the inter-lingual uncertainty made the situation more complex.[137] Here, again, the Court had to construe a meaning valid not only for the English phrase 'canalization and flood-relief works' but also for its equivalents in the other official language versions. Not surprisingly, it decided the case on the basis of teleological considerations relating to the purpose and the general scheme of rules of which the linguistic item at issue forms part.

Due to the differences observed, no sufficient overlap was held to exist which would have allowed the Court to determine a common meaning on the basis of solely linguistic arguments.[138] Given the divergence, the Court held that 'one must go to the purpose and general scheme of the directive'. The argument was then construed in the following terms:

> 30. According to [...] the directive, "project" means "the execution of construction works or of other installations or schemes" and "other interventions in the natural surroundings and landscape including those involving the extraction of mineral resources". [T]he directive is aimed at "projects likely to have significant effects on the environment by virtue inter alia of their nature, size or location". [It further] provides that the environmental impact assessment is to identify, describe and assess the direct and indirect effects of a project on human beings, fauna and flora, soil, water, air, climate and the landscape, material assets and the cultural heritage.
>
> 31. The wording of the directive indicates that it has a wide scope and a broad purpose. That observation alone should suffice to interpret [the provision in

136 C-72/95, *Kraaijeveld* [1996] ECR I-5403, para 29. For similar considerations, see case C-503/10, *Evroetil*, not yet reported, para 41.

137 Cf. Solan 2009a: 51. Here, he discusses another interesting case (100/84, *Commission v UK* [1985] ECR 1169) where the Court was asked to determine what constituted the essential part of a fishing operation. He notes that as a native English speaker, he really does not know whether fishing refers to pulling fish out of the water or catching fish on the line. See also Solan 2009b: 25.

138 Engberg 2004: 1158.

> question] as encompassing all works for retaining water and preventing floods and therefore dyke works even if not all the linguistic versions are so precise.
>
> 32. Even if, as argued by the Government of the Netherlands, dyke works consist in the construction or raising of the height of embankments in order to contain watercourses and avoid flooding, works retaining a static quantity of water, rather than a running watercourse, may have a significant effect on the environment within the meaning of the directive where they are liable permanently to affect the composition of the soil, flora and fauna or the landscape. Such works must therefore fall under the directive.

The Court's conclusion seems to be in accordance with the expressly mentioned objectives of the Directive and what can generally be understood as works for retaining water and preventing floods, and consequently dyke work along navigable waterways. But what does the decision mean from the perspective of multilingualism and legal certainty?

The ECJ resolved the meaning conflict of the different language versions by creating a new meaning that is identical in all language versions by referring to teleological reasoning.[139] This ensures that the interpretation forms a coherent whole with regard to the systematically surrounding concepts so that it does not create gaps in the wider legal framework.[140] If the Dutch version is taken separately, work on a dyke and flood-relief and canalization work may be distinguished from each other, as indeed the Dutch government argued. The latter are carried out to regulate water flow or for the benefit of river navigation. They change the character of the watercourse itself, or in other words, the quantity or quality of the water and the riverbanks and riverside, so that they have a considerable impact on aquatic flora and fauna. Dyke reinforcement work, on the other hand, consists of constructing or increasing the height of the embankment with sand or clay.[141]

Thus, when considering the Dutch version separately, prior knowledge connected with the word 'dyke' in a purely Dutch context would suggest that work on a dyke is distinguishable from canalization or flood-relief operations. However, after the Court's judgment in this case, the relevant criteria for the *particular purposes* of environmental impact assessment should be interpreted as meaning

139 Cf. Solan 2009b: 278–279. Solan suggests that language actually assists the ECJ in its task of interpreting EU law. This is so, he argues, because the goal of the Court is to construe statutes to effectuate the intent of the legislature and to further the goals of the enacted directive or regulation, so that the existence of so many equally authentic versions makes this task easier, since careful study of different translations of the same text is likely to lead to a deeper understanding of the text's essential meaning. In this respect, see also Solan 2009a.

140 Engberg 2004: 1159 in relation to case *Commission v UK* [1985] ECR 1169.

141 C-72/95, *Kraaijeveld* [1996] ECR I-5403, para 24.

that works on a dyke form part of a more general category of 'canalization or flood-relief' works.[142]

Hence, the Court has in fact added a new 'declarative knowledge chunk' and restricted the application of this chunk to the limited context of EU law. In fact, the ECJ did not say anything about what the word in question in Dutch might mean in general (or in the context of purely national law).[143] Instead, it created a new and specialized meaning which is applicable in the specific field of EU environmental impact assessment in accordance with its interpretive authority in the field.

How does this relate to legal certainty? Interpretation that does not follow the wording of one or more language versions, or more specifically, previous agreements among specialists with regard to the meaning of a specific word in a specific context, is *prima facie* problematic from the viewpoint of legal certainty.

While such an approach to interpretation may be considered problematic with regard to predictability in the sense of predictable outcomes in judicial proceedings, as was argued by the Dutch government in the *Kraaijeveld* case, legal certainty cannot be exhausted in predictability in this formal sense. Hence, legal certainty should not be solely tied to wording. Given this uncertainty, the wording functions as poor justification for an interpretation as it makes disagreement concerning meaning possible and often likely. Thus, recourse to arguments stemming from systemic and teleological considerations appears necessary not only for creating a new EU meaning covering the different language versions, but also for ensuring substantive legal certainty in the form of acceptable judicial decision-making. This cannot be achieved by reference to linguistic arguments alone because intra- and perhaps most importantly inter-lingual uncertainty complicate reconciling the meaning of different language versions.

Influencing meaning construction

In this section, the Court's influence on legal meaning construction is discussed by drawing parallels to the cases examined above. According to the Danish company in *Fonden Marselisborg Lystbådehavn*, when a Danish lawyer uses the word 'kjøretøjer' for the purpose of defining criteria for taxation, he would *a priori* interpret the word as meaning land-based transport, not boats.[144]

142 Similarly Engberg 2004: 1160.

143 See Engberg 2004: 1160. For similar considerations with regard to the need to determine an EU law meaning for the term 'licensee', see C-376/11, *Pie Optiek*, not yet reported, paras 32–34.

144 Case C-428/02, *Fonden Marselisborg Lystbådehavn* [2005] ECR I-1527, para 38. For similar conclusions for the German language version in a different legal context, case C-381/10, *Astrid Preissl*, not yet reported. Cf. Kjær 2008a: 262–265 on similar interpretive problems related to the provisions of the Sixth Directive.

However, after the decision of the Court, all language versions (including the concept referred to by the Danish word 'kjøretøjer') must be interpreted as meaning all means of transport, including boats, when used for the purpose of defining criteria for VAT. Similarly, in *Lietuvos geležinkeliai*,[145] the Court limited the meaning of 'motorized vehicles' in the particular context of import duties and VAT so as to exclude locomotives from the scope of the provision at issue.

Thus, in both instances, the ECJ provides a 'compliance guide',[146] including new knowledge about the meaning of the words which formed the kernel of the interpretive problem, to the national court whose task it is to subsequently apply the Court's authoritative interpretation in the national setting. However, this chunk of new knowledge concerns only the limited context of EU law: in this respect, the ECJ does not say anything about what the word used in the different language versions might mean in general in the official languages or in purely national legal situations.[147]

The Court's role in creating EU law meaning also results in a dichotomy between concepts used in national law and *sui generis* concepts of EU law.[148] From the perspective of attaining uniform interpretation and application of EU law throughout the EU, the dichotomy is not without problems. For national judges, this juxtaposition of meaning, which entails that the same words or expressions may be attributed different meanings depending on the applicatory context, results in an obvious quandary: in purely national settings, when EU law is not applicable, 'kjøretøjer' for example can still be interpreted as meaning land-based transport on wheels, or locomotives regarded as falling within the meaning of motorized vehicles. Here, the task of the national judge is an uneasy one: when differences between thus identified contextually conditioned meanings are subtle, the judge should nonetheless be able to (cognitively) distinguish situations where the case is governed by EU law meaning as opposed to (purely) national law meaning. In the long run, such a situation appears clearly untenable. This, again, places emphasis on the way the ECJ justifies its interpretive choices. It could be argued that if the ECJ succeeds in the task of convincing national courts of the acceptability of its interpretations, this is also the way these interpretations will allow for gradual infiltration of EU law concepts into national legal systems, thus also creating more uniformity on the level of national legal systems.[149]

145 Case C-250/11, *Lietuvos geležinkeliai*, not yet reported.

146 Davies 2012a: 81.

147 Similarly case 100/84, *Commission v United Kingdom* [1985] ECR 1169 and C-149/97, *The Institute of the Motor Industry v Commissioners of Customs and Excise* [1998] ECR 7053.

148 Kjær 2008a: 265.

149 Cf. Kjær 2004 on the role of discourse among the EU legal community in enabling integration.

As is clearly observable, parallels can be drawn with J.L.L. Austin's theory of illocutionary or speech acts.[150] In *Fonden Marselisborg Lystbådehavn*[151] and *Lietuvos geležinkeliai*,[152] the Court performs an illocutionary act by imposing a new meaning on the word 'vehicle' and 'motorized vehicle' and their equivalents in official language versions. For example, the Court's statement as to how the word should be applied in connection with VAT legislation imposes an obligation for national courts to follow this interpretation, irrespective of what the expression at issue might mean generally in the official language if interpreted separately in a national context.

This brings us back to the role of linguistic communities in defining meaning. With the help of Hart's famous example of 'no vehicles in the park', Schauer contends it is possible to differentiate between straightforward applications of a legal rule (in Hart's terms, the rule's core) and hard cases at the rule's edge.[153] According to Schauer's analysis, the way the word 'vehicle' is used in a particular linguistic community is what determines the standard meaning of the word 'vehicle'. The nucleus of the argument lies in the notion of 'linguistic *community*'. Certainly, that particular community may decide (unconciously) over time that the word 'vehicle' should instead refer to cats or pigs. In this respect, the meaning of a word or a sentence portrays its temporally conditioned function within the relevant linguistic community.[154]

However, meaning is not entirely or even largely a function of how individuals use language in specific situtations. Interestingly, no particular rule exists according to which we could not call a snowboard 'a tripod', although such a use would probably be criticized or otherwise sanctioned by other language users belonging to the same linguistic community. This is because we would have violated a rule reflecting linguistic practice. Although linguistic practices continuously change, enough short-term fixity exists for us to understand who is following the rules and who is breaking them, notwithstanding the long-term flexibility of those practices.[155] The same conclusion applies to legal language. However, this may hide the basic problem of language and the law: on the one hand, new sentences are understood, but on the other hand, no certainty exists as to the stability of meaning attributed to a sentence heard.

The obvious limits set by the relevant linguistic community aside, it seems doubtful whether a judge can, in practice, separate the literal meaning of a rule from its purpose.[156] This is in fact the nucleus of Fuller's counter-argument to Hart. In his response, Fuller raised the following hypothetical question: what if a

150 Austin 1975.
151 Case C-428/02, *Fonden Marselisborg Lystbådehavn* [2005] ECR I-1527.
152 C-250/11, *Lietuvos geležinkeliai*, not yet reported.
153 Hart 2012: 125–127. See also Schauer 2008: 1109–1110.
154 Schauer 2008: 1121.
155 Schauer 2008: 1122.
156 Tamanaha 2010: 170.

group of patriots sought to place in the park a functioning military truck as a war memorial?[157] Although in ordinary language the truck would count as a vehicle, within the context of application of the rule at hand, it was unclear whether a truck would, taking account of the purpose of the rule, fall within the scope of the rule. In essence, this can only be arbitrated on the basis of what is known about its legal context and how its deeper purpose is construed in that context.[158]

Certainly, the existence of hard cases does not mean that there are no clear cases: just as there are clear examples of, say, ankles and legs (although the borderline between the two is not clear at all), night and day, and vehicles, there are also clear cases in law. However, *potential* for vagueness always exists in language: this is the essence of 'open texture'.[159]

Even the most precise formulations carry the potential for vagueness so that no amount of precision can preclude the possibility of future (unforeseen) vagueness in context. In this respect, the difference between vagueness in the strict sense and open texture or open-endedness may be described as 'open texture is the possibility that even the least vague, the most precise, term will turn out to be vague'.[160] Understood this way, open-endedness is vagueness in the broad sense of the term.[161]

In this respect, Fuller's example captures the intricate problem of linguistic and legal indeterminacy we are concerned about. This is because it emphasizes the need for analyzing the provision at issue in context, in light of its (reconstructed) purpose. The kernel of judicial practice does not lie in determining 'literal meaning' which would exist separately from its broader context, but it is 'purpose, not unadorned literal meaning, that tells judges what falls within the core of the rule'.[162]

Certainly, the role of purpose-oriented reasoning closely relates to the moments of discretion in adjudication described in Chapter 1. On this view, the fact that the Court actively chooses among different solutions at various steps of its decision-making process implies that to influence meaning construction in national courts, it needs to explicate these choices. As the above-described debate on different types of vehicles suggests, this unavoidably means mapping out the underlying purposes and values on the basis of which the legal norm is construed *in context*.

Importantly, therefore, this brief excursion to the Hart-Fuller debate is also of significance in the context of EU law because Fuller was convinced that there are

157 Fuller 1958: 661–669.

158 Schauer 2008: 1111, who notes that Fuller's example was intended as a challenge to the idea that language would determine the core of a rule, as Hart called it.

159 Naturally, this is not to say that there would be a clear border between easy and hard cases, as Endicott points out. Endicott 2001: 379.

160 Schauer 1991: 35.

161 Endicott 2000: 37.

162 Tamanaha 2010: 168.

no rules that could be interpreted without looking at their purpose.[163] It is here that the example becomes particularly interesting within the context of the *Fonden Marselisborg Lystbådehavn* and *Lietuvos geležinkeliai* cases. When language versions and the subtle differences between their wording are examined, it is impossible to deduce the meaning of the text solely on the basis of wording. Rather, it is necessary to look at the provision's purpose in order to understand how the text should be interpreted. Of course, the Court's role in determining the 'correct' reading of the provision is based on its authority to impose its understanding of the EU legal system on national courts. Since acceptance appears only achievable through communication within the relevant linguistic community (here, the EU legal community, which in its most restrictive form consists of the Court and national courts), articulating the foundational purposes and values which guide the decision-making process form an inevitable aspect of the Court's armoury with which it can convince its audience of the well-foundedness of its interpretative choice.

Choosing among different meanings

The cases discussed above show how ordinary words and their indeterminacy in one or more language versions may have implications for the way in which EU law is interpreted. Apart from the indeterminacy of non-legal words and expressions, other recurring problems in interpreting EU law include different language versions, system-bound legal terms or concepts. These elements also add to the uncertainty in interpretation as differences in meaning stem from corresponding systemic disparities. While at the outset, language versions may appear equivalent, they might nonetheless carry diverse meanings because of differences between the national legal systems in which they are used.[164]

This is also a challenge for the Court although EU law provisions and EU law terms should, as a matter of principle, be interpreted autonomously from national concepts.[165] The idea of autonomous interpretation leaves the following question unanswered: is an autonomous 'EU interpretation' that disregards the interpreter's background knowledge and preconceptions possible? Certainly, the Connectionist model mapped above suggests that it would at least be possible to gradually change the way in which certain concepts and words are connected, and thus understood. This can be done if the interpreter is convinced of the acceptability of the new interpretation. In other words, in the case of EU law, the ECJ may guide the legal community in this operation through communicative reasoning. Before moving on to the issue of how such communication takes place, the issue of specialized meaning in the context of law is first explored.

163 Tamanaha 2010: 168. As Tamanaha notes, this may also be done unconsciously.

164 Cao 2007b: 76.

165 Cf. Prechal *et al.* 2008.

Creating specialized meanings that differ from ordinary, everyday meaning,[166] as in the above examples, may be regarded as problematic from the viewpoint of communication, since it makes the text and the subject area concerned less intelligible. However, to cope with the complexity of modern societies, specialization of meaning is necessary in contemporary legal systems.[167] Hence, in legal communication, meaning is discussed and determined.[168] Importantly, however, in the context of EU law, the communicative situations in which EU law provisions are interpreted and applied are multiplied compared to purely national settings. As the legal text does not carry meaning as an autonomous, context-independent entity, but rather meaning is created on the basis of the legal context at hand, the task of the Court is not to discover the meaning of the text as implied by linguistic arguments. Rather, it is to decide whether particular behaviour is in accordance with the rule that is argued to be the basis of the action. A text is only the basis on which a legal meaning is construed in a given situation.[169]

Essentially, the fact that in ordinary language (following the rules of a specific linguistic community) a car is plainly a vehicle, and it (usually) also counts as a vehicle in legal language, does not mean that law is restricted to the 'ordinary meaning' of ordinary terms. Indeed, in certain situations, law may use language that contains little if any meaning to a layperson, but this language may still have a 'plain' or 'ordinary' meaning within the law, for lawyers and judges.[170] As with words in everyday language, the meaning of legal words is determined by the rules of the relevant linguistic community, which in this case is the community of legal actors.

In this sense, Dworkin's idea of the connection between literary and judicial interpretation functions well in this context. He argues that just as in literary interpretation, in judicial interpretation courts should try to convince addressees of particular legal decisions of the soundness of the interpretation. Judges trying cases have to try to make the text (law) the best possible in the light of the purpose of the legal system; that is, in accordance with the political theory that guides the court's work. The theory includes, *inter alia*, substantive claims related to social or economic goals and principles of justice underlying the legal system in question.[171]

---

166 This is not to say that there would be any such clearly definable meaning as 'everyday meaning', as all language usage is indeterminate and contextual.

167 Endicott 2001: 382.

168 Engberg 2004: 1161, who argues that altering the meaning of lexical elements is not an optimal solution if no connection exists between the specialized meaning and the way in which the lexical element is used in other contexts.

169 Engberg 2002: 380 *et seq.*

170 Schauer 2008: 1123. Schauer refers to terms such as bailment, due process, and *res judicata* as examples of legal terminology that possess plain or ordinary meaning in law. Cf. Van Hoecke 2002: 140, who notes that in the legal context 'plain meaning' or 'ordinary meaning' is nothing other than *prima facie* meaning, determined by the context in which it appears, which may be used only if no counter arguments exist.

171 Dworkin 1985: 162, 172.

In other words, no such thing exists as 'ordinary' or 'plain' meaning to which judges could refer when interpreting a text in an individual case.[172] This may be regarded as contradictory with regard to what was said earlier about plain or ordinary meaning in law and language in general. A closer look reveals that this is not the case. Firstly, open-endedness of words does not entail that there could be no agreement as to what certain words mean. In fact, this is what the prototype theory claims from a cognitive perspective. From this perspective, it is correct to say, for instance, that a 'car' is a vehicle in the plain sense of the term. While it may be the case that a given object may be described as a vehicle, reference to language does not alone constitute a convincing argument; especially with a view to creating EU law meaning. This is because what is understood as the 'plain' or 'ordinary' meaning of a specific word may differ depending on the (legal) language in question. Secondly, therefore, what is decisive in determining the meaning of textual elements in particular cases is not whether the word or expression around which the interpretation centres may be interpreted in accordance with plain or ordinary meaning, but how these words should be understood *in relation to* the legal system.

The meaning chosen in individual cases depends, then, on the political morality that guides the Court's (and other courts') decision-making. This view follows mainly Dworkin's ideas about judicial interpretation. However, Dworkin's critic, Fish, who concentrates on the relationship between text and reader, opines that the only true meaning of a text is the one intended by the author.[173] Or, text means what its author intends, since intention exists prior to text: thus, no difference would exist between textual and purpose-oriented statutory interpretation, because those engaged in judicial interpretation are, by definition, trying to find out what the author intended by the text. However, it is a different matter altogether to determine exactly what that intention is.[174] But how and where can the Court find such an intention, in view of what was said about EU law-making in Chapter 1?

In this respect, the difference between *sender meaning* as opposed to *addressee meaning* comes in useful. While sender meaning refers to content attributed to a linguistic utterance to portray a message about reality, addressee meaning results from interpretation of a linguistic utterance by its addressee.[175] In the case of adjudication, it may be argued to constitute a form of *methodologically determined* addressee meaning attributed to a statute or other sources of law on the basis of conscious interpretation. As a result of this interpretive process, the message is placed in a broader systemic, contextual and teleological context.[176]

It is commonly accepted that adjudication is often based on other considerations than that of meaning. These include vague principles such as 'proportionality',

172 Endicott 1996: 697.

173 Fish 2005: 12 *et seq*. On the Dworkin-Fish debate, Glass 1986.

174 Fish 2005: 18.

175 Van Hoecke 2002: 128.

176 Van Hoecke 2002: 129.

a constant companion in the Court's analysis, that Fish calls 'stopping rules'. They tell the judge to stop looking for meaning.[177] Certainly, one could claim that judicial interpretation is not about finding the meaning of the text intended by its author(s) but rather about giving the relevant text, in the sense intended by Dworkin, the best possible interpretation with regard to the constraints of the legal system.[178] These constraints include values deeply rooted in society expressing the underlying rationality of the particular legal system. These elements are not of course objective. They refer to the court's normative understanding of the legal system that can be subject to disagreement.[179] In this sense, the 'stopping rules' to which Fish refers in fact come into play in judicial interpretation: they are included in the political theory that guides the interpretive process of courts.

Indeed, within the context of EU law, systemic and teleological considerations could be regarded as 'stopping rules'. When it becomes apparent that different language versions point to different conclusions, the ECJ judge cannot continue looking for the 'true meaning' of the text. Instead, on the basis of these legal mechanisms inherent in the EU legal system, an EU law meaning is constructed with reference to considerations such as the 'objectives and general scheme of the text and the purpose of the Treaty'.

Discursive legal certainty and judicial reasoning

The Court's judgments are generally intended for various addressees. After ending the meaning conflict between the parties by means of a judgment, the Court communicates a message to its addressees. In the context of preliminary references, which have received most attention in legal scholarship with regard to the dialogical[180] relationship between the Court and its national counterparts, the decision intends to end the uncertainty of national courts as to the meaning or validity of a specific provision of EU law. Thus, the parties to the case as well as national courts may be described as direct addressees of ECJ case law. It is therefore necessary to develop further the idea of the EU legal community.

177 Fish 2005: 12 *et seq*. Essentially, then, if we cannot know the intention, then law is based on an educated guess no matter which language it is expressed in. Cf. Sperber and Wilson 1995.

178 Glass: 205 on the two dimensions of fit that Dworkinian interpretative practice must satisfy: the first dimension consists of formal coherence and correspondence with existing legal rules and the second includes congruence with values and beliefs.

179 However, it would appear that the court's view with regard to the political theory that guides interpretation nevertheless often reflects the majority view.

180 Rosas 2007a: 6 *et seq*., who makes a distinction between five different categories of judicial dialogue in the EU. See also Claes 2006: 666, Groussot 2008: 934 *et seq*. See also case C-495/03, *Intermodal Transports BV v Staatssecretaris van Financiën* [2005] ECR I-8151, para 38.

Taking account of the Court's role as the guardian of uniformity in the EU legal system, its judgments may also be argued to be directed to the whole legal community. Adopting a broader perspective, the EU legal community would thus include national judiciaries and other legal actors which comprise parties and interveners such as the Commission, other EU institutions as well as Member States and also legal scholars. In a broader sense still, this community includes private actors, organizations and citizens. However, due to the importance of the preliminary ruling procedure in shaping EU law, it is argued here that national courts constitute the primary addressees of ECJ judgments.

This multi-layered understanding of the EU legal community translates into separate communicative spheres.[181] Indeed, as EU law is constantly moulded and developed in ECJ case law, these changes must be accepted in deliberative communication among the ECJ and its 'stakeholders';[182] that is, the EU legal community. Different communicative spheres are presented in Figure 3.1 below.

The first circle represents the communicative sphere where judgment is given as a result of communication between the parties, interveners and the ECJ. If the ECJ succeeds in offering convincing arguments in support of its decision, both the parties, interveners as well as national courts, primary addressees of preliminary rulings, might accept the decision. Positing the Advocates General (AGs) into this figure is somewhat problematic. On the one hand, as members of the Court, they form part of the inner circle of the ECJ itself. On the other hand, their opinions are not binding and may differ from the Court's judgment.

In this respect, the AGs may be argued to perform a twofold function in this context. Viewed from an external perspective, they form part of the Court, with their impartial and independent reasoned opinions adding to the discursiveness of ECJ decision-making by explicating in more detail issues related to the case decided by the Court: the opinions may in this respect be said to increase the persuasiveness of ECJ reasoning.[183] From an internal standpoint, however, AGs form part of the first circle of the Court's primary audience so that they need to be convinced, too. It should also be observed that this relationship is particularly dialectical: not only does the Court itself need to convince the AGs but the opposite also holds true. Generally, AGs' opinions reflect on previous ECJ case law so that if they are not convinced by ECJ judgments and the soundness of the reasoning, these reservations are often expressed in subsequent opinions, which in turn aim at convincing the Court.[184]

The second circle refers to the broader context of similar cases, thus closely connecting to the AGs' role at the ECJ. If previous case law is not followed, the

181 See Van Hoecke 2002: 176–177. Cf. Salmi-Tolonen 2005: 66 on the communicative strategy inherent in Advocates' General opinions.

182 Bengoetxea 2007: 55.

183 Lasser 2004: 347 *et seq.* See also Salmi-Tolonen 2005: 66–67.

184 Salmi-Tolonen 2005: 66.

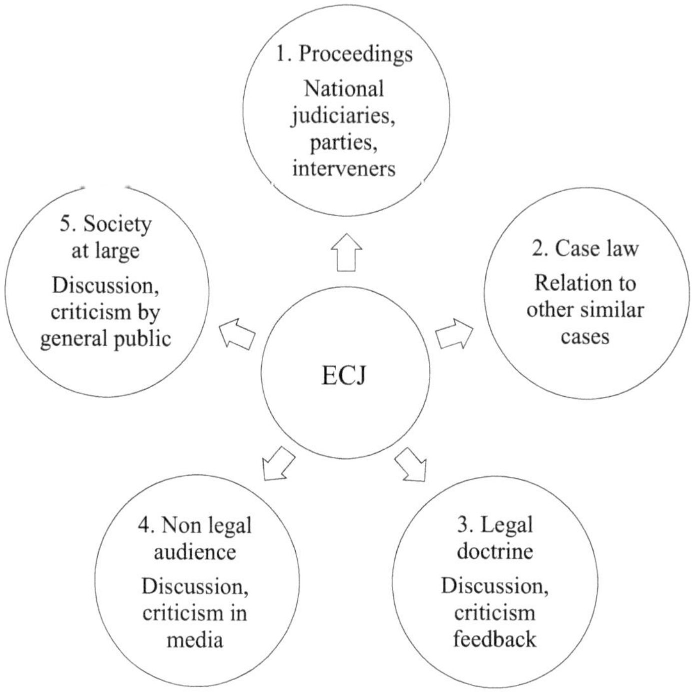

Figure 3.1 Communicative spheres of the Court's judgments

Court must in general give more in-depth reasons for that choice.[185] In this sense, ECJ judgments are in dialogical interaction with previous case law so that the acceptability of individual judgments is to a certain extent determined in relation to other similar cases. Consequently, ECJ decisions may also be discussed in legal doctrine and subsequently followed or overruled in future cases.

The third circle consists in discussion on ECJ case law in legal doctrine. In general, legal scholars comment on and criticize ECJ judgments that are deemed important. Consequently, they place these judgments in a broader context of case law. By the same token, legal scholars systematize the content of EU law.[186] Indeed, sometimes these comments influence decision-making in future cases. In this respect, legal doctrine constitutes a space for feedback where the (substantive issues of the) Court's judgments are evaluated and systematized with regard to other cases. From the viewpoint of multilingualism, it is interesting to note that discussion among EU legal scholars concerning ECJ judgments primarily occurs in

185 See *e.g.* case C-208/90, *Emmot* [1991] ECR I-4269 and subsequent case C-335/91, *Steenhorst-Neerings* [1993] ECR I-3475.

186 Similarly Tuori 2002: 320.

one of the 'big' languages, to a large extent in English.[187] This scholarly discourse on EU law occurs irrespective of constraints related to multilingualism. Does this mean that the practical importance of multilingualism is gradually diminishing? What will this mean for the *quality* of discourse?

The fourth circle represents cases in which the Court's judgments attract attention in the media so that they are discussed by a non-legal audience as well.[188] Finally, the fifth circle refers to society at large: in cases where judgments concern fundamental ethical or political questions (such as abortion,[189] terrorism[190] and immigration[191]), citizens may be closely involved with such cases.[192]

The great majority of cases are discussed in the first three communicative spheres whereby communication is limited to the community of legal professionals.[193] Legal certainty in its substantive form relates first and foremost to these three spheres, although not exclusively. In this respect, it seems plausible to argue that the more technical and individual the issue, the more limited is the interest for the broader community. However, in cases involving broad political significance (or even in technical matters with general importance as precedent), it is important that these cases are discussed in not only the first two but also the other three spheres.[194] The further one moves towards the general public and away from the spheres of communication involving legal professionals, the more problematic achieving general acceptable judicial decisions may be argued to be.[195]

187 Jääskinen 2008: 219. He notes that to a certain extent, legal doctrine is divided according to national and language borders while law journals published in English constitute an exception in this respect.

188 It could be argued that the well-known *Bosman* case (transfer of footballers) made the ECJ known to a wider public: see case C-415/93, *Bosman* [1995] ECR I-4921.

189 See *e.g.* case C-159/90, *Grogan* [1991] ECR I-4685.

190 See *e.g.* case C-402/05 P, *Kadi and Al Barakaat International Foundation v. Council and Commission* [2008] ECR I-6351 and C-340/08, *M and Others v. Her Majesty's Treasury* [2010] ECR I-03913.

191 See *e.g.* case C-261/08, *Zurita García and Choque Cabrera* [2009] ECR I-10143 and C-357/09 PPU, *Said Shamilovich Kadzoev (Huchbarov)* [2009] ECR I-11189.

192 Increasingly, as a result of media interest and the Internet in particular, society in general also plays an important part in the legal field.

193 Van Hoecke 2002: 177.

194 Van Hoecke 2002: 177–178.

195 In scholarship, acceptance of general doctrines of primacy and direct effect (*e.g.* Alter 2001: notably 64 *et seq.*, Stone Sweet 2004) devised by the Court have been discussed at length, but less attention has been paid to analysis of how, in concrete terms, the dialectic of EU courts mediates in relation to open norms such as proportionality. See Davies 2012a: 78. According to Davies, 'the question *how* the law is used becomes at least as important as *whether* it is used, and focus on acceptance can mislead' in the context of open norms which allow for national courts and the ECJ to focus on their respective tasks of interpretation and application.

The multifaceted communicative situation depicted above might be said to refer to what Madsen calls the 'external communication situation' of a judgment.[196] This description may be said to carry affinity with Kelsen's understanding of legal communication in general.[197] The sender is the lawmaker and direct addressees are lawyers, more specifically judges who have the authority to interpret the message sent by the lawmaker.[198] In this respect, problems related to multilingual legal communication are multiplied in the EU because the communicative situations are multiplied.[199] Whether the ECJ succeeds in convincing direct addressees of the judgment (the referring court and the parties to the dispute as well as interveners) of its interpretation, and furthermore, whether its interpretation will be generally accepted in the different Member States (through acceptance by the legal community in general), depends on how the decision is justified. At first glance, in the *Fonden Marselisborg* case, for example, the solution that boats also count as vehicles appears to be problematic from the viewpoint of formal legal certainty or, more specifically, from the viewpoint of predictability especially with regard to the Danish language version.

However, a closer look reveals deficiencies in this approach. Instead, predictable and transparent reasoning is of more central importance in the EU legal system, since a certain degree of indeterminacy (that is, uncertainty as to the result in legal adjudication) is actually needed in order for relatively static legal texts, such as statutes, to be applied to new situations. Rosas notes that 'values and general principles should emerge and evolve in a deliberative process, where judges and other decision-makers interact in a search for *general acceptability* [italics added]'.[200]

This search for acceptability closely relates to the Court's reasoning, the visible part of this deliberative process. In a multilingual legal system, the use of teleological reasoning to support interpretive decisions would appear to increase transparency with regard to normative choices made by the Court. This is particularly so, it is argued, in cases where the ECJ is confronted with ambiguous or conflicting language versions. In fact, the use of *telos* as the guiding principle of interpretation signifies that the ECJ (and subsequently, national courts) are not only bound by the wording and presumed (*ex post* reconstruction of the) intent of the lawmaker: *telos* further requires that the Court gives a more consistent

---

196 Madsen 2000: 164.

197 Kelsen 1979: 40. See also Šarčević 2000, who highlights the role of translators as mediators in multilingual legal communication.

198 While the general public may be said to merely represent indirect addressees of the message, the normative effects of legal texts nonetheless directly concern the activities of these indirect addressees; that is, citizens.

199 Šarčević 2000: 7.

200 Rosas 2007a: 15.

normative reading of the provision in question.[201] Yet it also leaves national courts with discretion in their applicatory task.

This is related to the distinction between justification and application discourses explained above. A discursive justification of valid norms ensures that the general following of a norm represents a universal interest.[202] A norm is justified if all participants could accept it because of the reasons stated. This requires that some ideal conditions of argumentation are fulfilled. These include rules of semantic consistency necessary in reasoning, rules for organization of a conversation, and rules ensuring free and equal participation of all those concerned.[203]

However, norms created in such a process of impartial justification are only *prima facie* applicable to a specific case. These general circumstances have to be completed with a 'full description' of the facts of the case. To achieve this requires a special discourse: application discourse. As soon as the participants enter this discourse, they have to leave that perspective of circumstances being equal in every situation which was presupposed with the validity of a norm. This argument is not directed against the validity of other, possibly colliding norms but only against their appropriateness in the case at hand: in other words, application discourse has to do with the appropriateness of a norm which can at the outset be applicable.[204]

Applying the distinction between justification and application discourse to the Court's role in the EU legal system, one could in fact argue that *telos* offers a way for the ECJ to engage in justification discourse: as a result of the 'incomplete' nature of the EU law-making process leaving questions of political significance unanswered, EU law is in need of further justification. What is more, in the particular context of the preliminary ruling procedure, the actual application discourse is posited on the national level due to the applicatory authority enjoyed by national courts. Although often venturing into making factual assertions, the Court's role in this judicial space is far more complex. Through the case at hand, it directs legal development within the EU: arguably, since EU legislation is based on diverging normative assumptions, translations and often intentionally vague language, the ECJ in its decision-making needs to engage not only in application discourse but also justification discourse.

Justification discourse requires that all interests are duly taken into consideration. Clearly, deciding general questions of EU law on the basis of individual cases, in particular in the preliminary ruling procedure, implies that questions of justification become relevant. Within the EU context, the preliminary ruling procedure in particular enables consideration of different interests in the process: not only parties to national proceedings before the referring court, but also

201 Maduro 2007: 10.

202 See also Habermas 1984: 75 *et seq.*

203 Habermas 1984: 97 *et seq.* See also Torres Pérez 2009: 119 on the prerequisites of a well-functioning judicial dialogue.

204 Günther 1989: 158–159.

the broader EU legal community are able to engage in the process. In this sense, it is not only a question of applying *prima facie* applicable norms to the case at hand but, rather, the ECJ must take into account the broader normative context of its decisions where even conflicting interests must be considered. Relevant interests are not confined to those of the parties to the national proceedings but also include EU policy interests defended by the Commission as well as Member State policy interests framed in observations submitted by Member State governments.[205] Therefore, instigating proceedings before the Court often results in a broader evaluation of the policy interests at stake, again justifying frequent recourse to purpose-oriented reasoning.

In a situation where a risk of incongruent language versions exists, the ECJ cannot fulfil its role as the linguistic authority harmonizing legal meaning in the EU context without reference to the overall purpose of the provision and of the systemic context in general. So in order for the ECJ to convince the legal community (national courts in the first instance), it needs arguments that do not have their basis in the meaning of individual language versions in order to make the interpretation feasible and acceptable despite differences between language versions.

While reference to wording would hide alternative normative readings and make debate impossible, teleological reasoning arguably contributes to a debate among alternative normative preferences in the interpretive process. In this sense, the AGs' role is one of particular significance from the perspective of justification: in their opinions, they discuss more broadly the systemic impact of individual decisions compared to the way those issues are discussed in ECJ judgments.[206] Hence, they give guidance not only to the Court but also to the wider legal community with regard to the deeper normative choices and teleological foundations of possible different interpretations in a specific case. In other words, the AGs play a pronounced role in providing an understanding as to how a particular decision fits into a given systemic and meta-teleological conception of the EU legal system.

On the one hand, in the actual judgment, teleological reasoning makes the reasoning more transparent, since it obliges the ECJ to make value choices explicit. On the other hand, from the viewpoint of communication, one could say

205 See, in this respect, Article 23 of the Statute of the Court of Justice. In cases where a reference for a preliminary ruling is related to an act originating from the Council or the European Central Bank or to an act adopted jointly by the European Parliament and the Council, these institutions are also notified of the case and have an opportunity to submit written observations. Interestingly, in cases governed by Article 267 TFEU, the reference is also notified to State parties to the EEA Agreement and the EFTA Surveillance Authority which also have the option to submit statements of case and written observations to the ECJ in cases concerning fields of application of the EEA Agreement. See also Jacobs 2003: 549.

206 On the AGs' discursive strategy, see Lasser 2004: 237.

that teleological reasoning opens the chosen interpretation to debate within the legal community. Indeed, as the substantive element of legal certainty is closely tied to acceptability of judicial decisions, it requires transparent reasoning, which in a multilingual legal system, it would appear, requires that the relevant purpose-oriented arguments and value choices that influenced the decision are stated explicitly.

Dialogue among courts

'Language has its true being only in dialogue, in coming to an understanding'.[207] This statement is equally true in the context of communication among EU courts. Indeed, language – understood as reasoning in the context of adjudication – may be used to negotiate a common understanding of law.[208]

As suggested in the previous sections, the ECJ may through its reasoning gradually change meanings which legal actors associate with specific words in the limited EU law context. This can only be done through communication among relevant legal actors: that is, through transparent judicial reasoning in which, *inter alia*, value and policy choices underlying inherently subjective interpretive processes are openly discussed. In this respect, achieving a genuine dialogue between the ECJ and national courts appears important so as to create a common cognitive basis for interpretation.[209]

In fact, the solution to the problem of diverging language versions encompassing different legal systems and cultures may lie in conceptualization. Accordingly, as the Connectionist model suggests, concepts used by people speaking different languages and forming part of different cultures will be most alike if people are designed to form the same or similar concepts from the same or similar experiences.[210] Put differently, the likelihood of identical concepts possesses both an innate component (our cognitive design) and a cultural one (how culture structures experience and represents it in that culture's language).[211]

It is most likely that creating common understanding and shared experience can be achieved in the preliminary ruling procedure based on Article 267 TFEU, since under that procedure the ECJ not only guides national courts in individual

207 Gadamer 2006: 443. See also Glass 1986: 209, who observes that Gadamerian and Heideggerian hermeneutics 'takes as primary not the subject that understands nor the object that is understood but the fact that both subject and object must stand within a pregiven historic and linguistic tradition'.

208 Kjær 2004: 395. Cf. Habermas 1984. See also generally on judicial dialogue Ordóñez-Solís 2007, Baez Seara 2008.

209 On the role of dialogue in judicial relations in Europe, Rosas 2007a: 15. See also Ordóñez-Solís 2007, Cartabia 2007 on judicial cooperation and dialogue in the global age. For an opposing view on the existence of a genuine dialogue among courts, see Alter 2001.

210 Solan 2009b: 19.

211 Engberg 2004.

cases, it also guides the application of EU law on a general level by interpreting it in relation to individual cases brought before it by national courts. Precisely for this reason, the need for *substantive* reasons is highlighted here, since these provide 'a thicker normative understanding of the law beyond the decision in the case at hand'.[212]

Although theoretically dialectical, the nature of the preliminary ruling procedure is admittedly such that participating courts are not on a level playing field; rather, it is for the ECJ to state the law and provide national courts with assistance as to the proper interpretation and application of EU legislation.[213] In this respect, Dani contends that 'the current state of judicial relationships is for many reasons far from the comfortable image of dialogue. Not only do many national [courts] seem reluctant to dismiss certain belligerent tones when it comes to EU issues, but also the Court [...] does not seem entirely convinced by the argument that it should abandon its unilateral style of adjudication and establish genuine and open relationships with its national interlocutors'.[214]

To be sure, the discourse situation in which communication between the courts takes place is not 'ideal' in that communication is not necessarily reciprocal and free from constraint; instead, it is based on the ECJ as the authoritative interpreter of EU law to 'dictate' meanings and give content to abstract and open-ended provisions of EU law.

At the same time, as current scholarly interest in constitutional pluralism clearly illustrates,[215] the relationship between the ECJ and national (constitutional) courts does not form a relation of direct vertical hierarchy in that the ECJ does not function as a court of appeal empowered to annul or modify national court judgments. Nor is there among scholars any unanimous reading with regard to how this relationship should be depicted in constitutional terms. However, discussion on constitutional pluralism extends beyond the scope of this book.

212 Maduro 2007: 9.

213 However, this is not to say that national courts always accept ECJ interpretations without reservation. For the most known examples, see German Constitutional Court decisions: Internationale Handelsgesellschaft v Einfuhr und Vorratsstelle für Getreide und Futtermittel, BVerfG 37, 271 (Solange I) and Wünsche Handelsgesellschaft, BvR 2, 197/83 (Solange II) and BVerfG 89, 155 (Maastricht). See also the German Constitutional Court judgment on the Lisbon Treaty of June 30, 2009, BVerfG 2 BvE 2/08. More recently, other Member State constitutional courts have joined the fray. For example, after the Court's ruling in case C-399/09 Landtová [2011] ECR I-5573, the Czech constitutional court declared the ECJ judgment ultra vires. Cf. Ojanen 1998: 313–319 on the Constitutional Court's approach that Ojanen describes as one of the phases of acceptance and antagonism. See also Claes 2006: 666 *et seq.* who notes that especially the principle of primacy of the EU frames the dialogue between the ECJ and national courts.

214 Dani 2009: 151.

215 See, in particular, contributions in Avbelj and Komárek 2012. For earlier discussion, *inter alia* Kumm 1999, Kumm 2005, Barber 2006 and Baquero Cruz 2008.

Be that as it may, from a purely discursive standpoint, the dividing line between interpretation and application is clearly 'perilously thin' so that the Court's willingness to occasionally provide national courts with solidly concrete answers or case-specific applicatory guidance sometimes gives this dialogue a multilateral tonality.[216] And indeed, as is well known, failure to respect ECJ interpretations or, in some cases, failure to request a ruling may constitute an infringement leading to proceedings before the ECJ or an action for damages brought by a private person against the Member State in question.[217]

So, why do we nonetheless insist on describing this judicial relationship in terms of a dialogue? Although judicial action can never be wholly free from strategic considerations oriented to consequences and steered by individual preferences – because bargaining and reasoning are unavoidably intertwined in actual instances of discourse[218] – there is no reason to exclude conceptualizing the interaction among the ECJ and national courts in terms of dialogue.[219] In this sense, the image of dialogue depicted here is firmly rooted in reality and not made from a strictly Habermasian standpoint.

Despite its shortcomings and despite the reluctance of some national (constitutional) courts to engage in dialogue,[220] the interaction between the ECJ and national courts (especially the lower courts) forms a dialectic where it is up to national courts to a) decide on the need for a reference, b) formulate the questions put to the court, c) determine the relevant facts, and d) apply the Court's interpretive stance to the particular circumstances of the case at hand. While the questions may sometimes be reformulated by the Court, it is at least in principle bound by the questions referred to it by national courts. Moreover, a national court may also suggest an answer or outline optional answers in its reference for a preliminary ruling.[221] In fact, in an information note on preliminary rulings, the ECJ has specifically encouraged national courts to suggest their own answer to questions referred.[222]

216 Craig and de Búrca 2011: 473–474.

217 For the shortcomings of the preliminary ruling procedure, Komárek 2010. Case C-6/90 and C-9/90, *Francovich and Bonifaci v Italy* [1991] ECR I-5357. See also the *Köbler* case, case C-224/01, *Gerhard Köbler* [2003] ECR I-10239, para 118 *et seq.* See also *inter alia* case C-453/00, *Kühne & Heitz* [2004] ECR I-837, paras 27 and 28. The *Kempter* case is also related to the issue, case C-2/06, *Willy Kempter* [2008] ECR I-0411, especially paras 57–60 and case C-495/03, *Intermodal Transports* [2005] ECR I-8151, para 38.

218 Elster 1998: 5–8.

219 Torres Pérez 2009: 132–133.

220 See for example Maduro 2012: 74 (note 32).

221 Rosas 2007a: 8. He notes that views expressed by the referring court may also in some cases be reflected in the actual ECJ judgment.

222 Information note on references by national courts for preliminary rulings (OJ 2009 C 297, p. 1). See also Article 94 of the Rules of Procedure of the Court of Justice (OJ 2012 L 265, p. 1).

Put differently, notwithstanding the admittedly manifold challenges that may be observed in this dialogue, as doctrinal discussion on constitutional pluralism aptly shows, the preliminary ruling procedure aims – in Gadamerian terms – at coming to an understanding among courts. This dialogue oriented towards mutual understanding takes place in a temporal continuum: it takes form 'over time, as courts from different states bring arguments before the ECJ, and the interpretive outcomes keep on being refined'.[223]

Chalmers' prescription to remedy the shortcomings of this dialectic is three-fold and stems from his call for constitutional tolerance.[224] First, it would require a national court requesting a preliminary ruling to devise an opinion that would not only set out its understanding of the national law and how the case should be resolved. The opinion would also explain how national law fits with European legal values. As national courts form part of a broader network of European courts, this opinion should, accordingly, provide a set of principled reasons for how the relationship between values could evolve.

Second, this dialogue would involve the Court in addressing points raised by the national court, giving reasons for where it agreed or disagreed with those points. As Chalmers puts it, 'in a community of values whose constituent elements include national values, there is a duty to explain the relationship between the two'.[225] Of particular significance would thus be the discursive articulation of relevant values and their mutual order of importance through the use of principles as commands to optimize. Together, the preliminary reference and the Court's judgment thus form opposing parts of a dialogue. Third, however, when the Court's solution is not accepted and disagreement persists, national constitutional courts would be free to deviate from the Court's judgment providing that they explain why their interpretation conforms to broader European values.[226] This reasoned disagreement could, in turn, convince the Court to adapt its future rulings accordingly. Similarly, Davies' emphasis on the national courts' mandate to *apply* the Court's interpretation in concrete cases illustrates how this discretionary space offers a tool for managing disagreement.[227]

Multifaceted, as the communicative spheres sketched above show, this dialogue not only concerns the referring court and the ECJ. On every reference to the ECJ, parties to national court proceedings, Member State governments as well as EU institutions are entitled to present written observations and take part in the hearing. Furthermore, the fact that the Court itself comprises judges and AGs from different Member States and with experience of diverse legal systems

223 Torres Pérez 2009: 139.

224 Chalmers 2004: 34–35. Similar tonalities of tolerance and cooperation can be perceived in Davies 2012a and Torres Pérez 2009.

225 Chalmers 2004: 34.

226 This comes close to what Weiler calls a 'new style of conversation' between national courts and the ECJ. See Weiler 2001: 226.

227 Davies 2012a.

means that this dialogue contains elements which certainly suggest responsiveness to differences inherent in those legal systems.[228]

Protection of fundamental rights serves as an example of the importance of preliminary ruling references for 'cross-fertilization'[229] of EU and national legal systems. After references from German courts on the matter, the ECJ developed a doctrine according to which fundamental rights were enshrined in the general principles of Community law and protected by the Court.[230] These references encouraged the ECJ to recognize protection of fundamental rights as forming part of the EU legal system.[231] In this sense, the ongoing dialogue among courts serves as a springboard for new developments within the EU legal system.

Although national courts are under the obligation to follow ECJ case law, the Court's guidance can be of a general character – and even contain silences that can be interpreted in minimalist terms[232] – which can in practice be argued to give leeway to national courts with regard to application of rules stated in the Court's case law. Within the context of judicial review, Komárek argues for a reassessment of the preliminary ruling procedure and for a differentiated approach which would not undermine the role of national judicial systems.[233] While it is true that providing authoritative guidance to national courts as to the correct understanding of the law can only be done by consistent and reasoned judgments of general significance to the development of EU law, it is important to note that the precondition for the success of preliminary rulings and also in broader terms for the coherent evolution of EU law and its uniform application throughout Europe is that domestic courts use it. 'If references dwindle, [EU] law will not evolve and the Court will lose authority'.[234]

Thus, without going into the details of the constitutionally loaded debate about judicial review, it is observed that in order to ensure that the Court's reading is accepted by these courts, a strong case exists that the ECJ needs to articulate values and general principles in its reasoning so that communication between the ECJ and national courts, as well as between the ECJ and the broader legal community, may develop concerning the best-reasoned outcome from the perspective of EU law. Additionally, values, principles and other substantive arguments in the Court's reasoning may be described as serving as 'road-signs and yardsticks'[235] on the basis of which stability, consistency, predictability and perhaps even coherence –

---

228 Jacobs 2003: 549.

229 Jacobs 2003: 548.

230 See, *inter alia*, Lockhart and Weiler 1995, de Witte 1999 and von Bogdandy 2000. For a recent contribution to the discussion, see Bryde 2010. On judicial dialogue in relation to fundamental rights, see Torres Pérez 2009.

231 Jacobs 2003: 549. See also Cartabia 2007: 4.

232 Sarmiento 2012.

233 Komárek 2011: 114–115.

234 Bengoetxea 2007: 57.

235 Rosas 2007a: 15.

in the sense of coherence in judicial reasoning – can be achieved. This is important not only with regard to the multilingual character of EU law, but also the particular characteristics of the Treaties expressing different (sometimes even conflicting) principles, objectives and purposes.

Although the EU Treaties are particularly purpose-oriented, one can argue that vagueness would not disappear with precise formulations.[236] Rather, it is a question of degree: formulations in different legal instruments can be more or less precise, but this does not make the Court's interpretive task any less significant from the viewpoint of deciding on EU legal meaning. The Treaties, as well as EU legislation in general, can be described as instruments lacking in precision, but the same can be said of many (national) constitutions and other legal instruments. While they do not perhaps express aims and purposes as clearly as the Treaties do, they typically contain general principles, fundamental rights and values.

Even without taking into account problems of multilingualism, the translated nature of EU law, the shortcomings of the political process and the pluralist nature of the EU legal system necessarily delegate to courts, and more particularly to the ECJ, the role of final arbiter of the normative content of EU legislation.[237] This highlights the importance of reasoning in judicial decisions in order to guarantee a sufficient degree of (democratic) control over decisions by courts. When the ECJ is faced with a choice between conflicting or ambiguous provisions, reference to *telos* opens the decision to debate in the legal community and thus contributes to communicative reasoning that represents the Court's interpretive process more accurately than reference to wording or presumed intent.

Agreement among the legal community

This section builds on the ideas presented above with regard to the different communicative spheres in which the Court's judgments operate. This section explores more closely the role of the *legal* community in understanding legal certainty.

Judgments concerning correct or incorrect use of language – that is, the concept of meaning in general – are based on community agreement.[238] In this context, the definition of community introduced by Finnis offers a helpful starting point: 'wherever there is, over an appreciable span of time, a co-ordination of activity by a number of persons, in the form of interactions, and with a view to a shared objective'.[239]

236 See Rosas 2006: 488. He notes that the Court's purpose-oriented approach to interpretation of EU law is not so much a conscious choice, but a consequence of the open-endedness of Treaty provisions.

237 Maduro 2007: 9. See also Stone Sweet 2012, who describes this development as a 'judicial coup d'état'.

238 Cf. Schauer 2008: 1121.

239 Finnis 1980: 153.

In the context of EU law, one could argue that the EU legal community must also be based on (at least) an implicit shared understanding of the objectives of the legal system. Cotterrell differentiates between different types of communities: traditional community (habitual, accidental or traditional forms of interaction); instrumental community (community aiming at a shared goal); community of belief (community sharing beliefs and values); and affective community (based on mutual affection among individuals belonging to this community).[240]

Here, the concept of *community* must be tied to law: what is relevant, then, is defining the concept of 'EU legal community'. Primarily, for the present dialectical purposes among courts, the notion of the EU legal community should be understood as comprising national judiciaries – who may subsequently use and reaffirm ECJ case law by applying it in other similar cases – and other legal actors (including parties and interveners, *i.e.* the Commission, other EU institutions, Member States as well as legal scholars as identified above). This strict understanding of 'the EU legal community' is plausible since legal professionals' understanding of values and policies that ought to govern judicial decision-making may be influenced more easily in comparison with conceptions on a deeper societal level.[241]

Although one might say that legal adjudication constitutes an elite discourse in which only 'authorized' actors directly participate, a strong case exists that citizens and other private actors may increasingly be taking part in this discourse due *inter alia* to easy access to case law on the Internet. For that reason, a need may arise to review the types of arguments used in order to ensure that judicial decisions are also accepted by the wider public.[242] However, for reconfiguring legal certainty on the basis of a dialogue between relevant specialists, the emphasis must remain on a strict understanding of a *legal* community, thus excluding the fourth and fifth communicative circles from the analysis.

In the context of the EU legal system, employing Cotterrell's distinction, the EU legal community mainly comprises instrumental elements and shared beliefs. Clearly, in order for the legal system to function, shared beliefs and values are indispensable (*e.g.* values related to fundamental rights, views on democracy and economy in the EU context). Traditionally, the European project has been conceptualized as one furthering certain objectives including the gradual establishment of an internal market, an obvious expression of the EU as an essentially instrumental community.[243] While problems related to integration may partly be explained by the lack of traditional community in the EU context (lack of a shared language), on the level of specialists, EU law and more specifically discourse among legal actors about the meaning of EU law and its intrinsic values may be argued to enhance the coming into being of an EU legal community that

240 Cotterrell 1997a: 80–81.
241 Van Hoecke 2002: 58–59.
242 Cf. Paso 2012: 35–36.
243 Similarly Davies 2012b: 271 and 281.

increasingly shares common denominators and interests as well as an understanding of values and beliefs in society.[244]

While Member State legal systems, legal cultures and legal languages certainly differ to different extents, existing common discourse – as manifested, *inter alia*, by judicial dialogue between the ECJ and national courts – on the meaning of EU law may instigate change both in national legal systems and national legal languages.[245] In this respect, judicial reasoning that succeeds in convincing the legal community in question about the correctness of interpretation assumes central importance. Previously, the context of legal discourse was firmly rooted within the borders of the nation state and the corresponding national legal system.[246] Given the emergence of the EU legal system, this discourse is no longer confined to national legal systems. Although Europeanization brings with it problems related to conflicting legal practices and differing legal languages, EU legal discourse may gradually contribute to changing national legal concepts and, more generally, legal languages so as to reflect this EU discourse in law.

Tying the notion of community to judicial reasoning and adjudication, the role of the legal community in determining the underlying values of a particular legal system implies that courts are in fact using a word correctly only if its use is in accordance with the way the pertinent majority of the legal community in question use the word.[247] That is, agreement among the relevant community (which in this case is the EU legal community) as to the 'correctness' of the interpretation (the meaning given to the words in question) and of the way in which the Court has deployed the relevant words for deciding the case such as 'vehicle', 'canalization' or 'flood-relief works'. Certainly, in such cases it would appear correct to say that no agreement exists, at least *a priori*, as to the meaning of the contested text. In this respect, it is for the Court to seek consensus among the relevant legal community.[248]

It is useful to note that the concept of 'consensus' discussed here links to the political theory of the court deciding cases in the Dworkinian sense. In fact, this approach presupposes that a political or ideological component exists in that consensus.[249] The political theory that guides judicial interpretation at the Court

244 Van Hoecke 2002: 31.

245 Goddard 2011: 124–127 on the limits of legal culture as a research tool due to its elusiveness as a concept. See also Cotterrell 2006: 88 on the linkage between legal culture and legal ideology.

246 Kjær 2004: 395.

247 Bix 1993: 39. See also Tamanaha 2004: 89 on the role of internalized values and beliefs of the judicial community in controlling indeterminacy in law.

248 Tontti 2004: 177 on how cases are categorized as hard or easy on the basis of prejudices and stereotypical cases. However, one can nonetheless say that this does not mean that there are no easy cases in law. Rather the 'easiness' of a case can be attributed to a (perhaps in some cases temporary) consensus of society or, in the case of law, of the relevant legal subset of society. See in this respect Bix 1993: 37.

249 Bix 1993: 38.

has to be accepted by the broader EU legal community in order to guarantee acceptance of ECJ case law as binding in Member States. Arguably, economic considerations (economic integration) can be seen to guide judicial interpretation at the ECJ. Thus, if the ECJ believes that the dominant purpose of the EU legal system, the goal it should serve, is economic, then earlier cases as well as future cases will be decided in a way that promotes economic goals. However, individual judges' opinions about the 'best interpretation' with regard to the underlying purpose of the legal system do not necessarily need to be the same.[250]

But, as there are no dissenting opinions in ECJ judgments, it would appear that even if some judges dissent from such a view about the function of EU law (economic goals as opposed to protecting fundamental rights, for example), the overall political theory that guides judicial interpretation and meaning-creation will not be affected.[251] The question remains, nonetheless, as to at what point the minority view about correct interpretation becomes relevant enough for it to be taken into account and change the way in which the purpose of the legal system is defined. Clearly, once the ideology[252] of the relevant subset of society changes, cases that are considered as 'clear' will subsequently change, too.[253]

Multilingualism is more often seen as a problem than an opportunity for the functioning of the EU legal system. In judicial interpretation at the ECJ, the central problem remains identical to that of any other legal system: how to reach mutual understanding between specialists by interpreting words and phrases. However, in the EU, the situation is somewhat more complex due to the number of languages involved. Thus, not only is there a discussion among specialists (lawyers) speaking the same mother tongue about how a specific word may be interpreted (intra-lingual indeterminacy), but additionally the problem exists of different languages in which meaning is generally distributed differently.[254]

As the analysis above concerning the *Fonden Marselisborg Lystbådehavn*[255] and *Lietuvos geležinkeli*[256] cases aims to illustrate, multilingualism adds to the uncertainty of any given language a new element of uncertainty which arises from inconsistency in the meaning of words in different language versions. This is by no means surprising, as in translation it is impossible to achieve absolute exactness or complete identity between source and target languages.[257] However,

250 Dworkin 1985: 162.

251 Torres Pérez 2009: 133, who explains how argumentation, even when based on self-interest, can possess a powerful restrictive function: courts 'not only need to be impartial, but also to appear to be so' so that dialogue among them can be argued to restrain recourse to individual interests.

252 Cf. Cotterrell 2006: 89 on legal ideology as generated and sustained in the interplay between legal practice and doctrine.

253 Bix 1993: 38.

254 Engberg 2004: 1137.

255 Case C-428/02, *Fonden Marselisborg Lystbådehavn* [2005] ECR I-1527.

256 C-250/11, *Lietuvos geležinkeliai*, not yet reported.

257 Cao 2007b: 71.

exact equivalence between language versions might not be necessary as long as agreement is assured among the legal community as to the correctness of the Court's interpretation. The presumed equivalence between the language versions on which the ECJ must base its interpretations exists, as noted in Chapter 1, for political purposes, with any other feature being irrelevant or subordinate to this essentially political aim.[258]

Arguably, multilingualism and linguistic equality between the official languages highlights the role of the Court in harmonizing meaning and creating internalized predictability within the legal system. Like coherence, which is often regarded as a central aspect of legal certainty, predictability forms a scale rather than a binary concept: that is, there can be more or less predictability in a given legal system at a given time. Harmonizing legal thinking and achieving a culture-bound common cognitive basis within the multilingual legal community of the Member States in the EU can best come about through transparent reasoning by the Court in favour of a given interpretation of a specific provision. In this respect, two types of legal uncertainty may be observed; 'whether the law will in fact be properly applied, and uncertainty about the content of the law'.[259] The claim of the legitimating function of transparent reasoning and dialogue attempts, in essence, to replace the first with the second. As Davies points out, the resulting uncertainty about content can be made acceptable by 'exposing the rationale behind it'.[260]

Since language versions do not necessarily convey a specific EU meaning when interpreted separately in a national context – which is often the case at least on the national level[261] – then the Court's task is to convince lawyers, parties and finally the general public through reasoning. This is best done by means of teleological reasoning whereby the purposes and aims of EU law take centre stage. While reference to linguistic arguments and other formal forms of reasoning hide discretion and preclude debate between 'the players' in the field of EU law as to the most suitable meaning of specific provisions in the EU context, teleological reasoning opens judicial decisions to debate with regard to the underlying values of the EU legal system.[262]

Additionally, teleological reasoning is asserted to offer the most effective method of reasoning from the point of view of creating a common cognitive basis irrespective of the language used. As noted above, change in how specific words are understood may occur through explicit change in meaning based on communicative experience. In the *Fonden Marselisborg Lystbådehavn* case, the change in meaning of especially the Danish word 'kjøretøjer' appears unavoidably to rely on acceptance by the (Danish) legal community of the new EU interpretation of the word that includes boats in the particular context of VAT exemptions. This

258 Koskinen 2000: 83.
259 Davies 2012b: 283.
260 Davies 2012b: 283.
261 Šarčević 2002: 261.
262 Maduro 2007: 14.

requires, however, that lawyers accept the Court's reasoning in the matter and therefore consciously change the way they use and interpret the word in the limited context of EU law.

Put differently, to impact on the meaning lawyers in the EU associate with specific words, the ECJ must guide the legal community in this process of changing routine understanding. As pointed out above, this form of guided change in meaning construction can be achieved through communicative reasoning; that is, by teleological, purpose-oriented arguments which do not hide behind the text. This communicative game – in which authorized specialists in the field may participate – may lead to creation among legal actors in the EU of a common cognitive basis which is needed for developing a truly multilingual legal system. This communicative game may be argued to form the most viable practice for ensuring more certainty in a system in which diversity and meaning potential of various language versions is not only a source of problems but also a source of new insights for those engaging in the communicative game.[263]

As formal legal certainty may indeed be undermined due to multilingualism and difficulties related to the incongruity of different language versions, emphasis should instead be placed on substantive legal certainty, which is here equated with substantive acceptability of judicial decisions. Especially in the EU, as distinct from many Member State legal systems, the role of the ECJ as an institution developing and creating law is of central importance. Thus, substantive acceptability of judicial decisions must be taken as a starting point when examining the issue of substantive legal certainty in the EU. If the legal community is not convinced by the interpretive stance taken by the Court, this appears to imply an equally reticent reaction with regard to content.

The subtleties of the Court's communicative practices necessarily affect the way in which a decision is received and whether it is followed. That is, whether the legal community accepts creation of EU law meanings that may run contrary to individual language versions and agreements on the meaning of those texts in national contexts depends on the Court's success in convincing addressees of the acceptability of the interpretation despite incongruence with their language version.

Therefore, it appears conceivable to enhance substantive acceptability primarily through open and transparent reasoning. While any attempt to eliminate subjectivity is unavoidably doomed to failure, because all human understanding is necessarily based on some degree of subjective appreciation, opening judicial reasoning on the level of the EU audience and thus immersing the relevant specialists in communicative reasoning means that the normative choices made by the Court become subject to debate. This debate, in turn, requires some reciprocity and exchange of views as to the correct (most suitable) interpretation with regard to the purpose of the text in question.

263 Engberg 2004: 1166.

Summing up

In this chapter, we deploy the Habermasian formulation of discourse ethics to reconfigure the notion of legal certainty. Rational argumentation about the correct meaning and content of EU law primarily occurs in the context of the preliminary ruling procedure. In this respect, the principle of discourse ethics functions as a critical standard against which we may evaluate the realities of this communicative interaction. Notwithstanding the idealistic underpinnings of this formulation and the only partial attainment of the requirements of rational discourse in adjudication, the dialogue among the ECJ and national courts constitutes the cornerstone of the present conceptualization of legal certainty. In essence, it is asserted that due to the unavoidable elusiveness of multilingual EU law, legal certainty may best be guaranteed through the interplay of procedural means (procedural certainty) and reasoning (rational acceptability). By not attempting to place EU law in the straitjacket of formal predictability, the virtue of this construction lies in its inherent ability to acknowledge the impact of intra-lingual as well as inter-lingual indeterminacy on legal certainty.

More particularly, discursive legal certainty sketched in this chapter shifts the focus away from static aspects of legal certainty and emphasizes the decisive importance of law's interpretive character. Law's interpretive nature, together with the contextuality of every instance of interpretation, raises the question of how legal certainty may be guaranteed if significant disagreement can arise as to what the law is and what it means. To remedy this problem, communication between the ECJ and its audience is suggested to possess decisive importance for ensuring that the dynamic requirements of legal certainty discussed in this chapter are met.

Notably, judicial reasoning that succeeds in convincing the relevant audience – the EU legal community consisting in particular of national judiciaries but also, if a broader perspective is taken, of other legal actors (including parties and interveners, *i.e.* the Commission, other EU institutions as well as Member States) – about the correctness of the Court's reading is of particular significance. This is because guided change in meaning construction takes place through convincing, rationally conditioned reasoning that may gradually influence legal languages so as to reflect this EU discourse in law.

Indeed, language is here understood as a dynamic phenomenon, as a constantly changing and developing means of communication that does not exist in a socio-political vacuum: statutory texts gain meaning in complex judicial interaction between text, sender and addressee which takes place in a particular legal and factual *context*. More specifically, they gain practical meaning in judicial discourse among courts. Of particular significance for EU law is that its meaning develops in individual cases decided by the Court; the acceptability of the Court's interpretations is then tested in national applicatory contexts. From the perspective of meaning construction across official languages, judicial reasoning forms the toolkit with which the Court may attempt to influence the process of understanding in which certain words, expressions, concepts and principles are automatically connected to a given meaning.

From this standpoint, multilingualism forms an additional challenge for communication. Therefore, compared to purely domestic systemic settings, the way Court judgments are construed has great impact. In this respect, although the Court's judgments are not solely intended for the legal elite, it is argued that a common EU law meaning can be generated and sustained through communicative reasoning, through a process where authorized, multilingual specialists (most notably the Court and its judicial audience in Member States) reach dialectical agreement on a particular interpretation. In that regard, this chapter again highlights the significance of the preliminary ruling procedure and the role of the courts participating in the described dialectic. A common cognitive basis among the EU legal community, a necessary prerequisite for agreement, can only develop through the use of convincing purpose-oriented arguments by which interpretation can be substantively justified to specialists in the field.

Taking account of the manner in which meaning is negotiated and generated through the Court's reasoning, this chapter puts forward the claim that acceptability of judicial decision-making is essentially achieved by means of deliberative communication. This does not imply *prima facie* agreement on meaning among specialists involved in discourse; instead, attaining agreement calls for communicative input from all participants. Put differently, it means that the Court's audience accepts the interpretation put forward in the case at hand as the most suitable one in that particular context on the basis of the Court's reasoning. In this sense, it is not a question of reaching consensus in the strict sense (whereby all EU legal actors would accept normative assumptions about EU law); instead, we are concerned about achieving a degree of agreement by means of communication among legal actors, and most importantly between the ECJ and national courts who possess the applicatory monopoly within the EU legal system, as to the most suitable interpretation with regard to the underlying values of the EU legal system enunciated by the Court in its reasoning.

In sum, acceptability cannot be achieved without communication. Primarily, negotiation as to the best-reasoned balance of interests at stake takes place between the ECJ and national courts in the context of preliminary rulings. Just as judicial adjudication is communicative, so is substantive legal certainty: rational acceptability arises from discursive judicial interaction among courts.

Chapter 4
Reconceptualizing legal certainty

Justification, audience and rhetoric

This chapter ties together the strands of argument presented above; it links the model of discursive legal certainty to rhetoric. In this respect, it builds on the concept of ideal particular audiences and evaluates the rhetorical possibilities available in the Court's reasoning and the implications of those strategies from the standpoint of acceptability.

As we have seen, the Court plays a central role in guaranteeing acceptability in the shape of substantive legal certainty.[1] The success enjoyed by the ECJ in ensuring substantive legal certainty, *i.e.* acceptability, is ultimately weighed against its ability to mediate agreement between those participating in the communicative game, specialists in EU law who participate in EU law discourse.

As the discussion in Chapter 3 demonstrates, reasoning is always directed to an audience. Here, it is asserted that the EU legal community, as defined above, forms an inevitable aspect of any attempt at describing the constituent elements of reasoning that ensure substantive legal certainty. The interrelationship between reasoning and audience builds on Perelman's theory of argumentation which suggests that rational argumentation is aimed at a universal audience to which all rational persons belong.[2] In this respect, we can observe similarities between that universal (ideal) audience and Habermasian discourse ethics which presupposes elimination of manipulation and self-interest in order for those participating in discourse to be placed on a level playing field.

The Habermasian consensus-based model of discourse lends itself with some difficulty to adjudication: conflict is constantly present in all phases of adjudication. Indeed, conflict forms an essential part of adjudication in that it occurs in a forum where different interpretations meet and compete.[3] This is why Habermas' model

---

1 More specifically, acceptability *requires* that judicial decision-making takes into account the fundamental normative principles of the legal system as well as the prevailing rationality. This is the so-called constituting relationship between the different levels of law: the deeper levels function as a legitimating element for the surface. See Tuori 2002: 183 *et seq.*

2 Perelman and Olbrechts-Tyteca 1971: 31 *et seq.*

3 See Tontti 2004: 35–37. Remodelling Dworkin's famous description of judicial decision-making as a chain-novel, Tontti suggests that the Dworkinian story of law depicts an ongoing process of conflicting interpretations where different readings compete to reach a position of 'hegemony' over other interpretations.

of discourse ethics and communicative action is asserted to function best as a regulative ideal against which the reality of judicial interaction may be tested. While imperfect, this interaction may nonetheless be conceptualized in terms of institutional dialogue that takes place between the Court and its audience.

For the purposes of conceptualizing judicial reasoning, Aarnio asserts that a particular concrete audience may be identified in a concrete argumentative situation. Because the rationality of the reaction of such an audience necessarily remains arbitrary, the notion of a particular ideal audience comes into play. Two criteria are needed for construing a particular ideal audience: firstly, discourse among participants must take place in accordance with the rules of rational discourse and, secondly, the members of a particular ideal audience should possess common values. Concretely, within the context of judicial discourse, a particular ideal audience is limited to the legal community in question.[4] In this respect, the audience identified by Aarnio is tied to a certain form of life that is defined culturally and socially.[5] In essence, to realize the aim of (rationally) acceptable judicial decision-making, the interpretive choices made by a court must be acceptable not only normatively but also rationally from the viewpoint of the particular ideal audience so that those choices are in accordance with the values of that particular community.[6] In this respect, soundness in the judicial context means rational acceptability supported by good reasons. The 'goodness' of any particular reasons ultimately reflects the systemic context in which reasoning takes place.[7]

In the following section, we flesh out the rhetorical tools with which the Court may attempt to convince the legally relevant audience consisting of the above-described EU legal community so that it may accept the interpretive choice made by the Court. To succeed in its task of convincing this contextually relevant audience, the Court needs to justify its decision so as to convince the audience of the soundness (rational acceptability) of the decision.

Rhetoric of judicial reasoning

Judicial reasoning operates in the realm of rhetoric. It forms part of so-called rhetorical discourse as opposed to symbolic and empirical discourse.[8] Judicial reasoning is indefinite not only because it uses essentially open-ended and indeterminate natural language but also because it includes assertions of value and belief that cannot be confirmed or refuted empirically. Because of the inherent indeterminacy of language with which law operates, definitions in

4 Aarnio 1987: 225.

5 Fish 1989: 298–305.

6 See also Dworkin 1986.

7 Cf. Habermas 1998: 226.

8 Rhetorical assertions and inferences are made in natural language: these assertions may possess existential pretensions, but they cannot be empirically confirmed or contested. Raymond 2009: 14–17. See also MacCormick 2005.

rhetorical discourse may be contested and assertions are open to a multiplicity of interpretations.[9] Indeed, no one can say what 'proportionate', 'fair trial', 'equality' or 'direct (and individual) concern' really mean in a way that would be accepted by everyone who uses these words.[10]

Here, the Court's reasoning is examined by employing rhetorical tools based on the Aristotelian distinction between strategies of persuasion, namely *logos*, *ethos* and *pathos*.[11] The first-mentioned *logos* arguments are intended to convince the audience intellectually whereas the second type of argument, *ethos*, is founded on the character or the credibility of the speaker. And lastly, *pathos* arguments appeal to emotion and are intended to persuade interlocutors.[12] However, persuasion – often an ugly term in law – must here be understood as the use of words as 'instruments of reasonable persuasion, where coercion appears only in the sense of the compelling force of an argument'.[13]

These rhetorical elements are intertwined and overlapping in actual reasoning so that many arguments possess qualities that may be categorized in different ways depending on the chosen perspective. That said, the Court's audience enjoys a focal role in this context: in the final analysis, it is the audience that sets the criteria for acceptance of an argument but also, in more general terms, of justification.

In this respect, a conceptual difference may be observed between convincing reasoning, on the one hand, and (rationally) acceptable judicial interpretations, on the other. The former is related to the rhetorical possibilities available in reasoning and the latter to the rationality and – ultimately – to the soundness of the proposed interpretation. However, in judicial interpretation, a close connection exists between convincing and acceptable judicial decision-making: they both relate to the outcome in a particular case.[14] Acceptability requires a degree of correspondence between the chosen outcome and the values of the particular ideal audience, but also its cognitive world view.[15] Additionally, in order for an interpretation to be acceptable, it must fulfil the requirements of rationality (consisting of L-rationality and D-rationality).[16] While generally (rhetorically) convincing (or indeed persuasive) argumentation is not necessarily rationally acceptable and vice versa, the difference remains a subtle one in adjudication: this is because convincing reasoning closely relates to the rationality of the decision.

9 Bengoetxea 1993: 218 *et seq*., MacCormick 2005: 121 *et seq*.

10 Raymond 2000: 5.

11 Cf. Perelman 1982.

12 Paso 2012: 16.

13 MacCormick 2005: 17.

14 Paso 2009: 353. In her dissertation, Paso uses rhetorical tools to analyze, *inter alia*, the Court's case law. For the distinction between rational and convincing argumentation, see Perelman 1982: 2–3. See also Paso 2012: 16.

15 Paso 2009: 352.

16 Aarnio 1987: 185–195.

Indeed, in the realm of law, rationality may be characterized as a prerequisite for acceptability.[17]

From the standpoint of rhetoric, convincing reasoning in the context of justifying judicial decisions begins with opening up the facts, applicable norms and legal sources used in the interpretive process. If this is not done, the outcome cannot be deduced from these premises.[18] Convincing judicial reasoning thus requires an explicit statement of applicable legal sources (authority reasons) and a description of the facts taken into account as well as reasons explained for their applicability in the case at hand (*logos*).[19] If the premises on which a judicial decision is based are left unarticulated, the reasoning rests on authoritative *ethos* arguments.[20]

Undoubtedly, authoritative arguments form the kernel of the Court's reasoning: in rhetorical terms, they may be categorized as *ethos* arguments, arguments that concern convincing the audience by the character of the author. *Ethos* arguments include not only authoritative rules and principles but also previous case law, and reference to scholarship. More particularly, in the Court's vocabulary, ethos arguments frequently translate not only into recourse to institutionalized *ethos* as 'settled' or 'well-established' case law but also into general principles of law.[21]

Additionally, many central arguments in the Court's judgments also possess traits which may be posited in the realm of *pathos*. They include arguments that are meant to persuade by appealing to the audience's emotions. For example, invariably repeating *ad verbatim* paragraphs from previous cases carries not only institutionalized, status-bound authority, it also reveals an expression of *pathos* as a result of tautology.[22] Similarly, the intermittently recurring meta-principles of effectiveness, uniformity, certainty and legal protection possess a highly persuasive tonality. Indeed, European 'legal integration has proceeded through persuasion, mutual empowerment and inter-court dialogue'.[23]

However, it is generally accepted that *logos* should form the kernel of judicial argumentation.[24] This is because it refers to the internal consistency of the message,

---

17 Paso 2009: 352. See similarly Weigand 2008: 241.

18 Paso 2009: 285.

19 Cf. Raymond 2000: 11, who argues that in debates in natural language, formal logic remains next to useless.

20 Paso 2009: 290 notes that ECJ reasoning is categorized by *ethos*. This depends on the fact that premises on which a decision is not based are often not articulated as well as use of expressions such as 'It follows…', 'The argument cannot be accepted…' See also Bengoetxea 1993: 233–262. It is often the case that the content of norms is not opened up and application of norms to the individual case is presented only briefly.

21 Paso 2012 for a reconstruction of rhetorical elements observed in the Court's case law.

22 Paso 2012: 23. See also Mattila 2006: 65–66.

23 Stone Sweet 2012: 201.

24 Paso 2009: 353. Cf. Raudenbush Olmsted 1991: 11, who notes that lawyers and judges aim to persuade by referring to arguments by example (including analogical reasoning).

to the clarity of the claim made, the logic of its reasons as well as the effectiveness of evidence given in its support. This is why the impact of *logos* on an audience is generally referred to as logical appeal.[25] Indeed, although precedent and general principles of law as well as reference to Treaty and Charter provisions undoubtedly form acceptable tools for justifying judicial decisions, their justificatory force is ultimately measured by how well their relevance and relationship is articulated by the Court with regard to the factual circumstances of the case at hand and to the legal framework. This is because rationally acceptable judicial decision-making requires use of legal sources and interpretive criteria generally acknowledged in the particular legal community as acceptable and applying them to the facts of the case.[26] The following section considers the interplay of different, often intertwined, rhetorical features in the Court's reasoning by focusing on how the Court employs fundamental rights arguments in justifying its decisions.

Fundamental rights in the Court's reasoning

Although acceptable and convincing argumentation may be conceptually distinguished, the two elements are intertwined in ECJ judicial reasoning. This issue is illustrated by reviewing the Court's reasoning in the *Schmidberger*[27] and *Omega*[28] cases which mark important steps in the Court's evolving approach to fundamental rights.

Firstly, in *Schmidberger*, the Austrian government granted permission for a demonstration to be organized on a closed motorway. At issue was the high level of pollution caused by heavy traffic in the Brenner Pass. For present purposes, it is sufficient to note that Schmidberger, a German transportation company, argued that allowing the demonstration to take place on the closed motorway was contrary to the free movement of goods. Because of the demonstration, Schmidberger was unable to transport goods from Germany through Austria to Italy.

The Court recognized the free movement argument in that it accepted that closing down the motorway did indeed restrict the free movement of goods. However, it also examined whether the restriction of the free movement of goods could be justified on the basis of freedom of expression and freedom of assembly. The Court analyzed the relation between Articles 10 (freedom of expression) and 11 (freedom of assembly) European Convention on Human Rights (ECHR) on the one hand, and free movement of goods guaranteed in the EC Treaty on the other.

25 Ramage *et al.* 2009: 81–82.
26 Aarnio 1987: 189–195.
27 Case C-112/00, *Eugen Schmidberger* [2003] ECR I-5659.
28 Case C-36/02, *Omega* [2004] ECR I-9609.

In short, the case turned on the correct balance to be struck between the pertinent fundamental rights and the fundamental freedom of free movement.[29] The Court confirmed that, in principle, protection of fundamental rights justifies a restriction on fundamental freedoms such as that of free movement and concluded, with regard to the facts of the case, that the restriction on the free movement of goods was justified so that the authorization given to the demonstration was deemed compatible with the Treaty provisions at issue.

Here, of special relevance is the justificatory direction undertaken by the Court.[30] The following extract contains an array of arguments that cannot escape the remit of *ethos* and *pathos*:

> 71. According to settled case-law, fundamental rights form an integral part of the general principles of law the observance of which the Court ensures. For that purpose, the Court draws inspiration from the constitutional traditions common to the Member States and from the guidelines supplied by international treaties for the protection of human rights on which the Member States have collaborated or to which they are signatories. The ECHR has special significance in that respect (see, inter alia, Case C-260/89 ERT [1991] ECR I-2925, paragraph 41; Case C-274/99 P Connolly v Commission [2001] ECR I-1611, paragraph 37, and Case C-94/00 Roquette Frères [2002] ECR I-9011, paragraph 25).
>
> [...]
>
> 73. It follows that measures which are incompatible with observance of the human rights thus recognised are not acceptable in the Community (see, inter alia, ERT, cited above, paragraph 41, and Case C-299/95 Kremzow [1997] ECR I-2629, paragraph 14).
>
> 74. Thus, since both the Community and its Member States are required to respect fundamental rights, the protection of those rights is a legitimate interest which, in principle, justifies a restriction of the obligations imposed by Community law, even under a fundamental freedom guaranteed by the Treaty such as the free movement of goods.

The *Omega* case considered whether German legislation banning the commercialization of a laser gun that could be used for simulated 'killing games' complied with the freedom to provide services. By reference to its judgment in *Schmidberger*, the Court confirmed that protection of fundamental rights in principle justifies a restriction on fundamental freedoms. While discussing the material issues in these cases falls beyond the scope of this book, it should be noted

29 Cf. Ojanen 1998: 134–135. See also Cartabia 2007: 5 and Williams 2010: 133–134 for a critical reading of the *Schmidberger* case.

30 Case C-112/00, *Eugen Schmidberger* [2003] ECR I-5659, paras 71–73. Indeed, classic cases in which the ECJ has referred to the ECHR are, *inter alia*, case C-260/89, *ERT* [1991] ECR I-2925, para 41; Case C-274/99 P, *Connolly v Commission* [2001] ECR I-1611, para 37, and case C-94/00, *Roquette Frères* [2002] ECR I-9011, para 25.

that in both cases the Court allowed the use of measures seeking to ensure respect for fundamental rights notwithstanding their negative impact on foundational principles of free movement.

In *Omega*, the gist of the Court's justification turned on ensuring respect for fundamental rights. This shared aimed allowed it to accommodate the national sensibilities and special characteristics of Member State legal systems. The following paragraphs illustrate:

> 33. It should be recalled in that context that, according to settled case-law, fundamental rights form an integral part of the general principles of law the observance of which the Court ensures, and that, for that purpose, the Court draws inspiration from the constitutional traditions common to the Member States and from the guidelines supplied by international treaties for the protection of human rights on which the Member States have collaborated or to which they are signatories. The European Convention on Human Rights and Fundamental Freedoms has special significance in that respect (see, inter alia, Case C-260/89 ERT [1991] ECR I-2925, paragraph 41; Case C-274/99 P Connolly v Commission [2001] ECR I-1611, paragraph 37; Case C-94/00 Roquette Frères [2002] ECR I-9011, paragraph 25; Case C-112/00 Schmidberger [2003] ECR I-5659, paragraph 71).
>
> 34. As the Advocate General argues [...], the Community legal system undeniably strives to ensure respect for human dignity as a general principle of law. There can therefore be no doubt that the objective of protecting human dignity is compatible with EU law, it being immaterial in that respect that, in Germany, the principle of respect for human dignity has a particular status as an independent fundamental right.
>
> 35. Since both the Community and its Member States are required to respect fundamental rights, the protection of those rights is a legitimate interest which, in principle, justifies a restriction of the obligations imposed by Community law, even under a fundamental freedom guaranteed by the Treaty such as the freedom to provide services [...].[31]

In fact, the language employed by the Court in both cases testifies a high level of *ethos* and *pathos* as tentatively suggested in the preceding section. As observed above, precedent functions as an authoritative *ethos* argument, if analogical use of cases mentioned is not justified by substantive reasons.[32] Put differently, the justificatory force in a legal context remains weak if no explanation is provided for why these cases are pertinent and what makes them similar to (or distinguishable from) the case at issue. In this respect, analogical reasoning based on previous case law may be framed as 'court-*ethos*'.[33]

---

31 Case C-36/02, *Omega* [2004] ECR I-9609, paras 33–35.

32 Similarly Paso 2012: 21 *et seq.*

33 Paso 2012: 21–22 and 25.

Indeed, just as in Aristotle's reasoning based on a specific logic of enthymemes (deduction) and paradigms (induction), the Court's reasoning also intertwines these elements. The first-mentioned refers to syllogisms based on often implied and not stated premises that are presumed to be true. However, they work only as long as the audience believes the underlying premise or is not opposed to a conclusion drawn on the basis of these premises for ideological reasons. The latter – paradigm – refers to reasoning by example that, in the context of law, generally takes the form of precedents.[34] What is also of importance is that judicial reasoning depends on legal systems and legal cultures so that neither reason nor persuasion can be universalized: they are influenced by the cultural background in which reasoning takes place.[35]

For example, in *Omega*, the applicant's argument according to which Articles 49 to 55 EC prevents the city of Bonn from prohibiting 'killing games' is acceptable only if we believe that these Articles (read in conjunction with the Court's case law) say so. The same problem of inconclusiveness of arguments also applies if we argue for the opposite conclusion. Equally, given the intermittently fluctuating factual context of individual judicial decisions, precedents can always be overruled (distinguished).

We also observe tautology (*pathos*) in the way the Court refers to case law. While this approach certainly ties individual cases to a longer line of cases and therefore may be argued to enhance consistency and coherence, it may nonetheless involve problems from the viewpoint of convincing the audience if the relevance of cases referred to is not elucidated (while not necessarily convincing, this 'authoritarian' style of reasoning may nonetheless be perceived as persuasive).[36]

Emphasizing the importance of fundamental rights in the EU legal system as well as the role of the ECHR not only relies on the (legal) authority of the argument, it also functions as a powerful means of convincing the audience of the soundness of the decision: this is because of the intimate linkage of fundamental rights to values underlying the legal system.[37] This being so, in *Omega* the Court proceeds with caution, seemingly reluctant to create a monolithic European standard as to how fundamental rights should be defined in Member States, thus paving the way towards a more differentiated approach to fundamental rights protection.[38]

34 Raymond 2000: 6.

35 Weigand 2008: 241.

36 Paso 2009: 354 argues that the ECJ often refers to relevant legal sources, principles and legislation without opening these arguments by explaining why they are relevant and what their content is. However, as a counter-argument, one could say that since the Court's audience consists of the EU *legal* community, it can be presumed that not every argument needs to be opened up and elaborated.

37 Sobotà 1994: 170–171.

38 For early examples, see case C-159/90, *The SPUC v Grogan* [1991] ECR I-4685. Cf. case *Open Door and Dublin Well Woman v Ireland* (application No 14234/88 and 14235/88), A246-A. See also Ojanen 2009: especially 1116 *et seq.*

Instead, the Court confines itself to confirming that the EU legal system aims to ensure respect for human dignity and emphasizes protection of fundamental rights on a general level so as to accommodate different national sensibilities. In concentrating on the proportionality of the national measure, the Court in fact omits to enquire into the substantive meaning of the right at issue.[39] In this respect, the 'principle rhetoric' employed by the Court is confined to the boundaries set by declarative *ethos* and *pathos*.[40]

However, keeping in mind the both linguistically and culturally divergent audience to which the Court directs its judgments maintaining its reasoning on an abstract and general level, the Court in fact allows leeway for different solutions in Member States.[41] By the same token, it also ensures acceptability in different legal systems and cultures based on a different transitive order of values. Indeed, it appears that in a community of diverging languages and cultures, leaving certain questions unanswered may sometimes prove an effective rhetorical strategy.

Because interpretations may be contested, the way judicial decisions are justified assumes key importance. Indeed, the raw material on which the Court relies is 'perpetually dissolving into ambiguity'.[42] The Court is faced with additional difficulty due to multilingualism. So, if each interpretation may be challenged, how can the ECJ convince its multilingual audience?

Certainly, as the above extracts suggest, general principles of law – including fundamental rights – enjoy an important function in the Court's reasoning.[43] Taking account of the entry into force of the Treaty on the Functioning of the European Union (TFEU) and the binding legal status given to the EU Charter, the EU Charter now carries the same legal value as the Treaties so that it forms part of the body of rules and principles on the basis of which the Court adjudicates.[44] Arguments based on fundamental rights therefore now possess a stronger connection to *logos*, since they can be tied to authoritative legal texts. However, given that arguments based on fundamental rights are easily accepted by an audience that has adopted a European (legal) culture and based to a great extent on protection of fundamental

39 Williams 2010: 134.

40 Paso 2012: 25.

41 See Conway 2008 on the high level of generality of the Court's style of reasoning.

42 Raymond 2000: 5.

43 Cf. Ojanen 1998: 133–138, who notes that even from early on, fundamental rights have played a role in ECJ argumentation. According to Ojanen, even during the period running from 1973 to 1983, fundamental rights formed primary and secondary balancers in ECJ argumentation. By this he means that they were either balanced against another right or a policy goal (primary balancer) or, alternatively, fundamental rights affected the choice between two or more plausible interpretations (secondary balancer).

44 See *e.g.* case C-400/10 PPU, *J. McB. v L. E.* [2010] ECR I-8965, especially para 50. Increasingly, the Court is faced with cases with a close connection to fundamental rights. Recently, the Court elucidated its position on the existence of an implementing measure which is required to trigger the application of the Charter. See, in particular, case C-617/10 *Åkerberg Fransson*, not yet reported.

rights, the value of those arguments in persuading this divergent audience is equally relatively high.[45] From the viewpoint of appealing to emotion, it appears that fundamental rights are particularly forceful.

As in Dworkin's chain-novel metaphor, reasoning that takes its cue from values and principles ties individual cases to a longer line of cases and explicates the underlying (social) theory guiding the Court's judicial decision-making process.[46] While arguments from fundamental rights may at best be valuable in achieving greater acceptability and in convincing the pertinent audience, they can remain vague and formal and therefore unsatisfactory in light of the dual requirement of convincing and acceptable reasoning, if they are not *substantially* tied to the case at hand.[47]

In this respect, an argument from principle becomes a *pathos* argument when the application criteria of those arguments are not explained. In such cases, no substantive connection is made between the particular case and the arguments given to support the outcome in that case.[48] Just as with *ethos* arguments based on the authority of the author (*e.g.* 'the Court has stated', 'as the Court has emphasized', 'It follows that'), *pathos* arguments remain fallible without an established connection between them and the factual situation to which they are applied. See Figure 4.1 below.

Importantly, while *ethos* and *pathos* may be effective means of persuasion, from a rhetorical viewpoint they are both – taken separately – incomplete. This is because neither type of argument shows that the argument itself is 'correct'. Essentially, *logos* involves providing factually accurate and logically meaningful reasons in support of the outcome. This is particularly important in the context of judicial reasoning. Indeed, to convince a linguistically pluralistic legal community of the soundness of a particular interpretation requires all three types of argument.[49] Drawing parallels to discussion concerning the modest notion of

45 Paso 2009: 255–259. See also MacCormick 2005: 20 on how a judicial decision can ultimately be justified by 'considerations of ideology extraneous to law'. Cf. Ojanen 2009, who argues that fundamental rights continue to represent the Achilles' heel of EU constitutionalism. Cf. McRudden 2000: especially 523.

46 Cf. Habermas 1998: 194–195.

47 Cf. Lasser 2004: 229–236. One possible way of explaining why the Court frequently settles for shorthand, magisterial argumentation is that ECJ judgments are always published together with AGs' opinions that may be seen as explanatory notes for ECJ rulings. See in this respect Lasser 2004: 347 *et seq*.

48 Paso 2009: 254.

49 Paso 2009: 362 suggests that arguments from comparative law may prove useful for the ECJ in convincing the audience in this dialogue. In that sense, she suggests that using a greater number of arguments from comparative law could result in a more nuanced dialogue and open ECJ judicial reasoning to a critical balancing of different arguments and views. See similarly Torres Pérez 2009: 141 *et seq*. Cf. Maduro 2007: 6, who argues that the Court should not use comparative law as a means of identifying what it believes to be the best legal solution in the abstract. The 'bottom-up' construction and legitimacy of EU

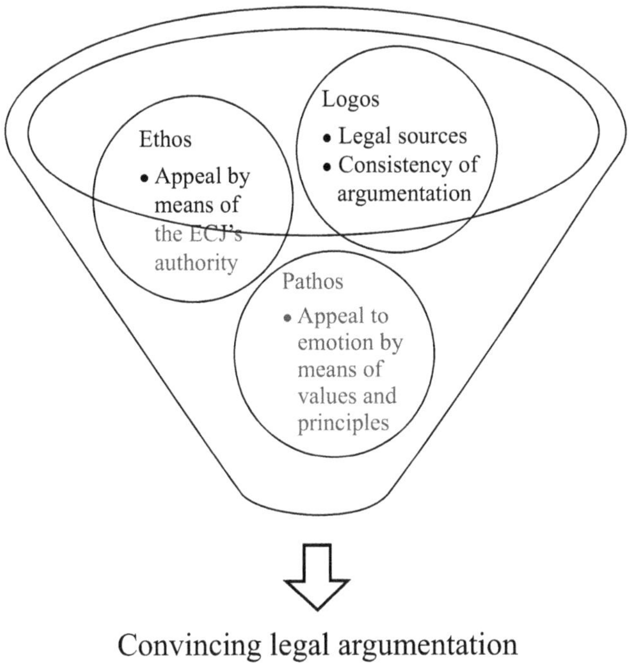

Figure 4.1 Building blocks of convincing judicial reasoning

coherence in judicial reasoning in Chapter 2, one could say that *logos* requires reasoning that proceeds without logical jumps from one premise to another. On this understanding, none of the different arguments is enough for rational acceptability if taken separately: although using arguments that appeal to emotion involves a risk of manipulation, they nonetheless offer a powerful argumentative tool.

Challenge of a multilingual audience

The Court is faced with an audience that is significantly wider and more diverse compared to that of national courts in Member States. The latter courts operate within a linguistically and culturally more homogeneous community. Whereas the

law, in which the ECJ enjoys a key role, requires that the ECJ respect common national legal traditions and not use comparative law to search for its preferred legal solution among different national legal systems. With regard to the Court's role in convincing a divergent audience, it seems plausible that comparative law functions best as an underlying starting point in the deliberative process, but not necessarily as an argument given to justify a specific outcome. This is so because comparison necessarily leads to choosing one legal solution instead of another: this may create a situation of inequality between Member State legal systems forming part of the EU legal system. See also Smits 2006: 537.

audience and the directly concerned addressees of national court judgments are generally the parties to proceedings, the role of the ECJ is significantly broader.

As observed above, the Court's multilingual audience sets limits on the justificatory force of certain types of argument, most notably those based on the wording of the text at issue. This is so not only because of discernible divergences in language versions but also because of the Court's largely monolingual model of reasoning. It is asserted that to surpass this challenge, the Court may validly deploy reasons that appeal not only to logic but also to emotions. Interestingly, appealing to emotion is generally associated with political, not judicial reasoning.[50] However, none of the rhetorical strategies should be strictly ruled out because of the special features of the EU legal system.

Certainly, in the context of linguistic plurality, it would be insufficient – at least from the perspective of substantive legal certainty – for the Court merely to state the law in authoritative style without referring to the underlying purposes for which a specific reading has been chosen over another. This is why teleological reasoning may be regarded as an important element in the Court's reasoning. Clearly, to distinguish judicial reasoning from, for example, political speech, it does not suffice alone without appropriately taking a cue from the relevant legal framework, nor does it mean that *legally* irrelevant issues need to be discussed.[51] As outlined above, this is because we cannot assume the existence of agreement among the EU legal community on meaning in the same way as in domestic systems. In such a situation, exposing the *ratio* of the decision is a way of increasing the transparency of the Court's decision-making and persuading its multilingual audience.

As noted above, in national legal systems, the number of legal actors participating in the process of constructing legal meaning is limited and, perhaps even more importantly, official languages are restricted in number. However, in the EU context, where the specialists taking part in the process of meaning harmonization do not share the same legal background and language, authoritative, deductive reasoning appears problematic. The *Fonden Marselisborg*[52]and *Lietuvos geležinkeliai*[53] cases reviewed in Chapter 3 illustrate this point.

An additional argument for employing different types of rhetorical strategy is the translated character of judgments and opinions: ECJ judgments and Advocates' General (AGs') opinions are also – with some exceptions – translated into all official languages (Irish being an exception for the time being). In the same way, EU legislative texts, judgments and opinions are also products of translation. As observed in Chapter 1, uncertainty as to the meaning of a text increases with the intervention of translation.

50 Paso 2009: 340.

51 Cf. Jääskinen 2008: 184.

52 Case C-428/02, *Fonden Marselisborg Lystbådehavn v Skatteministeriet* [2005] ECR I-1527.

53 C-250/11, *Lietuvos geležinkeliai*, not yet reported.

In this respect, it is relevant to inquire into what kind of arguments best translate into different languages (as well as legal cultures). Reasoning based on the aims and purposes of the legal system as well as on arguments related to value choices – such as fundamental rights – might be easier to translate into different languages and legal systems than, for instance, those based on language. Certainly, fundamental rights arguments will only gain further importance as a result of the binding status of the EU Charter. In this respect, it appears plausible to argue that purpose-oriented reasoning which exposes the underlying rationality guiding judicial decision-making at the Court may be regarded as particularly useful for attaining legal certainty in a situation where the Court is confronted with a multilingual audience. Although attempts to impose predictability on judicial decision-making in the present context undoubtedly remain futile, some degree of certainty may be achieved by making certainty a question of agreement among language users, or in this case, the legal community.[54]

In this respect, the Court's reasoning functions as the primary means of facilitating communication within the EU legal community: this discourse takes place over time and builds rational agreement as to the legal paradigm to be followed in interpreting EU law. Value discussions that take their cue from general principles or broad aims and purposes may also function as a basis for agreement within the EU legal community on sound judicial interpretation in accordance with the dominant legal paradigm.[55] Indeed, from the viewpoint of rhetoric and persuasion, reference to values and principles that take their cue from fundamental rights, for example, constitute sufficiently indeterminate and vague concepts so as to remain useful in new cases or in the face of changing public values.[56]

Certainly, individual judgments can generally be said simply to provide a solution for a specific case in minimalist terms. However, using general legal principles in adjudication generalizes adjudication, since principles may be discussed not only among the legal community, in particular, but also among the broader public.[57] In this respect, judicial reasoning functioning on the basis of articulated principles and values may be argued to have a greater possibility of acquiring broad agreement, consequently providing legal decisions with more institutional support. However, this requires that principles and values referred to in adjudication rely on a broad consensus in society or, at least, among the legal community. Realistically, without agreement on the underlying values of the

54 Engberg 2004: 1155, Schauer 2008: 1124.

55 Rosas 2007a: 15. See also Van Hoecke 2002: 171–172, who draws a distinction between structural and ideological legal principles. The former derive from the legal system itself whereas the latter refer to an ethical framework of law.

56 Raudenbush Olmsted 1991: 15.

57 Davies 2012: on proportionality review as a means of facilitating accommodation of diverging solutions in Member States.

legal system, securing institutional support for general principles as well as legal decisions based on these values appears a cumbersome task.[58]

From a discursive viewpoint, arguing from principles and values (as well as the objectives of the legal system) offers a clear advantage to linguistic reasoning. Both meaning and how values and principles are applied in concrete cases may be widely discussed among the legal community, in this way obtaining a stronger basis for legitimacy.[59] This is so because these meanings and applications can be said to justify the interpretation more profoundly than linguistic or systemic, essentially authoritative *ethos* arguments, which can be said to be less persuasive from a rhetorical standpoint. Indeed, the principle of loyal cooperation, and the need to guarantee the functioning of the democratic system as well as the overriding need to safeguard protection of fundamental rights, for example, possess high justificatory value in the context of a shared legal ideology.[60]

Problems related to linguistic arguments discussed in Chapter 1 are to a certain extent shared by systemic and teleological arguments. Once the *why* behind teleological or systemic arguments is left unarticulated or when principles and policies are deployed without giving them a concrete substantive meaning, these arguments remain rhetorically relatively weak.[61] In this respect, Conway criticizes the level of generality of ECJ reasoning.[62] For example, Conway suggests that ECJ interpretations are typically justified on the basis of abstracting broadly stated goals of effectiveness and integration coupled with a tendency to assert conclusions required by these goals without always adequately discussing alternative interpretations and conclusions.[63]

As noted above, the Court's reasoning may be described in terms of *meta-teleology*: even a brief perusal of the Court's case law illustrates how it frequently deploys a small number of recurring general, abstract purposes and principles.[64] Rhetorically, the Court's style of reasoning is undoubtedly authoritative both in style and in argument. Weiler, calling for more transparency, famously asserts that 'the Court should abandon the cryptic, Cartesian style which still characterizes many of its decisions and move to the more discursive, analytic, and conversational style [...] it is crucial that the Court demonstrate in its judgments that national

58 Van Hoecke 2002: 171. Indeed, this idea of arguing from principles that are shared by the community in question comes close to Dworkin's views. See Dworkin 1986 on political morality that underlies adjudication.

59 Van Hoecke 2002: 171, Torres Pérez 2009: 97 *et seq*.

60 Paso 2009: 275. See also Summers 1978 on the role of goal reasons in common law.

61 Paso 2009: 276. Cf. Bengoetxea 2007: 62 on the risks of taking transparency to extremes and on finding a balance between authority and transparency by means of quality indicators.

62 Conway 2012: 245.

63 Conway 2008: 804. See for a similar conclusion Paso 2009.

64 Lasser 2004: 211 *et seq*. See also Weiler 2001: 225.

sensibilities were fully taken into account. And it must amply explain and reason its decisions if they are to be not only authoritarian but also authoritative'.[65]

Indeed, the Court's style of reasoning has been described as 'magisterially authoritative and clipped in tone, impersonally collegial in style, and decidedly deductive in form'.[66] It has also been criticized for silencing unwanted voices.[67] While these problems are hardly contestable, at least one of their causes may be a practical one: the Court's reasoning brings together many different styles and cultures of judicial reasoning. What may also contribute to an impression of a distinctive 'Cartesian' style is that all versions other than the French one are translations and it might be a fact that not one of the judges deliberating in French is a native French speaker.[68]

To be sure, as the Court currently has 28 judges and eight (although the number will increase to 11) AGs from different Member States and legal cultures, it cannot be described as a monolithic entity: judges deliberate on the basis of draft judgments drawn up by the Judge-Rapporteur, to which each judge sitting in the formation concerned may propose changes. Moreover, the Court takes decisions by majority without publishing dissenting opinions.[69] Given these factors, it is not surprising that the Court's judgments can contain gaps or internal inconsistencies:[70] in this respect, the final product – the judgment – may reflect a compromise between different views hidden beneath an apparently calm surface, a judgment speaking with one single voice.[71]

Clearly, one of the most obvious advantages of dissenting opinions, which some authors call for, is that 'they force the majority opinion to be reasoned in an altogether more profound and communicative fashion. Dissent often produces the paradoxical effect of legitimating the majority because it becomes evident that alternative views were considered even if ultimately rejected'.[72] While discussing the virtues of dissenting opinions will remain a purely scholarly exercise, it may be asserted on a practical level that use of teleological, purpose-oriented reasoning might be seen as reflecting an attempt to employ the so-called 'discursive alternative justification' whereby the final outcome is based on interpretive choices made on the basis of different arguments: this model

65 Weiler 2001: 225.

66 Lasser 2004: 229.

67 Komárek 2011: 107–108 expresses particular concern with regard to a recent and regrettable development in the structure of the Court's judgments: to cut translation costs, the Court sometimes partly or altogether omits parties' submissions. See *e.g.* case C-392/04, *i-21 Germany* [2006] I-8559.

68 Bengoetxea 2011a: 11.

69 Perju 2009 contends that dissenting opinions would open up the Court's judicial reasoning to external deliberation.

70 See Lasser 2004, especially 233–236.

71 See Bengoetxea 2011b: 232–233 on employing the ECHR system as a comparator for analyzing how authority may be enhanced through discourse.

72 Weiler 2001: 225.

requires that different arguments are expressed, discussed and weighed against each other. On the basis of that discussion, choices are made for openly expressed reasons.[73]

While the Court's style often follows a type of deductive, discursively thin French model of justification where justification proceeds as a logical syllogism,[74] one can plausibly argue in favour of a more discursive style of reasoning in the EU context: this would entail an open discussion of different views expressed by parties and interveners before drawing any definitive conclusions. Indeed, the Court needs to strike a balance between many different competing values in its case law: balancing different values, policies and principles against each other means that no *prima facie* priority order among them may be established.[75] Because of the incommensurability of values such as environmental protection and economic freedoms, they 'cannot be aligned along a single metric'.[76] Purposive arguments thus provide the 'main tool to justify rationally choices between incommensurable goods'.[77] In such a situation, discursive, conversational reasoning could certainly contribute to a genuine dialogue among the EU legal community with regard to values and policies that underlie the legal system.

Clearly, seen from this perspective, teleology is not in itself problematic: rather, it turns on the question of how and to what extent aims and objectives mentioned in reasoning are connected to the factual background of the case at hand and balanced against other competing values, policies and principles. However, gaps that sometimes occur in the Court's reasoning relate – at least partly – to the particularities of the preliminary ruling procedure itself whereby the Court does not decide the case pending before the referring court, but instead gives – generally applicable – guidelines on the interpretation of EU law provisions on the basis of the questions referred to it.

Admittedly maintaining a high level of generality of reasoning, while helpful for sustaining a healthy dialogue among courts and consequently for providing referring courts sufficient leeway in application, reveals weakness from the standpoint of transparency and openness. Linguistic, systemic as well as teleological arguments remain in the empty sphere of *ethos* or *pathos* if they are not connected adequately with *logos* by explaining their connection to the case at hand and on what grounds these arguments are relevant for deciding the dispute.[78]

---

73 Summers and Taruffo 1991: 492–493. Cf. Paso 2009: 286 *et seq.* who notes that ECJ reasoning may be described as dialectical in the sense that the ECJ discusses different arguments presented by parties and interveners.

74 Cf. Raitio 2003: 315–316, Paso 2009: 303.

75 Kennedy 2010. Cf. Habermas 1998: 260–261.

76 Sunstein 1997: 238.

77 Moral Soriano 2003: 297.

78 Generally, ethos and pathos arguments are considered to be persuasive rather than convincing. See Perelman 1982: 2–3; Perelman and Olbrechts-Tyteca 1971: 26–31.

This is because in judicial reasoning, *logos* builds on reason, on the rationality of the arguments given to support a particular outcome.

Reasoning that proceeds on a high abstract level based on purposes and objectives induces difficulties from the standpoint of describing normative systems and justifying legal decisions by logical inferences.[79] Conversely, the approach based on *telos* seems justified from the viewpoint of a 'narrative' approach to law where legal argumentation is modelled on the practice of storytelling, similarly to Dworkin's chain-novel metaphor. In this respect, Bertea warns about the risks of the narrative approach, because it may be a source of uncertainty in law.[80]

Within the context of multilingual EU law in particular, opaque reasoning that additionally operates on such a high level of generality that it translates into disappearance of the connection between the facts of the case and the reasons articulated in support of the outcome can be perceived as problematic. However, the AGs' opinions might at least partially remedy the breach observed: this is because opinions are less authoritative in style and deductive in form, thus offering the relevant audience a more discursive account of the legal problem at hand. In this respect, Lasser contends that publication of AG opinions considerably reduces the formality of the Court's reasoning taken as a whole; the considerations expressed by the AGs contribute to a more discursive style of reasoning since an opinion, which may in certain cases function as an external dissenting opinion, 'significantly increases the transparent confrontation of perspectives that characterize ECJ decision-making'.[81] However, several factors attenuate the discursive impact of opinions. While they certainly exercise considerable normative effect, the Court is not under an obligation to follow the AG's independent legal opinions. Nor does the Court systematically have recourse to them in judgments.[82]

Quest for a shared legal paradigm

Law can be described as both an institution and a medium for social integration. The pan-European legal sphere, which takes shape in discourse among legal actors, is the domain where EU and national legal systems interact. Judicial adjudication forms a process where the different rationalities of these legal systems come into contact with each other and where agreement is sought between the underlying political moralities of these systems. The dialectics of judicial reasoning therefore offer a platform for negotiating rational agreement between legal actors (primarily

79 Cf. Posner 2008: 42 *et seq.*, who notes that judicial decisions cannot be regarded as logical operations where policy and other considerations would not be taken into account. See also Tamanaha 2009: 189.

80 Bertea 2005b: 387.

81 Lasser 2004: 350 and 354.

82 See also for criticism Lasser 2004: 351–360.

the ECJ and national courts) on the interpretive choices made.[83] As Torres Pérez observes, 'the fact that judicial action might be partly strategic does not mean that the claim of dialogue as a model of judicial interaction to construct the meaning of [law] should be rejected'.[84]

In accordance with the model of legal certainty proposed here, the need is highlighted for dialogue in the preliminary ruling procedure in which the ECJ can give guidance on the correct interpretation and subsequent application of EU law in national contexts.[85] This is because the EU legal community may be argued to be more receptive to changes introduced to their respective legal cultures and to accepting the legitimacy of those changes than the general public, for example.[86] Dialogue and mutual search for agreement among the EU legal community as to how and on the basis of what values and principles EU law should be interpreted as offering a means for influencing and harmonizing those values.

While procedural rights arguably ensure participants an equal possibility to present their arguments, this alone does not assure that the actual judicial decision fulfils any substantive requirement of rationality or acceptability. In this sense, procedural safeguards, if not coupled with discursive judicial reasoning, cannot alone succeed in achieving legal certainty in the substantive sense. Adjudication offers a forum where different views are negotiated in an institutionalized setting. Agreement among participants is presupposed with regard to the 'communicative rules' of this process. In this respect, an underlying aim to reach agreement may be discerned, if not on the case to be decided, then in the context of the procedural guarantees that aim to enable the parties to have their say.[87]

As Gadamer famously suggests, judicial decision-making is essentially dialectical: it may be described as a dialogue where different interpretations are discussed according to a given set of procedural rules.[88] Clearly, coercion cannot be wholly eliminated as it forms an integral part of adjudication: as a result of a judicial process, one reading of the law is imposed over others. This is why procedural guarantees assist in defining 'the equal consideration of the participants' interests as procedurally correct agreements'. Within the framework provided by procedural guarantees, we can aim at compromise that does not wholly satisfy the

83 According to Habermas, a European constitution does not work due to the lack of a shared *Lebenswelt* on the EU level. In this sense, he seems to favour a 'bottom-up' approach to European integration. Similarly, Torres Pérez 2009: 131–132.

84 Torres Pérez 2009: 132.

85 Preschal and van Roermund 2008: 20 note that the preliminary ruling procedure is a 'vital instrument for handling divergence and diversity' in that in this procedure 'national courts are instructed how to interpret and apply EU law'.

86 Van Hoecke 2002: 59. See also Bell 2001 for changes in lawyers' attitudes in Europe under influence from the EU and the ECHR.

87 Habermas 1998: 166–167.

88 Gadamer 2006: 363 on the dialectical relation between question and answer in the process of understanding.

communicative rationality of consensus where reasons convince participants in the same way.[89]

It is certainly a truism that when the Court pronounces judgment, it does not discuss it openly with the other parties involved. Indeed, the dialectic of the preliminary ruling procedure is indirect: dialogue is ingrained in judgments.[90] From the standpoint of EU law, dialogue is based on the authority of the ECJ as the 'highest' court in the EU to 'dictate' meanings and give content to abstract provisions of EU law. However, the Court's monopoly in interpreting EU law and consequently to decide on the meaning of EU law presupposes input from national courts. To maintain its authority, the Court, through its judgments, and more specifically, its reasoning, must convince national courts of interpretive choices made during the decision-making process.

Seen from this perspective, legal certainty does not require that every person interprets legal texts in an identical manner without communicating with others. Rather, it entails engagement in a communicative process that allows for mutual accommodation of values and goals within 'an overreaching community constituted by partly separate but interdependent national and supranational legal orders, whose fundamental norms are not hierarchically ordered'.[91] The test is therefore to ask whether agreement on an interpretation may be reached among the authorized experts and not whether everyone would reach the same interpretation in all imaginable situations. Constructing legal meaning that is valid in all languages requires that relevant specialists agree that the interpretation proposed by the Court is suitable and can thus be accepted.[92] This means that although no common legal language exists within the EU, a common legal discourse on EU law enables dialogue among legal actors that may result in consensus through convincing argumentation.

In this respect, Kjær contends that while linguistic relativity and radical untranslatability of languages makes full inter-lingual understanding improbable, language nonetheless functions as a means by which mutual understanding may occur.[93] Put differently, intercultural dialogue – here, within the remit of the preliminary ruling procedure – makes understanding possible and it is precisely through this dialogue that legal actors can strive to agree on the underlying value basis of the legal system, thus harmonizing different cultures and world views inherent in language.

Indeed, following the regulative principle of judicial decision-making, judicial interpretations should possess the support of the majority in a rationally reasoning legal community.[94] Therefore, substantive acceptability depends on the reactions

89 Habermas 1998: 167.
90 Rosas 2007a: 4.
91 Torres Pérez 2009: 181.
92 Engberg 2004: 1165.
93 Kjær 2008b: 151.
94 Aarnio 1987: 226–227.

of other courts. In this dialectic, both the reasoning as well as the end result of proceedings are subject to control by other courts. Certainly, reasons for following the Court's reading may vary. As the present book does not attempt to describe the actual reasons for national courts complying with the Court's judgments, the analysis of acceptability must be understood in normative terms. The purpose is therefore to devise a normative account of the building blocks of acceptability through a dialogue-based approach.

Stressing the plurality of international, European and national norm-givers and norm-appliers, Rosas underlines the importance of European values and principles as parameters guiding interpretation.[95] Since the Court lacks coercive means for ensuring compliance, values and principles may be seen as a means of tying together pluralistic societies and ensuring a degree of predictability and stability within the EU legal system. The role of the ECJ in the European context in articulating and interpreting those values and principles appears to be becoming all the more important. Values and principles that guide decision-making in courts constitute appropriate yardsticks and parameters not only for the court deciding the case but also for the wider, pluralistic and multilingual legal community as they reveal the community's political morality.

In this sense, values and principles articulated in judicial decisions constitute a medium that other courts and the wider legal community may use in order to evaluate ECJ judgments. Ideally, in accordance with the regulative ideal of discourse ethics, values and principles that guide adjudication should emerge and develop in a process where courts and other legal actors interact.[96] The success of this deliberative process in the EU context is essentially based on the Court's ability to communicate to the scrutiny of the legal community the underlying values and principles in its decisions by means of its reasoning.

Adopting Tontti's terminology, it may be said that in order to win the dialectical battle for hegemony of interpretation,[97] the ECJ must – through its judgments – continuously convince its audience of the acceptability of its case law. The above discussion on fundamental rights in the context of the Court's reasoning illustrates the role of conflict and power in the context of judicial dialogue. A potential conflict may be discerned between views as to how to reconcile, on the one hand, fundamental rights as guaranteed in national legal systems – and after entry into force of the TFEU, in the EU Charter – with fundamental freedoms as guaranteed in the Treaties, on the other. Additionally, the delicate issue of hierarchy between, for example, national supreme courts and the ECJ is closely tied to the issue of fundamental rights and use of power in the dialogue among these

95 Rosas 2007a: 1.

96 Rosas 2007a: 15. See similarly Maduro 2010 on the role of more contextual reasoning at the ECJ.

97 Tontti 2004: 35.

courts.[98] More specifically, the issue relates to the power struggle often described as occurring between these courts with regard to the question of which European court should function as the final arbiter of issues involving broad constitutional significance.[99]

As dialogue among European courts as to the suitable level of fundamental rights protection attests, conflicting views certainly exist in the dialogue between the ECJ and national courts.[100] To be sure, without engagement in communication, neither common values nor a shared legal paradigm may emerge. Judicial dialogue enables inter-judicial exchange of arguments in which the content of common values underlying the pluralist framework constituted by the EU legal system may be negotiated.[101] Thus, ensuring acceptability of judicial decision-making presupposes mutual willingness to engage in dialogue about the value basis for adjudication. Indeed, as the constitutional tenets and their mutual priority order in the EU polity are essentially contestable and subject to contrasting readings, the dialogue constitutes the source of acceptability for interpretive outcomes.[102]

In fact, on the basis of the above analysis, a case could be argued that in order to succeed in convincing national courts of its decisions, the ECJ needs to refer to a 'legal paradigm'[103] or underlying social theory that may be internalized by the EU legal audience with relative ease. It might be asserted that although the *Schmidberger* and *Omega* cases attest to the economic undercurrent of ECJ reasoning – due undoubtedly to the essentially economic foundation on which the EU has been gradually constructed and the questions that may be put to the Court within the remit of its jurisdiction – protection of fundamental rights has made its way to the very core of EU constitutionalism.[104] Taking account of the incessantly increasing importance afforded to fundamental rights protection in the EU legal system, it might be contended that these form part of the Dworkinian underlying political morality on which the legal system is built.

However, unlike many domestic contexts, the underlying rationality of the EU legal system cannot be accurately explained by reference to fundamental rights:

98 See Torres Pérez 2009 on pan-European judicial dialogue in the field of fundamental rights.

99 See *e.g.* Kumm 1999, Claes 2006, cf. Rosas 2007a.

100 See, *e.g.* German Constitutional Court judgment on the Lisbon Treaty of June 30, 2009, BVerfG, 2 BvE 2/08. See also a special issue of the German Law Journal (10, 2009) on the Lisbon judgment. See also Cunha Rodriguez 2010: 94 on the dialectic in which the Court's fundamental rights case law has developed. See also Littlepage 2008: 3, who analyzes how transnational judicial dialogue has played an important role in, *inter alia*, the field of fundamental rights: judicial dialogue creates a feedback mechanism for interacting courts.

101 See similarly Weigand 2008: 252.

102 Similarly Torres Pérez 2009: 183.

103 For elements constituting a legal paradigm, see in particular Van Hoecke and Warrington 1998: 514–515.

104 See *inter alia* Alemanno 2004, Avbelj 2004. See also Jääskinen 2008: 149.

indeed, due to the instrumental nature of EU constitutionalism (furthering goals defined in the Treaties), fundamental rights do not constitute a clear-cut foundation on which balancing different interests could *automatically* be based.[105] To illustrate, the well-known cases *Viking Line*[106] and *Laval*[107] are reviewed.

Priority orders and legal paradigms: the challenge of incommensurable interests

The Court is faced with an increasing number of cases marked by conflicts between fundamental rights and fundamental freedoms, as well as between different fundamental rights. Accession of new Member States to the EU in 2004 provided the factual and political framework for the *Viking Line*[108] and *Laval*[109] cases. Both cases offer fruitful ground for discussion since the Court was in both called on to strike a balance between fundamental freedoms (services and establishment) and fundamental rights.

In the *Viking Line* case, Viking Line – a Finnish shipping company – owned and operated a passenger and cargo ferry between Helsinki and Tallinn, with a primarily Finnish crew benefiting from a collective agreement negotiated by the Finnish Seamen's Union (FSU). Following Estonia's accession, Viking Line announced that it would operate one of its ships from Estonia; to achieve the desired competitive advantage, it wished to re-flag the ship at issue from Finland with a view to entering into a new collective agreement with a trade union established in Estonia. Fearing that this would lead to deteriorated working conditions and terms, the FSU called for a union blockade of Viking Line and obtained the support of the International Transport Workers' Federation (ITF). Viking Line challenged the legality of this action. Within the preliminary ruling procedure, the Court was asked, in essence, to determine whether the now Article 49 TFEU applies in this context and whether collective action constitutes a restriction on freedom of establishment under that Article.

Briefly, holding that the above-described factual circumstances may constitute a restriction on the freedom of establishment enshrined in Article 49 TFEU, the Court confirmed the applicability of the Treaty Article to collective action initiated by a trade union or a group of trade unions against an undertaking to force it to enter into a collective agreement when the terms of that agreement are liable to deter it from exercising its freedom of establishment. Applying well-established criteria, the Court held that, as a matter of principle, in order to be justified, such a

105 See also Ojanen 2009 who describes fundamental rights as the 'Achilles' heel' of EU constitutionalism.

106 Case C-438/05, *Viking Line* [2007] ECR I-10779.

107 Case C-341/05, *Laval* [2007] ECR I-11767.

108 Case C-438/05, *Viking Line* [2007] ECR I-10779.

109 Case C-341/05, *Laval* [2007] ECR I-11767.

restriction – here a fundamental right – must pursue a legitimate aim of overriding public interest and conform to the requirement of proportionality.[110]

As closer scrutiny of the case reveals, the kernel of the case lies in establishing a fair balance between different interests protected under EU law; that is, the 'internal market characterised by the abolition, as between Member States, of obstacles to the free movement of goods, persons, services and capital' and 'a policy in the social sphere'.[111] The gist of the issue put to the Court, as AG Maduro points out, is to determine to 'what ends collective action may be used and how far it may go. This touches upon a major challenge for the [EU] and its Member States: to look after those workers who are harmed as a consequence of the operation of the common market, while at the same time securing the overall benefits from intra-Community trade'.[112] In other words, at issue was striking a fair balance (reflecting the underlying rationale of the EU legal system) between the conflicting interests involved: between a fundamental freedom and a fundamental right.[113]

In the *Laval* case, Laval un Partneri, a Latvian construction company, posted workers from Latvia to work on Swedish building sites. Laval and the Swedish building and public works trade union initiated negotiations to conclude a collective agreement for the building sector. Laval's refusal to sign an agreement resulted in a blockade of the building site initiated by the trade union. As a consequence, Laval instigated proceedings and sought a declaration concerning the unlawfulness of the collective action and for compensation for damage suffered. The Court was called to interpret now Articles 18 TFEU and Article 56 TFEU as well as Directive 96/71/EC.[114]

While acknowledging the status of the right to take collective action as a fundamental right and as a general principle of EU law, the Court held that such a right cannot override other interests at stake, including the fundamental freedoms whose safeguarding it ensures.[115] As a consequence, the right of trade unions of a Member State to take collective action to force undertakings established in other Member States into negotiations – with a view to establishing more favourable terms and conditions of employment with regard to the minimum protection guaranteed by Directive 96/71 – hinders undertakings from carrying out construction work in Sweden, and therefore constitutes a restriction on the

110 Case C-438/05, *Viking Line* [2007] ECR I-10779, especially paras 55 and 66.

111 Case C-438/05, *Viking Line* [2007] ECR I-10779, paras 77–79, especially para 78.

112 Case C-438/05, *Viking Line* [2007] ECR I-10779, Opinion of AG Maduro, para 60. See also para 23.

113 Cf. Von Bogdandy 2000: 1326.

114 Directive 96/71/EC of the European Parliament and of the Council of 16 December 1996 concerning the posting of workers in the framework of the provision of services (OJ 1997 L 18, p. 1).

115 See similarly *e.g.* case C-346/06, *Rüffert* [2008] ECR I-1989.

freedom to provide services.[116] On the basis of detailed analysis of Directive 96/71, the Court held that the collective action at issue in the national proceedings was not justified on the basis of an overriding public interest.

Bound by systemic constraints set by established case law and the legislative framework, the Court established the priority order pertinent in the EU legal system by placing particular emphasis on free movement.[117] While these cases may be explored from the viewpoint of social dumping and the emergence of fundamental social rights in the EU context, they also raise a more theoretical question concerning the legal paradigm governing the interpretation of EU law.

Taking account of the systemic context in which the Court reviews the compatibility of national measures with EU law, it is certainly no surprise that the need to guarantee respect for fundamental freedoms formed the premise on which the analysis of restrictions was construed. Indeed, the Court operates within the framework set by the Treaties. Because safeguarding protection of fundamental freedom operates at the very core of this system, the pertinent question to which an answer was sought from the Court was to what extent fundamental rights may justify restrictions on those freedoms and not the other way around. While the Court clearly decided these cases in accordance with Dworkin's chain-novel metaphor by keeping to the prevailing paradigm of EU law – that of granting special significance to protection of fundamental freedoms in relation to fundamental rights – the question of whether the arguments presented convince national courts of the Court's interpretation is nonetheless worthy of discussion from the viewpoint of judicial dialogue.

Although traditionally the rationality of the EU legal system has been closely tied to protection of fundamental freedoms instead of fundamental rights,[118] the increasing complexity of issues heard by the Court means that Member State legal systems become increasingly intertwined with that of the EU – not least after entry into force of the TFEU, adding to the Court's jurisdiction questions with intimate linkage to protection of fundamental rights.[119] What is clear is that the ranking order between these freedoms and rights is not clear-cut:[120] rather, their mutual priority order is determined over and over again in each individual case.[121]

116 Case C-341/05, *Laval* [2007] ECR I-11767, paras 91, 93–95 and 99.

117 See in this respect Raitio 2010: 570. See similarly case C-369/96, *Arblade* [1999] ECR I-8453.

118 For an overview of this development, see Ojanen 1998.

119 ECJ jurisdiction has extended significantly after the pillar structure disappeared with entry into force of the TFEU. Consequently, the ECJ now also possesses general jurisdiction to give preliminary rulings in the area of freedom, security and justice.

120 A further source of ambiguity is the inclusion of a number of economic freedoms in the Charter, namely in Articles 15 (Freedom to choose an occupation and the right to engage in work), 16 (Freedom to conduct a business) and 17 (Right to property).

121 For recent case law, see *e.g.* case C-92/09, *Volker und Markus Schecke and Eifert* [2010] ECR I-11063, especially paras 45–51. Fundamental rights enshrined in the EU Charter are considered in relation to the function of fundamental rights in society so that

As Douglas-Scott points out, the concept of fundamental rights in the European landscape fluctuates: so many things have been framed as fundamental rights that the concept lacks any real content.[122]

Be that as it may, given the ever-growing range of questions covered by EU law and heard at the Court that do not naturally follow 'internal market logic', the dialogue between the ECJ and national courts is asserted to gain all the more importance. Arguably, in such a situation, fundamental rights dialogue may offer a tool for enhancing mutual understanding.[123] As von Bogdandy contends, they may 'provide a strong, visible, incontestable *raison d'etre*, [...], given the technicality of the common market and its policies'.[124]

Essentially, a strong case exists that in order for national courts to *accept* ECJ interpretations as valid, a mutual understanding as to the underlying values and principles guiding decision-making – not a relationship based solely on conflict and power – should exist between these courts. Persistent disagreement among European courts further highlights the need for nuanced reasoning based *inter alia* on fundamental rights: these reasons, as suggested above, could form a foundation for dialogue based increasingly on consensus that relates to values ingrained in the legal system.[125]

The regulative ideal of discourse explains the need for inter-judicial communication aiming at consensus with regard to underlying values of the legal system and should be of key importance in a legal system consisting of differing normative assumptions. Multilingualism particularly contributes to the importance of communication as a part of judicial decision-making. While this discursive account of judicial interaction does not resolve the persistent difficulty created by indeterminacy, it furthers understanding about the values underlying interdependent EU and domestic legal spheres and consequently fosters convergence. Indeed, discourse directs interaction towards achieving mutual understanding with regard to the goals and purposes of the legal system. Linguistically, it enables creation of EU law meanings that may differ from established meanings in the context of national legal systems when reciprocity is accepted. As Engberg suggests, this dialogue 'presupposes an open mind on all sides [which includes] the possibility of convincing the Court that their new meaning is not a good solution'.[126]

The Court plays a central role in managing interpretive conflict within the pluralistic and multilingual EU legal system. If reasons that take their cue from the underlying rationale of the legal instrument at issue are explicitly articulated

---

limitations on the exercise of rights contained in the EU Charter may be imposed under conditions laid down in Article 52(1) of the EU Charter. See also Rosas and Armati 2010: 190, Raitio 2010: 575. Cf. Habermas 1998: 254–255.

122 Douglas-Scott 2002: 435.

123 Similarly Williams 2010: 328.

124 Von Bogdandy 2000: 1308.

125 For similar ideas, see Cartabia 2007: especially 4. Cf. Raitio 2010: 570–575.

126 Engberg 2004: 1166.

and differing arguments involved are carefully weighed to establish the required priority order, they provide the Court's audience with concrete information on the basis of which it is possible to judge whether or not the chosen interpretation is the most suitable one in the EU context. Thus, the imperative of giving reasons that justify a particular interpretive outcome furthers reflexivity and allows those participating in discourse to 'regard the outcome as a shared product of collective deliberation'.[127]

Legal culture: a context enabling communication

Legal culture is an essentially contested concept.[128] While analyzing legal culture in great detail falls outside the scope of this book, it is nonetheless necessary to make some comments about the possibility of talking about EU legal culture. This is because of the interconnectedness between the concepts of audience and culture.

An essential element in the theory of communicative action, culture enables communication. Legal culture may be described as a specific professional culture that provides legal actors with necessary prejudices for communication in the legal field.[129] Indeed, understanding language as a means of communication entails that language is seen as a tool for communication among a social group: those who belong to this group also participate in its culture. Thus, what may be communicated within a particular language (or in this case, within different languages in which EU legal discourse occurs) depends on the social group in question and on the culture to which language users belong.[130]

On this view, culture forms part of shifting contexts in which language users use language so that the relationship between language and culture is one of reciprocity: language shapes culture and vice versa. In this respect, culture forms a variable background for communication.[131] In this sense, legal culture forms part of the discursive basis of law. In this respect, Bengoetxea describes legal culture as tradition that constitutes *Vorverständniss* which enables interpretation and makes speaking about the hermeneutic circle possible.[132]

In fact, diversity and incongruence in interpreting the same text may to a certain extent be attributed to divergences in juridical practices (that is, how law

127 Torres Pérez 2009: 182.

128 Nelken 1997: 1–2.

129 Tuori 2007: 68. See also Jääskinen 2008: 216.

130 Kjær 2004: 381. This view is based on a pragmatic view of language. See in this respect *e.g.* Fairclough 1992. For critical discourse analysis, Fairclough and Wodak 1997. Contrary to the pragmatic approach to language, structuralist theories see language as a stable system of meaning that mirrors culture. See *e.g.* Whorf 1956.

131 Kjær 2004: 381. Cf. Smits 2007 who speaks of legal culture as 'mental software' that may change over time.

132 Bengoetxea 1993: 132. See also Tuori 2007: 68–70.

is applied and interpreted by lawyers), not to legal culture *per se*. Importantly, it is possible to argue that EU Member States share – at least to a certain extent – a legal culture.[133] This depends on how legal culture is defined.

According to a sceptical account of the conditions enabling the emergence of a European legal culture, lawyers belonging to different legal cultures, even within the EU, cannot understand each other due to fundamentally different *mentalités* relating to their particular legal culture. On this view, culture forms an integral part of a particular society and its history.[134] However, adopting a more optimistic stance and applying a broader view on legal culture, we can say that European legal systems belong to the same Western legal culture: although these legal systems differ, divergence is observable, in particular, on the surface level of law. Looking more closely at the deeper structure of law reveals that basic legal principles and notions of justice are similar in European legal systems. This suggests that, for instance, although concepts of *contrat* and *contract* may contain different approaches to contract formation for civil and common law lawyers, these differences nonetheless occur on the law's surface, not on the level of legal culture.[135]

Clearly, shared legal culture (in the sense of a professional legal culture concerning the EU legal community understood in a strict sense) appears to form a prerequisite for an EU legal community to function. Because it possesses a close linkage to a specific community, culture may be said to consist of a 'world view', 'ideology' and 'habits' in their mutual interaction.[136] Although law is based on general values and world views in a particular society, law also shapes them: they develop a particular *legal* culture. In this sense, legal culture is not a given set of values and norms, but rather it develops in a communicative process in which members of the community in question take part in preserving or changing that culture.[137] Adopting this broader understanding of legal culture, one could say that because the fundamental understanding of law is similar in different European legal cultures, relatively undisturbed communication among lawyers belonging to different legal systems cannot be excluded.[138]

To a large extent, legal culture expresses the culture of a professional group, that of lawyers (internal legal culture). More generally, legal culture also includes widespread views on, for example, justice and equity, attitudes of citizens towards

---

133 Jääskinen 2008: 217. See also Letto-Vanamo 1998a: 57. Cf. Kjær 2004.

134 Most notably Legrand 1996, Teubner 1998.

135 Van Hoecke and Warrington 1998. Cf. Prechal and van Roermund 2008: 3, 5 distinguishing more traditions inside the paradigmatic division between civil and common law traditions.

136 Van Hoecke 2002: 57. For criticism concerning the vagueness of the notion of 'culture', see Cotterrell 1997b: 15–16.

137 Van Hoecke 2002: 57.

138 Kjær 2004: 387.

legal rules and institutions (external legal culture).[139] However, in the context of the discursive model of legal certainty, what is of particular significance is the legal culture prevailing within the ECJ and national judiciaries, who maintain the applicatory monopoly in the preliminary ruling procedure, but also other legal actors taking part in EU legal discourse (*e.g.* parties, interveners, legal scholars).

The idea of law's basic suppositions supports the idea that a shared legal culture exists among the ECJ and national courts.[140] In this respect, by referring to Harris, Jääskinen distinguishes between momentary and non-momentary legal systems. Accordingly, the basic suppositions shared by lawyers are non-momentary. They form the basic concepts that enable us to think about law as a consistent field of normative meaning. This can be achieved by referring to sources of law according to certain principles that express principles of legality and constitutionalism. These principles are based on a shared conception of courts as normative institutions that resolve social conflicts. The shared basic concept of law enables communication and understanding among legal systems.[141]

This shared understanding among EU Member State legal systems of what constitutes law in its non-momentary form offers a foundation for conceptualizing a common legal culture. In this sense, a shared understanding about law functions as the context in which EU legal discourse, including dialogue among courts, takes place. Van Hoecke and Warrington give an interesting account of issues on which a certain degree of convergence must exist in order to enable one to speak about a common legal culture within a specific legal community.[142]

Firstly, a common legal culture implies a shared understanding of what law is: the legal community in question must share a legal paradigm.[143] However, as the discussion above illustrates, conceptualizing a shared legal paradigm in the EU context might be somewhat problematic: this is so because in EU law, values, policies and principles that guide judicial decision-making are not necessarily ranked in the same order as in national contexts. To be sure, the emergence and permeation of the EU legal system with fundamental rights may gradually contribute to the emergence of a shared legal paradigm valid across systemic boundaries of national and EU law. In other words, a common legal culture implies convergence with regard to a concept of law, a specific understanding of its relationship with other social norms. Seen from this perspective, a common legal culture includes a specific paradigm for balancing between values, principles and policies. Secondly, a shared theory of valid legal sources underlies a common legal culture. This theory includes issues related to a hierarchy of legal sources,

139 Van Hoecke 2002: 58.

140 Harris 1979: 70. See also Jääskinen 2008: 218, Van Hoecke and Warrington 1998: 514–515.

141 Jääskinen 2008: 217.

142 Van Hoecke and Warrington 1998: 514–515.

143 Aarnio 1984. See also Dworkin 1986.

resolving problems of collision between legal sources and roles attributed to various legal professions within the legal system.[144]

Thirdly, then, a methodology of law must exist. This methodology includes both law-making and adjudicating. With regard to adjudication, this primarily consists of a theory of interpretation: how much discretion judges possess in deciding cases and which methods of interpretation may be used in reaching a particular outcome. Fourthly, the legal community within which a common legal culture exists requires a shared theory of reasoning. This theory comprises questions such as the following: 'What counts as a good reason?' and 'Which strategies for reasoning are acceptable?' In other words, to what extent are extra-legal (economic, political, social, and ideological) reasons perceived as acceptable?[145]

Fifthly, Van Hoecke and Warrington refer to a theory of law's legitimacy. A legal community with a common legal culture shares a view on the following questions. Why is law binding? Is formal validity enough or must law comply with the substantive values of society so as to be binding? Finally, the community concerned must share basic values and a world view. More specifically, this common ideology refers to a shared view on the role of law in society, on which problems constitute *legal* problems to be resolved by means of law.[146]

Certainly, it may be said that, for the most part, EU Member States share a similar (but by no means *identical*) view on the above issues. Together these elements form a paradigm describing a legal system.[147] While the existence of divergence among Member State legal systems cannot be rebutted, it is asserted here that *sufficient* shared understanding about the above elements does exist with regard to EU law *per se*. This appears to hold true, at least with regard to the EU legal community participating in EU legal discourse.

In a national legal system, different sub-cultures include, for instance, communities of legal academics, public lawyers and private lawyers. Similarly to national legal culture, *sub*-cultures may also be distinguished on the EU level. Accordingly, the EU legal system could be said to comprise the above shared elements without denying the existence of parallel national sub-cultures that continuously interact with EU legal culture. Though often different on the surface, these sub-cultures share underlying features that explain why a dialogue among them is possible. Additionally, it explains why the Court may, through its reasoning, influence national courts and consequently create greater acceptability

144 Van Hoecke and Warrington 1998: 514.

145 Van Hoecke and Warrington 1998: 514.

146 Van Hoecke and Warrington 1998: 514–515. European, and in a broader sense Western, legal cultures share a similar view of law founded on a rationalist and individualist understanding of the relationship between the individual and society. Moreover, this implies a positivist idea according to which it is valid irrespective of its moral content (except for extreme cases, such as Nazi law). Additionally, law is seen in instrumental terms: it is not a spontaneously emerging social order but rather a system for steering and organizing society.

147 Van Hoecke and Warrington 1998: 515.

through this dialogue. Clearly, without a basic conception of what constitutes an acceptable legal argument, for example, it seems unlikely that greater legal certainty may be ensured by means of judicial reasoning.

Therefore, a sufficient degree of overlap between the basic components of legal systems exists within EU Member States and the EU itself so as to enable communication across these legal systems. Shared understanding on the basic, non-momentary tenets of EU law enables communication, thus enabling EU legal discourse without a common language. In this sense, a common legal culture takes shape within the confines of a professional culture which, in turn, accommodates necessary prejudices that enable communication on EU law.

A common history built on the tradition of Roman law functions as a possible explanation for these affinities and shared understandings on the above issues. In this context, it is important to note that the period of national legal systems extends back only over a relatively short period in the history of pan-European law: prior to the modernization period founded on the emergence of national legal systems, law was essentially based on law taught in European universities and applied by the highest courts; this was the (shared and generally applicable) *ius commune*. In addition to a common Roman law, the role of fundamental rights has left its mark in shaping political communities and civil society in current EU Member States.[148]

Drawing from this brief review, it may be concluded that although on the law's surface, so-called black letter law may diverge between EU Member States, on deeper levels (legal culture and ideology), a common past plays a more significant role. Clearly, although the EU legal system incorporates many legal (sub-)cultures, a common past and traditions may be argued to facilitate communication among the different languages in which these cultures are expressed.[149]

Finally, in forming a legal culture, the role of elites, *i.e.* the legal community understood in the strict sense, plays an important role. Here, the significant role attributed to courts in assuring legal certainty in the EU legal system highlights the importance of elites. In this sense, a legal culture necessary for the model of discursive legal certainty to function, a shared understanding among the legal community of the issues listed above, may prove sufficient – not necessarily extending among the members of society in more general terms.[150]

148 Letto-Vanamo 1998a: 57–58, Letto-Vanamo 1998b: 4–9. Cf. Tontti 2001: 41, who notes that speaking of *ius commune* is a simplification that does not take adequately into account the heterogeneity of the past of European legal culture.

149 See for interesting similarities between the English and German legal systems, Van Hoecke and Warrington 1998: especially 516–519: differing statutes as well as ways in which a decision is reasoned may nonetheless result in the same practical result.

150 See Letto-Vanamo 1998a: 56, who notes that identity is developed by elites and then spread to society at large. Cf. Van Hoecke 2002: 59.

Interaction between EU and national audiences

Legal culture as a hermeneutical preconception can be described in terms of a non-propositional life-form.[151] This life-form is the basis of legal language games and propositional world views in the legal context: it enables communication between lawyers. As we have seen, on a deeper, systemic level, shared basic ideas about law and its underlying principles may be discerned among Member State legal systems. Following Aarnio, audiences demarcate contexts in which judicial reasoning and justification occur within the shared life-form.

The pluralist framework provided by interaction between national and EU legal systems involves two distinct contexts of interpretation: the EU legal community is polarized between the EU and national audiences. The EU context consists of lawyers working at the ECJ, other EU institutions, and lawyers working on the national level with matters related to EU law. These EU law specialists constitute, in Aarnio's terminology, a concrete particular audience. This audience shares a relatively coherent world view on a conceptual and normative level. Within this audience, judicial reasoning and justification are exclusively based on EU law. Ultimately, this framework for discourse is set by the Court.[152]

On the national level, however, the Court does not determine the remit for judicial reasoning and justification. Observing that national audiences have only partly 'internalized' a world view that distinguishes the EU audience from other legal audiences such as those of national legal systems, Jääskinen suggests that this occurs as a result of two factors.[153] EU law is only expressed in one language in the Member States: because EU law permeates national law and becomes an organic part of the domestic legal system, this interpretive context offers a distorted view of EU law. What is more, EU law mainly gives impulses to national law whereas the opposite is less common: national courts have less influence on ECJ case law. Although convergence of the internalized aspects of EU law in national contexts is only partial, this divergence appears less detrimental to cross-systemic communication than the incongruence observable with regard to the impact of purely national elements of the domestic system.[154]

With regard to EU law, differences do not lie on the surface level of legislation but rather on the level of legal systems: variation occurs as to how basic concepts of EU law are understood in Member States. Seen from this perspective, the interaction between Western contemporary legal cultures enables Europeanization, absorption of EU law elements into national legal systems. However, as noted above, the EU audience differs from national audiences. Additionally, the world views shared by the relevant audiences are not identical. These differences explain why a degree of recalcitrance to change exists, why national legal systems attempt

151 Aarnio 1987: 215–220.

152 Jääskinen 2008: 218.

153 On the internal aspect of law, see Hart 2012: 243.

154 Jääskinen 2008: 220.

to limit the effects of the Europeanization process seen as a danger for cohering national legal systems.[155]

Legal systems contain similar, yet not unconditionally shared, non-momentary elements.[156] Certainly, as the previous section suggests, an intimate linkage between Member State legal cultures exists: without 'organic' interconnectedness, the occurrence of EU legal discourse would be an impossibility. However, it is possible to distinguish between EU and national audiences. Firstly, on the EU level, the particular audience consists of the Court, EU lawyers and other lawyers working on the national level with questions related, *inter alia*, to preparation of EU legislation, its implementation and its application in both the private and public sectors.[157] Secondly, it appears arguable that national audiences only partly overlap with the EU audience. Indeed, Jääskinen's analysis suggests that no significant overlap – at least on a theoretical level – between these audiences can be perceived.[158]

However, a common EU law uniting EU and national audiences remains conceivable through communicative reasoning which enables creation of a common cognitive basis among lawyers working in the field. With regard to the EU audience, the ECJ enjoys a key role in defining the relevant arguments within this legal sphere. Whether the Court's interpretation is successful in extending its effect to national audiences depends ultimately on the degree to which the Court's reasoning is convincing and perceived as rationally acceptable, first by the EU legal community, then by lawyers working in other fields of law and finally by the broader linguistic community.[159] The latter two belong to the particular national audience. In accordance with the regulative ideal of discursive, the process of widening acceptance of an interpretive choice taken within the boundaries of the EU audience is only possible via discursive reasoning. Clearly, such communication presupposes receptiveness on all sides of the communicative game, including the Court in that it might need to accept that its proposed solution is not necessarily the most viable solution.

This discursive model possesses an intimate linkage to the way specialized meaning evolves in other contexts; indeed, it also appears a plausible solution for creating EU law meanings which depend on individual languages. The need to bring audiences closer to each other by means of discourse can be linked to differentiation between levels of the law. When the Court interprets EU legislation and gives it an EU law meaning, this occurs on the law's surface. It does not directly affect deeper levels in law. In this context, Tuori's notion of sedimentation comes in useful.[160] If the Court's interpretation is also accepted on the national

155 Jääskinen 2008: 220.

156 Harris 1979: 111. Cf. Tontti 2004: 35–37.

157 Jääskinen 2008: 218–220.

158 Jääskinen 2008: 220.

159 Engberg 2004: 1166.

160 Tuori 2007: 167 *et seq*. See also Tuori 2002: 199 *et seq*.

level, these interpretations can, then, gradually become a part of legal culture through the sedimentation process. From this viewpoint, communication appears in fact to be a central issue in discussing ways of gradually creating a uniform EU legal system.

To succeed, the process of incorporating the two particular audiences therefore necessitates communication. In national legal systems where only one relevant audience exists, authorized specialists possessing more discretion impose meaning on words and expressions in legal contexts. In these contexts, the impact of communication remains limited, because the process of meaning creation is limited with regard to the number of participants sharing the same legal culture.

Because the pluralist EU framework may be divided into the EU audience and 28 national audiences, creating EU legal meaning which is accepted within both audiences requires that a communicative situation is established where a dialogue between relevant parties – especially national courts and the ECJ – is possible. Certainly, a dialogue reaching beyond the formal boundaries of national and EU audiences is necessary for such communication. For the Court, this involves judicial reasoning that reaches beyond the linguistic, to purpose-oriented considerations that are not fixed on wording and text. Through this discursively open judicial reasoning, addressees of the Court's judgments reach a better understanding of the normative content of the decision, the Court's normative preferences and of the policies, principles and values that guide judicial decision-making in the context of EU law.

Without such an understanding, national courts will with difficulty be able to evaluate the merits of the interpretive choice made. Discursive judicial reasoning that is here argued to be founded on transparent, purpose-oriented reasoning will gradually foster agreement among those interpreting and applying EU legislation. Without such agreement as to, on the one hand, the purposes and goals to be achieved and on the other hand, the way in which those goals and purposes should be balanced in individual cases, it is difficult to pursue harmonization in a legal system consisting of over 20 official languages.

Admittedly, strategic considerations that manifest themselves in the form of policy choices and decisions regarding the relevant aims and objectives of given legal texts cannot be wholly disregarded in adjudication. As noted above, for Habermas, such situations are not covered by communicative action: they are not situations in which the participants aim at mutual understanding and agreement. An element of coercion certainly exists in any instance of adjudication. Within the preliminary ruling procedure, this manifests itself in that the Court imposes a specific reading on other participants, certain interests and goals on the addressees. From the viewpoint of the EU legal system, it is the Court's view of the legal system that is ultimately decisive. While communicative action that presupposes the ideal speech situation represents an idealization of reality, inter-subjective agreement concerning norms and values may be attained within the limited context of the EU legal community.

The connection between legal certainty and judicial reasoning might be described as a circular process by which transparent judicial reasoning and legal certainty gradually stabilize one another and thus give a more precise and predictable content to EU law. This is possible if we accept the view expressed by Maduro in discussing leading ECJ cases:

> the Court's case law may be fitted into a particular normative theory of judicial adjudication; one that conceives of legal interpretation as a process bounded by rules but also recognises that rules only acquire meaning in their context of application. This requires a more contextual form of judicial reasoning and greater awareness of the institutional choices involved in judicial deliberation. Once one recognises that law changes even when the legal texts remain unchanged then one should expect (and, sometimes, welcome) variations in the case law of courts. The role of the [Court] is bound to change not only to reflect changes in the legal rules but also changes in their context of application and in the institutional alternatives to the Court in the development of EU law (including the political process and national courts).[161]

Within the context of the EU legal system, it is argued that the discursive model of legal certainty which calls for mutual agreement among the EU legal community as to the most suitable interpretation of EU legislation in the light of the legal system as a whole entails a prerequisite in terms of agreement between the relevant actors as to the values that underlie the legal system. In other words, it is insufficient for the model of discursive legal certainty to function merely that the participants in the communicative game belong to the same subset of society (judges, lawyers), but, rather, they must also share ideas about the values that adjudication is understood to promote and secure. In this sense, judicial decision-making based on deliberative communication among the EU legal community functions as a stabilizing framework for future decisions and offers a means of testing agreement.[162]

Summing up

This chapter explored the model of discursive legal certainty by focusing on the role of the audience in judicial reasoning. Rules of rational discourse orient discourse among members of an ideal particular audience. On the other hand, the members of a particular audience adhere to common values: within the context of legal discourse, a particular ideal audience is limited to the legal community in question. In this respect, to realize the aim of (rationally and substantively) acceptable judicial decision-making, it seems important that interpretive choices

161 Maduro 2010: xvii–xviii.

162 Cf. Van Hoecke 2002: 66.

made by the court in question are accepted not only normatively but also rationally by the particular audience. Acceptance requires that these interpretations conform to the values of that particular community. So, the issue is whether the particular, *legally* relevant audience accepts the decision in question.

In this respect, fleshing out the rhetorical strategies deployed by the Court enables us to establish the requirements set for achieving acceptability through reasoning; the decision needs to be both rational and reasonable. Drawing from Aristotelian rhetoric, elements typically present in ECJ judicial reasoning are categorized by means of the distinction between arguments based on logic or reason, on the character of the speaker, and on emotion. Exploring the Court's reasoning from the perspective of rhetoric underlines the need not only for authoritative, but also for discursive reasoning. The Court's reasoning possesses traits that may be at some variance with elements generally associated with judicial reasoning: while these are undoubtedly deductive and often discursively meagre, we can discern elements that contribute not only to rational acceptability but also to rhetorical persuasion.

Although uncertainty as to meaning is unavoidable, in domestic settings, the limited number of languages involved in this process facilitates reaching mutual understanding. While the underlying problem remains similar in the EU context, the need to reconcile over 20 official languages appears to exacerbate this issue of uncertainty: in addition to problems encountered in relation to judicial interpretation within one language, problems related to differences in languages distributing meaning differently must be taken into account. Certainly, relative stability of meaning in the context of national legal systems presupposes a certain division of labour between those with authority and those without: legal concepts used in national legal systems are relatively stable due to the fact that only a limited number of specialists, *i.e.* primarily judges, possess the necessary authority to decide what legal texts mean. Because the number of specialists participating in the communicative process of meaning construction in the EU is significantly wider, the way interpretive choices are communicated to those participating in the communicative game assumes key importance.

To understand how the model of discursive legal certainty may function, the chapter also addressed the question of whether it is feasible to speak about a common EU legal culture. Adopting a broad notion of legal culture that only requires partial convergence of relevant sub-cultures, it is asserted that legal culture provides the EU legal community with the necessary prerequisites for communication that enable, in particular, judicial interaction. Similarly, the Court's audience, the EU legal community, consists of two diverging contexts – the EU and domestic level – which contain elements of incongruity. Fostering understanding among the confines of these contexts remains conceivable through communicative reasoning which enables creation of a common cognitive basis among the Court's audience.

In fact, although only partial convergence of legal cultures and audiences appears possible, dialogue between the ECJ and national courts in relation to how the underlying value basis for interpreting EU law should be construed offers a means of influencing and harmonizing those values. In this respect, the chapter argued that the model of discursive legal certainty defended assumes the gradual emergence of a shared legal paradigm through judicial reasoning. Use of fundamental rights as arguments is asserted to offer a medium for negotiating common ground across intersecting national legal systems. Although disagreement may persist, it does not devalue the importance of dialogue.

Hence, if the ECJ succeeds in convincing the audience of the acceptability of its interpretation, it enhances acceptability of both its interpretation and the legal system on a more general level. Certainly, one could say that in order for the ECJ to succeed in changing the underlying prejudices of national courts towards interpreting EU law in national contexts, the Court needs arguments that appeal not only to logic but also to values. In this sense, understanding legal certainty as a discursive process by which the EU legal community may accept the Court's interpretations and follow them in national contexts paves the way for a substantive understanding of legal certainty that takes into account the context-sensitive and discretionary nature of judicial decision-making.

Conclusion

This book set out to examine the concept of legal certainty in multilingual EU law. The overreaching theoretical point of reference was a two-dimensional understanding of legal certainty according to which it consists of both formal and substantive elements: predictability and acceptability. Formal predictability implies that law is static, independent from other social practices. It is pre-established and pre-settled so that its interpretation may be framed as predictable. Substantive acceptability refers to the more flexible aspect of law and judicial decision-making. It corresponds to the reflexivity, fluidity and context-sensitivity of adjudication. These two distinct and sometimes even contradicting values coalesce into the concept of legal certainty.

Given the added uncertainty related to rule application which stems from multilingualism, looking beyond the text of individual language versions may often prove necessary to construct the meaning of EU law. Working from that premise, this book developed a model of discursive legal certainty which places emphasis on acceptability of judicial decision-making and communication among the EU legal community.

Open-ended norm sentences expressed in one or several languages leave room for interpretation so that deciding on one interpretation over another is the result of an active decision-making process. These interpretive choices must be justified in order to assure their acceptability. Certainly, arguments based on language possess a rather weak justificatory force in any legal system. However, the role of language is particularly problematic in the EU context where law is expressed in over 20 official language versions. Intra-lingual uncertainty is topped with inter-lingual uncertainty. Consequently, different language versions are reconciled in the Court's case law.

From the standpoint of acceptability, multilingualism places particular emphasis on the way the Court's judgments are justified. Of particular significance is that the EU legal community (consisting of national judiciaries – who subsequently use and reaffirm ECJ case law through its application in other similar cases on the national level – and other legal actors), the particular audience of ECJ judgments, accepts the chosen interpretation as sound in the context of EU law.

However, the Court is faced with an audience that is not only considerably more divergent than audiences in national settings, but also multilingual. In this respect, limiting reasoning to authoritative legal sources (authority reasons) is argued to offer insufficient support for justification. In the context of linguistic plurality where looking at language versions separately may result in incongruent readings, the imperative of acceptability places all the more emphasis on teleological reasoning.

A judicial decision is not regarded as formally rational if it is not based on authority reasons applicable to the situation in question: if this is not the case, it will not be sufficiently justified. However, from the viewpoint of substantive legal certainty, this appears insufficient. To ensure legal certainty, judicial decisions should also fulfil the imperatives of substantive rationality, of acceptability, so that each of the premises needs to be justified as well. Elucidating the underlying *telos* may prove an adequate starting point for justifying judicial decisions in a multilingual legal system for several reasons.

Teleological reasoning, understood as referring to reasoning that expresses the underlying value basis on which ECJ decisions are based, is asserted to enhance deliberative communication among the EU legal community and, in particular, between the ECJ and national courts. For the discursive model of legal certainty, the Court and national courts constitute the pertinent participants in this communicative practice. Certainly, teleological reasoning that takes into account not only the purposes of the text but also the underlying aims of the legal system in general offers reflexivity in relation to changes in society. Such reasoning engages the Court in more discursive reasoning in that it provides an explanation as to why one specific interpretation is chosen over another. In particular, this purpose-oriented approach appears necessary and justified in the context of linguistic plurality.

As multilingualism requires moving beyond the words of individual language versions, or at least not taking the text at face value, legal certainty understood as stability and predictability of judicial decision-making may, at most, be described as a necessary fiction: taking account of the interplay of facts and (multilingual) norms underpinning judicial decision-making at the Court, no such absolute certainty about law exists that would follow from straightforward application of determinate legal provisions. In this respect, formal legal certainty remains relative. However, a degree of certainty in judicial decision-making may be guaranteed by means of procedural rules ensuring that participants in proceedings possess an equal possibility to express their views on the question at issue. Procedural safeguards thus further establishment of a stable space for legal discourse: in the preliminary ruling procedure, procedural rules offer a systemic framework for rational discourse among courts. Additional predictability may be achieved within the context of judicial decision-making through transparent, predictable argumentation that follows pre-established interpretive criteria which stabilize expectations for those participating in discourse.

The model of discursive legal certainty does not claim to eliminate uncertainty in judicial decision-making: rather, it adheres to the view that legal certainty constitutes a process whereby agreement on meaning is negotiated through communication. Similarly to national legal systems, EU legal meaning – which may differ from conventional legal meanings attributed to specific words, expressions and concepts in national legal systems – develops in discourse: it is the result of communication among authorized specialists.

While reconfiguring the concept of authority in the context of EU law falls outside the scope of this book, the model of legal certainty devised here suggests that a similar communicative approach to authority could also be applied in the context of ECJ adjudication. In this regard, even the Court's authority could be linked to transparency and sincerity and be conceptualized in terms of discursive practices. Because legal concepts develop in communication, it would be helpful to gain insight into the Court's internal communicative processes, speech situations and discursive practices.

Because such an insight is not available to the external eye, the preliminary ruling procedure offers the main arena for this discourse: in this procedure, where the meaning of fuzzy and vague multilingual legislation is negotiated, the Court may be able to modify the way national judiciaries interpret legal texts. However, this modification of routine understanding presupposes acceptance. Therefore, of particular importance is that the Court's audience may be convinced of the acceptability and correctness of the interpretive choices made. Hence, the model of discursive legal certainty sets emphasis in particular on deliberative communication among courts – namely, the ECJ and national courts in the context of the preliminary ruling procedure.

In this respect, substantive legal certainty in the context of multilingual EU law may be conceptualized as circular in character. As a result of open, purpose-oriented judicial reasoning, acceptability is determined by deliberative communication that proceeds as a circle: substantive acceptability requires that judicial decisions are, as a result of communication, accepted by the EU legal community as both rationally and substantively acceptable. Concretely, their acceptability depends on whether these judicial decisions are subsequently reaffirmed by national judiciaries in other similar cases. If further specifications or clarifications are required by national courts, case law will answer these questions on the basis of new preliminary references. In this respect, ECJ judicial decision-making helps to stabilize expectations about EU law by means of discourse. To function, the model requires that underlying values and policies guiding judicial decision-making are expressed in reasoning. Indeed, by unveiling these preferences and subjecting them to critical evaluation, it seems possible to reach agreement on the purposes and aims of the legal system over time.

Emphasizing the role of communication implies a conscious shift from universalizable, predictable judicial decision-making to concrete, context-sensitive adjudication that takes the particularities of each case into account. Discursive legal certainty therefore develops in the dialectic between the Court's reasoning and the EU legal community's expectations as to how EU legal provisions should be interpreted on the basis of values and policies that underpin the EU legal system. Seen from this perspective, multilingualism may represent a possibility for dialogue among legal systems, legal rules and legal principles as well as their underlying values and policies, instead of a risk to legal certainty.

Although this book employed the regulative ideal of discourse as a critical standard for analysis, it does not claim that communication among legal actors would result in universally applicable criteria of acceptability or a generally shared value basis. Rather, it attempted to devise a model for describing the requirements for acceptance of the Court's judicial decision-making within its audience, the EU legal community. By way of communication, in discourse, the EU legal community may come to agreement as to the purposes and aims underlying the legal system which orient judicial decision-making.

Therefore, while referring to authority reasons and following a certain predetermined formula in justification together with predictable procedural rules may be seen as possessing a stabilizing effect in the context of judicial decision-making, the importance of substantive and discursively open judicial reasoning is underlined. This is so because just as in Dworkin's chain-novel metaphor, policies and principles – such as, increasingly, fundamental rights – may be deployed in the dialectic between the ECJ and national courts as guidelines for interpreting EU law provisions in accordance with a particular 'political morality' underlying the legal system. This may require not only openly articulating values and principles but also canvassing and articulating alternative solutions, as well as elucidating the connection established between the arguments employed and the factual circumstances of the case at hand.

Understood this way, reasoning that takes its cue from values and principles is a tool for tying individual cases to a longer line of cases and for elucidating the underlying values guiding ECJ judicial decision-making. That legal sphere of judicial decision-making constitutes a domain where the EU and national legal systems interact. Through communication among the EU legal community, it is a process where the different rationalities of these legal systems come into contact with each other and where agreement between the underlying values of these systems is sought. Expressing substantive reasons in justifying decisions may be said to enhance adequate rational consensus regarding the underlying value basis of the EU legal system in order to assure substantive legal certainty.

Finally, multilingualism adds a layer of complexity to communication, but does not form an obstacle for assuring legal certainty. On the one hand, as the cases discussed in this book illustrate, multilingualism may indeed result in increased uncertainty as to the meaning of legal texts. On the other hand, the continuous dialogue between the ECJ and national courts within the preliminary ruling procedure, in particular, but also between the ECJ and other legal actors – which takes place irrespective of multilingualism – secures legal certainty on a different level.

Legal certainty thus develops in a circular process whereby the Court's decisions – justified by reference to accepted criteria of interpretation – are subject to control by the EU legal community. In this process, agreement is sought with regard to the underlying values and policies of the EU legal system. To a certain extent, while emphasis remains on legal certainty as substantive acceptability, it may be said that this process also stabilizes expectations, without guaranteeing absolute certainty as to outcomes, by means of procedural rules and reasoning. Discursive legal certainty thus takes shape in deliberative communication among legal actors which fosters agreement among persons of diverse backgrounds, values and languages.

Bibliography

Aarnio, A. 1984. Paradigms in legal dogmatics. Toward a theory of change and progress in legal science, in *Theory of Legal Science. Proceedings of the Conference on Legal Theory and Philosophy of Science, Lund, Sweden, December 11–14 1983*, edited by A. Peczenik, L. Lindahl, and B. van Roermund. Dordrecht: D. Reidel, 25–38.

Aarnio, A. 1987. *Rational as Reasonable. A Treatise on Legal Justification.* Dordrecht: D. Reidel.

Aarnio, A. 1997. *Reason and Authority. A Treatise on the Dynamic Paradigm of Legal Dogmatics*. Dartmouth: Ashgate.

Ajani, G. and Rossi, P. 2006. Multilingualism and the coherence of European private law in *Multilingualism and the Harmonisation of European Law*, edited by B. Pozzo and V. Jacometti. The Hague: Kluwer Law International, 71–93.

Alemanno, A. 2004. À la recherche d'un juste équilibre entre libertés fondamentales et droit fondamentaux dans le cadre du marché intérieur: quelques réflexions à propos des arrêts Schmidberger et Omega. *Revue du droit de l'Union européenne*, 2004(4), 709–751.

Alexy, R. 1989. *A Theory of Legal Argumentation: The Theory of Rational Discourse as Theory of Legal Justification.* Translated by R. Adler and N. MacCormick. Oxford: Clarendon Press.

Alexy, R. and Peczenik, A. 1990. The concept of coherence and its significance for discursive rationality. *Ratio Juris*, 1990(3), 130–147.

Alexy, R. 1992. *Begriff und Geltung des Rechts*. Freiburg: Karl Alber.

Allan, T. 1999. The rule of law as the rule of reason. *Law Quarterly Review*, 115(2), 221–244.

Allan, T. 2001. *Constitutional Justice. A Liberal Theory of the Rule of Law.* Oxford: Oxford University Press.

Alter, K. 2001. *Establishing the Supremacy of European Law: The Making of an International Rule of Law in Europe*. Oxford: Oxford University Press.

Amtenbrink, F. 2012. The European Court of Justice's approach to primacy and European constitutionalism – preserving the European constitutional order?, in *The European Court of Justice and the Autonomy of the Member States*, edited by H. Micklitz and B. de Witte. Cambridge: Intersentia, 35–64.

Arnull, A. 2006. *The European Union and its Court of Justice*. 2nd edition. Oxford: Oxford University Press.

Arnull, A., Dashwood, A., Ross, M., Wyatt, D., Spaventa, E. and Dougan, M. 2006. *Wyatt and Dashwood's European Union Law*. 5th edition. London: Sweet & Maxwell.

Austin, J. 1975. *How to Do Things with Words*. Edited by J. Urmson and M. Sbisà. 2nd edition. Cambridge, Mass.: Harvard University Press.

Avbelj, M. 2004. European Court of Justice and the question of value choices: Fundamental human rights as an exception to the freedom of movement of goods. *Jean Monnet Working Paper*, 6/04. Available at: http://centers.law.nyu.edu/jeanmonnet/archive/papers/04/040601.pdf [accessed: 4 October 2012].

Baez Seara, D. 2008. Pluralism regained – Book review: D. Ordoñez-Solís, El cosmopolitismo judicial en una sociedad global: globalización, derecho y jueces, Navarra, Thomsom-Aranzadi, 2008. *European Journal of Legal Studies*, 2(1), 387–401.

Baquero-Cruz, J. 2008. The legacy of the Maastricht-Urteil and the pluralist movement. *European Law Journal*, 14(4), 389–422.

Barber, N. 2006. Legal pluralism and the European Union. *European Law Journal*, 12(3), 306–329.

Bell, J. 2001. *French Legal Cultures*. London: Butterworths.

Bengoetxea, J. 1993. *The Legal Reasoning of the European Court of Justice. Towards a European Jurisprudence*. Oxford: Clarendon Press.

Bengoetxea, J. 1994. Legal system as a regulative ideal. *Archiv für Rechts und Sozialphilosophie – Beiheft; Praktische Vernunft und Rechtsanwendung*, 53(4), 65–80.

Bengoetxea, J., MacCormick, N. and Moral Soriano, L. 2001. Integration and integrity in the legal reasoning of the European Court of Justice, in *The European Court of Justice,* edited by G. De Búrca and J. Weiler. Oxford: Oxford University Press, 43–85.

Bengoetxea, J. 2007. Quality standards in judicial adjudication. The European Court of Justice, in *Festschrift für Heike Jung*, edited by H. Müller-Dietz, E. Müller, K.-L. Kunz, H. Radtke, G. Britz, C. Momsen and H. Koriath. Baden-Baden: Nomos, 47–62.

Bengoetxea, J. 2011a. Multilingual and multicultural legal reasoning: The European Court of Justice, in *Linguistic Diversity and European Democracy*, edited by A.L. Kjær and S. Adamo. Farnham: Ashgate Publishing, 97–122.

Bengoetxea, J. 2011b. Review of 'Beyond Words: the European Court of Justice and Legal Certainty in Multilingual EU Law by Elina Paunio'. *Tidskrift Utgiven av Juridiska Föreningen iFinland*, 147(2), 224–233.

Bertea, S. 2005a. Looking for coherence within the European Community. *European Law Journal*, 11(2), 154–172.

Bertea, S. 2005b. The arguments from coherence: Analysis and evaluation. *Oxford Journal of Legal Studies*, 25(3), 369–391.

Berteloot, P. 1999. Le droit à la langue de l'Union européenne, in *Langue et Droit: XVe Congrès International de Droit Comparé: Collection des Rapports*, edited by E. Jayme. Bruxelles: Bruylant, 345–362.

Beyer, C. 1990. Vad är rättssäkerhet?, in *Festskrift till Gotthard Calissendorff*, edited by L. Thorsson and S. Unger. Stockholm: Nordstedts Juridik, 11–37.

Bix, B. 1993. *Law, Language, and Legal Determinacy*. Oxford: Oxford University Press.

Bix, B. 2003. Can theories of meaning and reference solve the problem of legal indeterminacy? *Ratio Juris*, 16(3), 281–295.

Bobek, M. 2006–2007. The binding force of Babel: The enforcement of EC law unpublished in the languages of the new member states. *Cambridge Yearbook of European Legal Studies*, 9, 43–80.

Bobek, M. 2007–2008. On the application of European law in (not only) the courts of the new member states: 'Don't do as I say'? *Cambridge Yearbook of European Legal Studies*, 10, 1–34.

Breyer, S. 2005. *Active Liberty: Interpreting Our Democratic Constitution*. New York: Knopf.

Bryde, B. 2010. The ECJ's fundamental rights jurisprudence – a milestone in transnational constitutionalism, in *The Past and Future of EU Law: The Classics of EU Law Revisited on the 50th Anniversary of the Rome Treaty*, edited by M. Maduro and L. Azoulai. Oxford: Hart Publishing, 119–130.

Campana, M.-J. 2000. Vers un langage juridique commun en Europe? *European Review of Private Law*, 8(1), 33–50.

Cane, P. 2010. *The Hart-Fuller Debate in the Twenty-First Century*, edited by P. Cane. Oxford: Hart Publishing.

Cao, D. 2007a. *Translating Law*. Clevedon: Multilingual Matters.

Cao, D. 2007b. Inter-lingual uncertainty in bilingual and multilingual law. *Journal of Pragmatics*, 39(1), 69–83.

Cappelletti, M. 1987. Is the European Court of Justice running wild? *European Law Review*, 12(1), 3–17.

Carmen África, M. 2005. Re-presenting the 'Real': Pierre Bourdieu and legal translation. *The Translator*, 11(2), 259–275.

Cartabia, M. 2007. 'Taking dialogue seriously': the renewed need for a judicial dialogue at the time of constitutional activism in the European Union. Jean Monnet Working Paper, 12/07. Available at: http://centers.law.nyu.edu/jeanmonnet/papers/07/071201.pdf [accessed: 4 October 2012].

Chalmers, D. 2004. The dynamics of judicial authority and the constitutional treaty, in *Altneuland: The EU Constitution in a Contextual Perspective*, edited by J. Weiler and C. Eisgruber, Jean Monnet Working Paper 5/04. Available at: http://www.jeanmonnetprogram.org/papers/04/040501-14.html [accessed: 25 November 2011].

Charlesworth, H. 2010. Human rights and the rule of law after conflict, in *The Hart-Fuller Debate in the Twenty-First Century*, edited by P. Cane. Oxford: Hart Publishing, 43–61.

Christensen, R. and Sokolowski, M. 2002. Wie normativ ist Sprache? Der Richter zwischen Sprechautomat und Sprachgesetzgeber, in *Sprache und Recht. Jahrbuch des Instituts für Deutsche Sprache. Jahrbuch 2001*, edited by U. Haß-Zumkehr. Berlin: De Gruyter, 64–79.

Claes, M. 2006. *The National Courts' Mandate in the European Constitution*. Oxford: Hart Publishing.

Conway, G. 2008. Levels of generality in the legal reasoning of the European Court of Justice. *European Law Journal*, 14(6), 787–805.

Conway, G. 2012. *The Limits of Legal Reasoning and the European Court of Justice*. Cambridge: Cambridge University Press.

Coppel, J. and O'Neill, A. 1992. The European Court of Justice: taking rights seriously? *Common Market Law Review*, 29(4), 669–692.

Cotterrell, R. 1997a. *Law's Community: Legal Theory in Sociological Perspective*. Oxford: Clarendon Press.

Cotterrell, R. 1997b. The concept of legal culture, in *Comparing Legal Cultures*, edited by D. Nelken. Aldershot: Dartmouth, 13–31.

Cotterrell, R. 2006. *Law, Culture and Society: Legal Ideas in the Mirror of Social Theory*. Aldershot: Ashgate.

Coulmas, F. 1991. European integration and the idea of the national language. Ideological roots and economic consequences, in *A Language Policy for the European Community. Prospects and Quandaries*, edited by F. Coulmas. Berlin: De Gruyter, 1–43.

Craig, P. 2003. Constitutional foundations, the rule of law and supremacy. *Public Law*, 11(1), 92–111.

Craig, P. and de Búrca, G. 2011. *EU Law. Text, Cases, Materials*. 5th edition. Oxford: Oxford University Press.

Craig, P. 2012. Competence and Member State autonomy: Causality, consequence and legitimacy, in *The European Court of Justice and the Autonomy of the Member States*, edited by H. Micklitz and B. de Witte. Cambridge: Intersentia, 11–34.

Cunha Rodriguez, J. 2010. The incorporation of fundamental rights in the community legal order, in *The Past and Future of EU Law: The Classics of EU Law Revisited on the 50th Anniversary of the Rome Treaty*, edited by M. Maduro and L. Azoulai. Oxford: Hart Publishing, 89–97.

Dani, M. 2009. Tracking judicial dialogue – the scope for preliminary rulings from the Italian constitutional court. *Maastricht Journal of European and Comparative Law*, 16(2), 149–170.

Davies, G. 2012. Activism relocated. The self-restraint of the European Court of Justice in its national context. *Journal of European Public Policy*, 19(1), 76–91. (Davies 2012a)

Davies, G. 2012. Constitutional disagreement in Europe and the search for pluralism. *Constitutional Pluralism in the European Union and Beyond*, edited by J. Komárek and M. Avbelj. Oxford: Hart Publishing, 269–284. (Davies 2012b)

Defeis, E. 2007. Human rights and the European Court of Justice: an appraisal. *Fordham International Journal*, 31(5), 1104–1117.

Deflem, M. 1996. Introduction: Law in Habermas's theory of communicative action, in *Habermas, Modernity and Law*, edited by M. Deflem. London: Sage

Publications. Available at: http://deflem.blogspot.fi/1996/06/introduction-law-in-habermass-theory-of.html [accessed: 4 October 2012].

Dehousse, R. 1998. *The European Court of Justice*. Houndmills: Macmillan Press.

Derlén, M. 2007. *A Castle in the Air. The Complexity of the Multilingual Interpretation of European EU law*. Umeå: Umeå University.

Derlén, M. 2009. *Multilingual Interpretation of European Union Law*. Alphen aan den Rijn: Kluwer Law International.

De Witte, B. 1999. The past and future of the European Court of Justice, in *The EU and Human Rights*, edited by P. Alston. Oxford: Oxford University Press, 859–897.

Dicey, A. 1952. *Introduction to the Study of the Law of the Constitution*. 9th edition. London: Macmillan.

Dorf, M. 2003. Legal indeterminacy and institutional design. *New York University Law Review*, 78(3), 875–981.

Dougan, M. 2012. Judicial activism or constitutional interaction? Policymaking by the ECJ in the Field of Union Citizenship, in *The European Court of Justice and the Autonomy of the Member States*, edited by H. Micklitz and B. de Witte. Cambridge: Intersentia, 113–147.

Douglas-Scott, S. 2002. *Constitutional Law of the European Union*. London: Longman.

Dragone, S. 2006. The quality of Community legislation and the role of the European Commission legal revisers, in *Multilingualism and the Harmonisation of European Law*, edited by B. Pozzo and V. Jacometti. The Hague: Kluwer Law International, 99–106.

Dworkin, R. 1977. *Taking Rights Seriously*. Cambridge, Mass.: Harvard University Press.

Dworkin, R. 1985. *A Matter of Principle*. Oxford: Oxford University Press.

Dworkin, R. 1986. *Law's Empire*. London: Fontana Press.

Elster, J. 1998. Introduction, in *Deliberative Democracy*, edited by J. Elster, Cambridge: Cambridge University Press, 1–18.

Endicott, T. 1996. Linguistic indeterminacy. *Oxford Journal of Legal Studies*, 16(4), 667–697.

Endicott, T. 2000. *Vagueness in Law*. Oxford: Oxford University Press.

Endicott, T. 2001. Law is necessarily vague. *Legal Theory*, 7(4), 379–385.

Endicott, T. 2005. The value of vagueness. *Vagueness in Normative Texts*, edited by V.K. Bhatia, J. Engberg, M. Gotti and D. Heller. Bern: Peter Lang.

Engberg, J. 2002. Legal meaning assumptions – What are the consequences for legal interpretation and legal translation? *International Journal for the Semiotics of Law*, 15(4), 375–388.

Engberg, J. 2004. Statutory texts as instances of language(s): Consequences and limitations on interpretation. *Brooklyn Journal of International Law*, 29(3), 1135–1166.

European Parliament. 2009. *Codecision and Conciliation: A Guide to How the Parliament Co-legislates under the Treaty of Lisbon*. [Online: the European

Parliament] Available at: http://www.europarl.europa.eu/code/information/guide_en.pdf [accessed: 4 October 2012].

Fairclough, N. 1992. *Discourse and Social Change*. Cambridge: Polity Press.

Fairclough, N. and Wodak, R. 1997. Critical discourse analysis, in *Discourse as Social Interaction. Discursive Studies: A Multidisciplinary Introduction*, edited by T. Van Dijk. Vol. 2. London: Sage, 258–284.

Finnis, J. 1980. *Natural Law and Natural Rights*. Oxford: Clarendon Press.

Fish, S. 1989. *Doing What Comes Naturally: Change, Rhetoric, and the Practice of Theory in Literary and Legal Studies*. Durham: Duke University Press.

Fish, S. 2005. There is no textualist position. *San Diego Law Review*, 42(2), 629–650.

Frändberg, Å. 1996. 'Begreppet rättsstat', in *Rättsstaten – Rätt, Politik och Moral*, edited by F. Sterzel. Uppsala: Iustus Förlag, 21–41.

Frändberg, Å. 2000–2001. Om rättssäkerhet. *Juridisk Tidskrift*, 2, 269–280.

Fuller, L. 1958. Positivism and fidelity to law – A reply to Professor Hart. *Harvard Law Review*, 71(4), 630–672.

Fuller, L. 1969. *The Morality of Law*. New Haven: Yale University Press.

Gadamer, H.-G. 2006. *Truth and Method.* 2nd, revised edition. Translation revised by J. Weinsheimer and D. Marshall. London: Continuum.

Gallas, T. 2006. Understanding EC law as "diplomatic law" and its language, in *Multilingualism and the Harmonisation of European Law*, edited by B. Pozzo and V. Jacometti. The Hague: Kluwer Law International, 119–128.

Garzone, G. 2000. *Legal Translation and Functionalist Approaches: A Contradiction in Terms?*, Paper to the International Colloquium on Legal Translation: History, Theory/ies and Practice, Geneva, Switzerland, 17–19 February 2000. Available at: http://www.tradulex.com/Actes2000/Garzone.pdf [accessed: 4 October 2012].

Gémar, J.-C. 1995. *Traduire, ou, L'art d'interpréter: langue, droit et société : éléments de jurilinguistique. Tome 2, Application: traduire le texte juridique.* Québec: Presses de l'Université du Québec.

Gémar, J.-C. 2002. Le plus et le moins-disant culturel du texte juridique. Langue, culture et équivalence. *Meta*, 47(2), 163–176.

Glanert, S. 2008. Speaking language to law: The case of Europe. *Legal Studies*, 28(2), 161–171.

Glass, A. 1986. Dworkin, Fish and legal practice. *Bulletin of the Australian Society of Legal Philosophy*, 10(3), 203–224.

Glétzl, A. 2007. Lost in translation; EU law and the official languages – problem of the authentic text. Paper to the Centre for European Legal Studies, 2007, 1–11. Available at: http://www.cels.law.cam.ac.uk/events/Glezl.pdf [accessed: 4 October 2012].

Goddard, C. 2009. Fishing with new nets in familiar waters: a legal linguistic foray into comparative law, legal culture and legal ideology. *Lapland Law Review*, (1) 1, 122–143. Available at: http://www.ulapland.fi/loader.aspx?id=3ec94a2d-857b-4ed5-9c3c-bac04b58bbb3 [accessed: 27 December 2012].

Groussot, X. 2006. *General Principles of Community Law.* Groeningen: Europa Law Publishing.

Groussot, X. and Minssen, T. 2007. Res Judicata in the Court of Justice case-law: Balancing legal certainty with legality. *European Constitutional Law Review*, 3(3), 385–417.

Groussot, X. 2008. Spirit, are you there? – Reinforced judicial dialogue and the preliminary ruling procedure. *Europarättslig tidskrift*, 10(4), 934–966.

Guggeis, M. 2006. Multilingual legislation and the legal-linguistic revision in the Council of the European Union, in *Multilingualism and the Harmonisation of European Law*, edited by B. Pozzo and V. Jacometti. The Hague: Kluwer Law International, 109–117.

Günther, K. 1989. A normative conception of coherence for a discursive theory of legal justification. *Ratio Juris*, 2(2), 155–166.

Gustafsson, H. 2002. *Rättens polyvalens: en rättsvetenskaplig studie av sociala rättigheter och rättssäkerhet*. Lund: Lunds Universitet.

Habermas, J. 1984. *The Theory of Communicative Action. Vol. 1: Reason and the Rationalization of Society*. Translated by T. McCarthy. Boston: Blackwell Publishing.

Habermas, J. 1987. *The Theory of Communicative action. Vol. 2: Lifeworld and System: a Critique of Functionalist Reason.* Translated by T. McCarthy. Cambridge, Mass.: Polity Press.

Habermas, J. 1990. *Moral Consciousness and Communicative Action*. Translated by C. Lenhardt and S. Nicholsen. Cambridge, Mass.: MIT Press.

Habermas, J. 1993. *Justification and Application: Remarks on Discourse Ethics*. Translated by P. Cronin. Cambridge, Mass.: MIT Press.

Habermas, J. 1998. *Between Facts and Norms – Contributions to a Discourse Theory of Law and Democracy*. Translated by W. Rehg. Boston: Blackwell Publishing.

Habermas, J. 2001. Why Europe needs a constitution. *New Left Review*, 11, 5–26.

Habermas, J. 2003. On law and disagreement: Some comments on 'interpretive pluralism'. *Ratio Juris*, 16(2), 187–194.

Hakala, P. 2006. Legislative process from a Parliament perspective – Past practice in 11 languages and current challenges in 20, in *Multilingualism and the Harmonisation of European Law*, edited by B. Pozzo and V. Jacometti. The Hague: Kluwer Law International, 147–164.

Harris, J. 1979. *Law and Legal Science. An Inquiry into the Concepts Legal Rule and Legal System*. Oxford: Clarendon Press.

Hart, H. 2012. *The Concept of Law*. 3rd edition. Oxford: Clarendon Press.

Hartley, T. 1996. The European court, judicial objectivity and the Constitution of the European Union. *The Law Quarterly Review*, 122 (1), 95–109.

Hartley, T. 2010. *The Foundations of European Community Law: an Introduction to the Constitutional and Administrative Law of the European Community*. 7th edition. Oxford: Oxford University Press.

Harvey, M. 2002. What's so special about legal translation? *Meta*, 47(2), 177–185.

Hayek, F. 1973. *Law, Legislation and Liberty: A New Statement of the Liberal Principles of Justice and Political Economy. Volume 1: Rules and Order*. London: Routledge & Kegan Paul.

Hermans, T. 1999. *Translation in Systems*. Manchester: St. Jerome.

Herrmann, T. 1996. Die mentale Repräsentation von Konzepten, Wörter und Figuren, in *Konzepte, Bedeutungskonzepte: Theorie und Anwendung in Linguistik und Psychologie*, edited by J. Grabowski, K. Schweizer and R. Graf. Opladen: Westdeutscher Verlag, 120–153.

Holmes, O. 1897. The path of the law. *Harvard Law Review*, 10(8), 457–478.

Husa, J. 2009. Konstitutionalismin mahdottomuus? *Lakimies*, 107(7-8), 1141–1153.

Itzcovich, G. 2009. The interpretation of Community law by the European Court of Justice. *German Law Journal*, 10(5), 537–560.

Jääskinen, N. 2008. *Eurooppalaistuvan Oikeuden Oikeusteoreettisia Ongelmia*. Helsinki: Helsingin yliopisto.

Jackson, B. 1995. *Making Sense in Law.* Liverpool: Deborah Charles Publications.

Jackson, B. 1996. *Making Sense in Jurisprudence.* Liverpool: Deborah Charles Publications.

Jacobs, F. 2003. Judicial dialogue and the cross-fertilization of legal systems: The European Court of Justice. *Texas International Law Journal*, 38(3), 547–556.

Jans, J. 2000. *European Environmental Law*. Groningen: Europa Law Publishing.

Jans, J., de Lange, R., Prechal, S. and Widdershoven, R. 2007. *Europeanisation of Public Law*. Groningen: Europa Law Publishing.

Jareborg, N. 1992. *Straffrättsideologiska Fragment*. Uppsala: Iustus Förlag.

Kelsen, H. 1979. *Allgemeine Theorie der Normen*. Wien: Manz Verlag.

Kennedy, D. 2010. *Social Rights as Human Rights*. Paper to Seminar: The Future of the European Legal Culture, Helsinki, Finland, 12 May 2010.

Kinnunen, T. 2006. *Käännös Oikeudenkäyntiaineistona: Lakitekstien Tulkinta Oikeuskäsitteiden Kääntämisen Näkökulmasta*. Tampere: Tampere University Press.

Kjær, A.L. 2000. On the structure of legal knowledge. The importance of knowing legal rules for understanding legal texts, in *Language, Text and Knowledge: Mental Models of Expert Communication*, edited by L. Lundquist and R. Jarvella. Berlin: De Gruyter, 127–161.

Kjær, A.L. 2004. A common legal language in Europe?, in *Epistemology and Methodology of Comparative Law*, edited by M. Van Hoecke. Oxford: Hart Publishing, 377–398.

Kjær, A.L. 2008a. Recontextualization of concepts in European legal discourse, in *Dialogue and Rhetoric*, edited by E. Weigand. Amsterdam: John Benjamins, 251–266.

Kjær, A.L. 2008b. Introduction: Language as barrier and carrier of European legal integration, in *Paradoxes of European Legal Integration*, edited by H. Petersen, A.L. Kjær, H. Krunke and M. Rask Madsen. Aldershot: Ashgate Publishing, 149–156.

Kjær, A.L. 2010. Nonsense: the Cilfit Criteria Revisited – From the Perspective of Legal Linguistics, in *Europe – The New Legal Realism: Essays in Honour of Hjalte Rasmussen*, edited by H. Koch, K. Hagel-Sørensen, U. Haltern and J. Weiler. Copenhagen: Djøf Publishing.

Klatt, M. 2008. *Making the Law Explicit. The Normativity of Legal Argumentation*. Oxford: Hart Publishing.

Komárek, J. 2010. In the Court(s) We Trust? On the Need for Hierarchy and Differentiation in the Preliminary Ruling Procedure, in *Shaping the Rule of Law Through Dialogue. International and Supranational Experiences*, edited by F. Fontanelli, G. Martinico and P. Carrozza, Groningen: Europa Law Publishing, 89–118.

Korkea-aho, E. 2011. *New Governance and the EU Courts – The Experimentalist Architecture of Judicial Decision-Making*. Helsinki: University of Helsinki.

Koskinen, K. 2000. *Beyond Ambivalence. Postmodernity and the Ethics of Translation*. Tampere: Tampereen yliopistopaino.

Koskinen, K. 2008. *Translating Institutions. An Ethnographic Study of EU Translation*. Manchester: St. Jerome.

Krämer, L. 2003. *EC Environmental Law*. 5th edition. London: Sweet & Maxwell.

Kraus, P. 2008. *A Union of Diversity. Language, Identity and Polity-Building in Europe*. Cambridge: Cambridge University Press.

Kress, K. 1999. Coherence, in *A Company to Philosophy of Law and Legal Theory*, edited by D. Patterson. Oxford: Blackwell Publishing, 533–552.

Kumm, M. 1999. Who is the final arbiter of constitutionality in Europe? *Common Market Law Review*, 36(2), 356–381.

Kumm, M. 2005. The jurisprudence of constitutional conflict: constitutional supremacy in Europe before and after the Constitutional Treaty. *European Law Journal*, 11(3), 262–307.

Lasiński-Sulecki, K. and Morawski, W. 2008. Late publication of EC law in languages of new member states and its effects: Obligations on individuals following the Court's judgment in Skoma-lux. *Common Market Law Review*, 45(3), 705–725.

Lasser, M. 2004. *Judicial Deliberations: A Comparative Analysis of Judicial Transparency and Legitimacy*. Oxford: Oxford University Press.

Legrand, P. 1996. European legal systems are not converging. *International and Comparative Law Quarterly*, 45(1), 52–81.

Legrand, P. 1997. The impossibility of 'legal transplants'. *Maastricht Journal of European and Comparative Law*, 4(2), 111–124.

Legrand, P. 2008. Word/World (of primordial issues for comparative legal studies), in *Paradoxes of European Legal Integration*, edited by H. Petersen, A.L. Kjær, H. Krunke and M. Rask Madsen. Aldershot: Ashgate Publishing, 185–213.

Leiter, B. 2007. *Naturalizing Jurisprudence: Essays on American Legal Realism and Naturalism in Legal Philosophy*. Oxford: Oxford University Press.

Letto-Vanamo, P. 1998a. *Oikeuden Eurooppa: Luentoja Oikeushistoriasta*. Helsinki: Helsingin yliopisto.

Letto-Vanamo, P. 1998b. *Eurooppa Oikeusyhteisönä: Yhteistyön Haasteet ja Mahdollisuudet*. Helsinki: Helsingin yliopisto.
Levenbook, B. 1984. The role of coherence in legal reasoning. *Law and Philosophy*, 3(3), 355–374.
Lindroos-Hovinheimo, S. 2006. What the law says? Reflections on literal interpretation. *No Foundations: Journal of Extreme Legal Positivism*, 2, 56–65.
Lindroos-Hovinheimo, S. 2012. *Justice and the Ethics of Interpretation*. Abingdon: Routledge.
Littlepage, K. 2008. *Transnational Judicial Dialogue and the Rising Influence of European Courts*, Annual Meeting of the ISA's 49th Annual Convention: Bridging Multiple Divides, San Francisco, CA, USA, 26 March 2008. Available at: http://www.allacademic.com/meta/p251172_index.html [accessed: 4 October 2012].
Luhmann, N. 2004. *Law as a Social System*. Oxford: Oxford University Press.
Lyons, J. 1977. *Semantics. Vol. 1*. Cambridge: Cambridge University Press.
MacCormick, N. 1984. Coherence in legal justification, in *Theory of Legal Science. Proceedings of the Conference on Legal Theory and Philosophy of Science, Lund, Sweden, December 11–14 1983*, edited by A. Peczenik, L. Lindahl and B. van Roermund. Dordrecht: D. Reidel, 235–252.
MacCormick, N. 1994. *Legal Reasoning and Legal Theory*. Oxford: Clarendon Press.
MacCormick, N. 1998. Powers and power-conferring norms, in *Normativity and Norms: Critical Perspectives on Kelsenian Themes*, edited by S. Paulson and B. Litschewski-Paulson. Oxford: Oxford University Press, 493–506.
MacCormick, N. 1999. *Questioning Sovereignty. Law, State, and Nation in the European Commonwealth*. Oxford: Oxford University Press.
MacCormick, N. 2005. *Rhetoric and the Rule of Law*. Oxford: Oxford University Press.
MacCormick, N. and Summers, R. 1991. Interpretation and justification, in *Interpreting Statutes. A Comparative Study*, edited by N. MacCormick and R. Summers. Aldershot: Dartmouth, 511–544.
McLeod, I. 2004. Literal and Purposive Techniques of Legislative Interpretation: Some European Community and English Common Law Perspectives. *Brooklyn Journal of International Law*, 29(3), 1109–1134.
McRudden, C. 2000. Common law of human rights?: Transnational judicial conversations on constitutional rights. *Oxford Journal of Legal Studies*, 20(4), 499–532.
Madsen, D. 2000. 'Communicative situations as reflected in text structure. On legal text production and background knowledge' in *Language, Text, and Knowledge. Mental Models of Expert Communication*, edited by L. Lundquist and R. Jarvella. Berlin: De Gruyter, 163–187.
Maduro, M. 2003. Contrapunctual law: Europe's constitutional pluralism in action, in *Sovereignty in Transition*, edited by N. Walker. Oxford: Hart Publishing, 502–537.

Maduro, M. 2007. Interpreting European Law: Judicial adjudication in a context of constitutional pluralism. *European Journal of Legal Studies*, 1(2), 1–21.

Maduro, M. 2010. Introduction: the past and future of EU law, in *The Past and Future of EU Law: The Classics of EU Law Revisited on the 50th Anniversary of the Rome Treaty*, edited by M. Maduro and L. Azoulai. Oxford: Hart Publishing, xiii–xx.

Maduro, M. 2012. Three claims of constitutional pluralism, in *Constitutional Pluralism in the European Union and Beyond*, edited by J. Komárek and M. Avbelj. Oxford: Hart Publishing, 68–84.

Mäenpää, O. 2001. *Eurooppalainen Hallinto-oikeus*. Helsinki: Kauppakaari.

Mathijsen, P. 2010. *A Guide to European Union Law: As Amended by the Treaty of Lisbon.* 10th edition. London: Sweet & Maxwell.

Mattila, H. 2006. *Comparative Legal Linguistics*. Aldershot: Ashgate.

Mattli, W. and Slaughter, A. 1996. Constructing the European Community legal system from the ground up: the role of individual litigants and national courts, *Jean Monnet Working Paper*, 6/96. Available at: http://centers.law.nyu.edu/jeanmonnet/archive/papers/96/9606ind.html [accessed: 4 October 2012].

Maxeiner, J. 2006–2007. Legal certainty: A European alternative to American legal indeterminacy? *Tulane Journal of International and Comparative Law*, 15(2), 541–607.

Maxeiner, J. 2008. Some realism about legal certainty in the globalization of the rule of law. *Houston Journal of International Law*, 31(1), 27–46.

Moral Soriano, L. 2003. A modest notion of coherence in legal reasoning. A model for the European Court of Justice. *Ratio Juris*, 16(3), 296–323.

Moreso, J. 1998. *Legal Indeterminacy and Constitutional Interpretation.* Translated by R. Zimmerling. Dordrecht: Kluwer Academic Publishers.

Morijn, J. 2006. Balancing fundamental rights and common market freedoms in Union law: Schmidberger and Omega in the light of the European Constitution. *European Law Journal*, 12(1), 15–40.

Müller, F., Christensen, R. and Sokolowski, M. 1997. *Rechtstext und Textarbeit.* Berlin: Duncker & Humblot.

Nelken, D. 1997. Comparing legal cultures: An introduction, in *Comparing Legal Cultures*, edited by D. Nelken. Aldershot: Dartmouth, 1–9.

Newmark, P. 1982. The translation of authoritative statements: a discussion, in *Langage du Droit et la Traduction. Essais de Jurilinguistique*, edited by J.-C. Gémar. Québec: Linguatech Collection Langues de spécialité, Conseil de la langue française. Available at: http://www.cslf.gouv.qc.ca/bibliotheque-virtuelle/publication-html/?tx_iggcpplus_pi4%5bfile%5d=publications/pubf104/f104p2ch3.html [accessed: 4 October 2012].

Nuotio, K. 2003. Valikoivia huomioita Aulis Aarnion analyyttisesta hermeneutiikasta, in *Oikeusteoreettisia Katkelmia,* edited by K. Nuotio. Helsinki: Suomalainen lakimiesyhdistys, 143–177.

Ojanen, T. 1998. *The European Way. The Structure of National Court Obligation under EC Law*. Saarijärvi: Gummerus.

Ojanen, T. 2003. The times they are a-changin' – the reaction of European courts, in *Nordic Cosmopolitanism: Essays in International Law for Martti Koskenniemi*, edited by J. Petman and J. Klabbers. Leiden: Martinus Nijhoff Publishers/Brill Academic Publishers, 181–205.

Ojanen, T. 2007. Tavaroiden vapaa liikkuvuus EU-oikeuden nykytilassa, in *EU-oikeuden Perusteita II. Aineellisen EU-oikeuden Aloja ja Ulottuvuuksia*, edited by T. Ojanen and A. Haapea. Helsinki: Edita, 91–128.

Ojanen, T. 2008. Ratio ja voluntas EU-oikeudessa, in *Demokraattisen Oikeuden Ehdot: Kritiikki, Politiikka, Kulttuuri. Kaarlo Tuorin 60-vuotisjuhlakirja*, edited by S. Hurri. Helsinki: Tutkijaliitto, 220–231.

Ojanen, T. 2009. Perus- ja ihmisoikeudet – eurooppalaisen konstitutionalismin Akilleen kantapää? *Lakimies*, 107(7–8), 1106–1124.

Ordóñez-Solís, D. 2007. European judges in a global society: Power, language and argumentation. *European Journal of Legal Studies*, 1(2), 1–30.

Ost, F. 2009. *Traduire. Défense et Illustration du Multilinguisme*. Paris: Fayard.

Paso, M. 2009. *Viimeisellä Tuomiolla. Suomen Korkeimman Oikeuden ja Euroopan Yhteisöjen Tuomioistuimen Retoriikka*. Hämeenlinna: Lakimiesliiton kustannus.

Paso, M. 2012. The Court of Justice of the European Union as a rhetorical actor. *Maastricht Journal of European and Comparative Law*, 19(1), 12–36.

Paunio, E. 2007. Ympäristönsuojelu ja tavaroiden vapaa liikkuvuus perusoikeuksien näkökulmasta EU:ssa. *Lakimies*, 105(6), 889–909.

Paunio, E. and Lindroos-Hovinheimo, S. 2010. Taking language seriously: An analysis of linguistic reasoning and its implications in EU Law. *European Law Journal*, 16(4), 395–416.

Peczenik, A. 1989. *On Law and Reason*. Dordrecht: Kluwer Academic Publishers.

Peczenik, A. 1995. *Vad är rätt? Om demokrati, rättssäkerhet, etik och juridisk argumentation*. Stockholm: Nordstedts Juridik.

Perelman, C. 1982. *The Realm of Rhetoric*. Translated by W. Kluback. Notre Dame: University of Notre Dame Press.

Perelman, C. and Olbrechts-Tyteca, L. 1971. *The New Rhetoric: A Treatise on Argumentation*. Translated by J. Wilkinson and P. Weaver. Notre Dame: University of Notre Dame Press.

Perju, V. 2009. Reason and authority in the European Court of Justice. *Virginia Journal of International Law*, 49(2), 307–377.

Phelan, D. 1997. *Revolt or Revolution: the Constitutional Boundaries of the European Community*. Dublin: Sweet & Maxwell.

Pollicino, O. 2004. Legal reasoning of the Court of Justice in the context of the principle of equality between judicial activism and self-restraint. *German Law Journal*, 5(3), 283–317.

Posner, R. 2008. *How Judges Think*. Cambridge, Mass.: Harvard University Press.

Pozzo, B. 2006. Multilingualism, legal terminology and the problems of harmonising European private law, in *Multilingualism and the Harmonisation of European Law*, edited by B. Pozzo and V. Jacometti. The Hague: Kluwer Law International, 3–20.

Prechal, S. and van Roermund, B. 2008. Binding unity in EU legal order: An introduction, in *The Coherence of EU Law. The Search of Unity in Divergent Concepts*, edited by S. Prechal and B. van Roermund. Oxford: Oxford University Press, 1–20.

Prechal, S., Senden, L., van Roermund, B. and Vandamme, T. 2008. Experiences from professional practice: Some steps towards empirical research, in *The Coherence of EU Law. The Search of Unity in Divergent Concepts*, edited by S. Prechal and B. van Roermund. Oxford: Oxford University Press, 23–43.

Pym, A. 1992. *Translation and Textual Transfer. An Essay on the Principles of Intercultural Communication.* Frankfurt am Main: Peter Lang.

Pym, A. 1998. Transferre non semper necesse est. *Quaderns. Revista de traducció*, 1, 88–93. Available at: http://usuaris.tinet.cat/apym/on-line/intercultures/1998_transferre.pdf [accessed: 4 October 2012].

Raban, O. 2010. The fallacy of legal certainty: Why vague legal standards may be better for capitalism and liberalism. *Boston University Public Interest Law Journal*, 19(2), 175–192.

Raitio, J. 2003. *The Principle of Legal Certainty in EC Law*. Dordrecht: Kluwer Academic Publishers.

Raitio, J. 2008. The principle of legal certainty as a general principle of EU law, in *General Principles of EC Law in a Process of Development: Reports from Conference in Stockholm, 23-24 March 2007, organized by the Swedish Network for European Legal Studies*, edited by U. Bernitz, J. Nergelius and C. Cardner. Alphen aan den Rijn: Kluwer Law International, 47–73.

Raitio, J. 2010. *Eurooppaoikeus ja Sisämarkkinat*. 2nd edition. Helsinki: Talentum.

Ramage, J., Bean, J. and Johnson, J. 2009. *Writing Arguments. A Rhetoric with Readings*. 8th edition. New York: Longman.

Rasmussen, H. 1986. *On Law and Policy in the European Court of Justice: A Comparative Study of Judicial Policy-making*. Dordrecht: Martinus Nijhoff Publishers.

Rasmussen, H. 1993. *Towards a Normative Theory of Interpretation of EU Law*. Copenhagen: Copenhagen Political Studies Press.

Rasmussen, H. 1998. *The European Court of Justice*. Copenhagen: GadJura.

Rasmussen, H. 2003. *EU-ret i Kontekst*. 5th edition. Copenhagen: GadJura.

Raudenbush Olmsted, W. 1991. The uses of rhetoric: indeterminacy in legal reasoning, practical thinking and the interpretation of literary figures. *Philosophy and Rhetoric*, 24(1), 1–24.

Rawls, J. 1995. *Political Liberalism. Expanded Edition.* New York: Columbia University Press.

Raymond, J. *The Limits of Logic in Legal Argumentation*. Paper to the International Colloquium on Legal Translation: History, Theory/ies and Practice, Geneva, Switzerland, 17–19 February 2000. Available at: http://www.tradulex.com/Actes2000/raymond.pdf [accessed: 4 October 2012].

Raymond, J. 2009. *Legal Existentialism: Reasoning Beyond Reason in the Law*. Paper to the Conference: Judicial Reasoning: Art or Science?, Australian Academy of Forensic Sciences, ANU College of Law, National Judicial College of Australia, February 2009. Available at: http://njca.anu.edu.au/Professional%20Development/programs%20by%20year/2009/Judic%20Reas%20papers/Raymond%20Legal%20Existentialism.pdf [accessed: 4 October 2012].

Raz, J. 1979. *The Authority of Law*. Oxford: Clarendon Press.

Raz, J. 1994. The relevance of coherence, in *Ethics in the Public Domain. Essays in the Morality of Law and Politics*, Oxford: Clarendon Press, 277–325.

Reich, N. 2005. *Understanding EU Law: Objectives, Principles and Methods of Community Law*. 2nd edition. Antwerp: Intersentia.

Ricci, G. 2006. Controlled multilingualism in parliamentary practice, in *Multilingualism and the Harmonisation of European Law*, edited by B. Pozzo and V. Jacometti. The Hague: Kluwer Law International, 131–146.

Ricoeur, P. 1966. *Freedom and Nature: The Voluntary and the Involuntary*. Translated by E. Kohák. Evanston: Northwestern University Press.

Rosas, A. 2003. The legal sources of EU fundamental rights: A systemic overview, in *Une communauté de droit—Festschrift für Gil Carlos Rodríguez Iglesias*, edited by N. Colneric, D. Edward, J.-P. Puissochet and D. Ruiz-Jarabo Colomer. Berlin: BWV Berliner Wissenschafts-Verlag, 87–102.

Rosas, A. 2006. The European Court of Justice: sources of law and methods of interpretation, in *The WTO at Ten: The Contribution of the Dispute Settlement System*, edited by G. Sacerdoti, A. Yanovich and J. Bohanes. Cambridge: Cambridge University Press.

Rosas, A. 2007a. The European Court of Justice in context: forms and patterns of judicial dialogue. *European Journal of Legal Studies*, 1(2), 1–16.

Rosas, A. 2007b. The European Court of Justice and fundamental rights: yet another case of judicial activism?, in *European Integration through Interaction of Legal Regimes*, edited by C. Baudenbacher and H. Bull. Oslo: Universitetsforlaget, 33–63.

Rosas, A. and Armati, L. 2010. *EU Constitutional Law. An Introduction*. Oxford: Hart Publishing.

Rosch, E. 1973. Natural categories. *Cognitive Psychology*, 4(3), 328–350.

Salmi-Tolonen, T. 2005. Persuasion in judicial argumentation: the opinions of the Advocates General at the European Court of Justice, in *Persuasion Across Genres: a Linguistic Approach*, edited by H. Halmari and T. Virtanen. Amsterdam: John Benjamins, 59–104.

Sankari, S. 2011. *Legal Reasoning in Context. The Court of Justice on Articles 17 and 18 EC (20 and 21 TFEU) 2000–2008*. Helsinki: Juvenes Print.

Šarčević, S. 1997. *New Approach to Legal Translation*. The Hague: Kluwer Law International.

Šarčević, S. 2000. *Legal Translation and Translation Theory: a Receiver-oriented Approach*. Paper to the International Colloquium on Legal Translation:

History, Theory/ies and Practice, Geneva, Switzerland, 17–19 February 2000. Available at: http://www.tradulex.com/Actes2000/sarcevic.pdf [accessed: 4 October 2012].

Šarčević, S. 2002. Problems of interpretation in an enlarged European Union, in *L'interprétation des Textes Juridiques Rédigés dans Plus d'une Langue*, edited by R. Sacco. Paris: l'Harmattan, 239–272.

Sarmiento, D. 2012. The silent lamb and deaf wolves. Constitutional pluralism, preliminary references and the role of silent judgments in EU Law, in *Constitutional Pluralism in the European Union and Beyond*, edited by J. Komárek and M. Avbelj. Oxford: Hart Publishing, 285–317.

Scalia, A. 1997. *A Matter of Interpretation. Federal Courts and the Law*. Princeton: Princeton University Press.

Schauer, F. 1991. *Playing by the Rules. A Philosophical Examination of Rule-Based Decision-Making in Law and in Life.* Oxford: Clarendon Press.

Schauer, F. 2008. A critical guide to vehicles in the park. *New York University Law Review*, 83(4), 1109–1134.

Schermers, H. and Waelbroeck, D. 2001. *Judicial Protection in the European Union*. 6th edition. The Hague: Kluwer Law International.

Schirato, T. and Yell, S. 2000. *Communication and Culture*. London: Sage Publications.

Schübel-Pfister, I. 2005. Enjeux et perspectives du multilinguisme dans l'Union européenne: après l'élargissement, la 'babélisation'? *Revue du Marché commun et de l'Union européenne*, 488, 325–333.

Smith, S. 2000. Taking law seriously. *University of Toronto Law Journal*, 50(2), 241–259.

Smits, J. 2006. Comparative law and its influence on national legal systems, in *The Oxford Handbook of Comparative Law*, edited by M. Reimann and R. Zimmermann. Oxford: Oxford University Press, 477–512.

Smits, J. 2007. Legal culture as mental software, or: how to overcome national legal culture?, in *Private Law and the Many Cultures of Europe*, edited by T. Wilhelmsson, E. Paunio and A. Pohjolainen. Alphen aan den Rijn: Kluwer Law International, 141–151.

Sobotà, K. 1994. Logos, ethos, pathos – A quantitative analysis on arguments and emotions in law, in *Retorik och Rätt: Sett genom Tio Författares Ögon*, edited by M. Mellqvist and M. Persson. Uppsala: Iustus Förlag, 155–172.

Solan, L. 2005. Vagueness and ambiguity in legal interpretation. *Vagueness in Normative Texts*, edited by V.K. Bhatia, J. Engberg, M. Gotti and D. Heller. Bern: Peter Lang.

Solan, L. 2009a. Statutory interpretation in the EU: the Augustinian approach, in *Translation Issues in Language and Law*, edited by D. Stein, F. Olsen and A. Lorz. Houndmills: Palgrave Macmillan, 35–54.

Solan, L. 2009b. Interpretation of multilingual statutes by the European Court of Justice. *Brooklyn Journal of International Law*, 34(2), 277–302.

Sperber, D. and Wilson, D. 1995. *Relevance: Communication and Cognition*. 2nd edition. Oxford: Blackwell Publishing.

Steiner, G. 1998. *After Babel. Aspects of Language and Translation*. 3rd edition. Oxford: Oxford University Press.

Stone Sweet, A. 2004. *The Judicial Construction of Europe*. Oxford: Oxford University Press.

Stone Sweet, A. 2012. The judicial coup d'état and the problem of authority, in *The Past and Future of EU Law: The Classics of EU Law Revisited on the 50th Anniversary of the Rome Treaty*, edited by M. Maduro and L. Azoulai. Oxford: Hart Publishing, 201–210.

Summers, R. 1978. Two types of substantive reasons: The core of a theory of common-law justification. *Cornell Law Review*, 63(5), 707–788.

Summers, R. and Taruffo, M. 1991. Interpretation and comparative analysis, in *Interpreting Statutes. A Comparative Study*, edited by N. MacCormick and R. Summers. Aldershot: Dartmouth, 461–510.

Sunstein, C. 1995. Problems with rules. *California Law Review*, 83(4), 953–1026.

Sunstein, C. 1996. *Legal Reasoning and Political Conflict*. Oxford: Oxford University Press.

Sunstein, C. 1997. Incommensurability and kinds of valuation: some applications in law, in *Incommensurability, Incomparability, and Practical Reason*, edited by R. Chang, Cambridge: Harvard University Press, 234–254.

Sunstein, C. 1999. *One Case at a Time. Judicial Minimalism on the Supreme Court*. Cambridge, Mass.: Harvard University Press.

Tamanaha, B. 2004. *On the Rule of Law. History, Politics, Theory*. Cambridge: Cambridge University Press.

Tamanaha, B. 2009. A concise guide to the rule of law, in *Relocating the Rule of Law*, edited by G. Palombella and N. Walker. Oxford: Hart Publishing, 3–16.

Tamanaha, B. 2010. *Beyond the Formalist-Realist Divide: The Role of Politics in Judging*. Princeton: Princeton University Press.

Temple Lang, J. 2000. Legal certainty and legitimate expectations as general principles of law, in *General Principles of European Community Law*, edited by U. Bernitz and J. Nergelius. The Hague: Kluwer Law International, 163–184.

Teubner, G. 1998. Legal irritants: Good faith in British law or how unifying law ends up in new divergences. *Modern Law Review*, 61(1), 11–32.

Tontti, J. 2001. European legal pluralism as a rebirth of Ius commune. *Retfærd*, 24(4), 40–54.

Tontti, J. 2004. *Right and Prejudice. Prolegomena to a Hermeneutical Philosophy of Law*. Aldershot: Ashgate.

Torres Pérez, A. 2009. *Conflicts of Rights in the European Union – A Theory of Supranational Adjudication*. Oxford: Oxford University Press.

Tridimas, T. 2006. *The General Principles of EU Law*. 2nd edition. Oxford: Oxford University Press.

Tridimas, T. 2011. Primacy, fundamental rights and the search for legitimacy, in *The Past and Future of EU Law: The Classics of EU Law Revisited on the 50th Anniversary of the Rome Treaty*, edited by M. Maduro and L. Azoulai. Oxford: Hart Publishing, 98–105.

Tuori, K. 2002. *Critical Legal Positivism*. Aldershot: Ashgate.

Tuori, K. 2003. Om rättssäkerhet och sociala rättigheter (samt mycket annat). *Tidsskrift for Rettsvitenskap*, 115(3), 341–365.

Tuori, K. 2007. *Oikeuden ratio ja voluntas*. Helsinki: WSOYPro.

Tuori, K. 2011. *Ratio and Voluntas: The Tension between Reason and Will in Law*. Farnham: Ashgate.

Twining, W. and Miers, D. 1999. *How to Do Things With Rules: A Primer of Interpretation*. 4th edition. London: Butterworths.

Twining, W. 2008. Surface law, in *Paradoxes of European Legal Integration*, edited by H. Petersen, A.L. Kjær, H. Krunke and M. Rask Madsen. Aldershot: Ashgate Publishing, 157–183.

Urban, N. 2000. One legal language and the maintenance of cultural and linguistic diversity. *European Review of Private Law*, 8(1), 51–57.

Usher, J. 1998. *General Principles of EC Law*. London: Longman.

Van Calster, G. 1997. The EU's tower of Babel – The interpretation by the European Court of Justice of equally authentic texts drafted in more than one official language. *Yearbook of European Law*, 17(1), 363–393.

Van Hoecke, M. and Warrington, M. 1998. Legal cultures and legal paradigms: Towards a new model for comparative law. *International and Comparative Law Quarterly*, 47(3), 495–536.

Van Hoecke, M. 2002. *Law as Communication*. Oxford: Hart Publishing.

Varga, C. 2000. Validity. *Acta Juridica Hungarica*, vol. 41(3–4), 155–166.

Villa, V. 1990. Normative coherence and epistemological presuppositions of justification, in *Law, Interpretation and Reality. Essays in Epistemology, Hermeneutics and Jurisprudence*, edited by P. Nerhot. Dordrecht: Kluwer Academic Publishers, 431–449.

Von Bogdandy, A. 2000. The European Union as a human rights organization? Human rights and the core of the European Union. *Common Market Law Review*, 37(6), 1307–1338.

Walker, N. 2009. The rule of law and the EU: necessity's mixed virtue, in *Relocating the Rule of Law*, edited by G. Palombella and N. Walker. Oxford: Hart Publishing, 119–138.

Wasserfallen, F. 2010. The judiciary as legislator? How the European Court of Justice shapes policy-making in the European Union. *Journal of European Public Policy*, 17(8), 1128–1146.

Watson, A. 2000. Legal transplants and European private law. *Electronic Journal of Private Law*, 4(4). Available at: http://www.ejcl.org/44/art44-2.html [accessed: 4 October 2012].

Weigand, E. 2008. Towards a common European legal thinking: a dialogic challenge, in *Paradoxes of European Legal Integration*, edited by H. Petersen,

A.L. Kjær, H. Krunke and M. Rask Madsen. Aldershot: Ashgate Publishing, 235–252.

Weiler, J. 1999. The constitution of the common market place: Text and context in the evolution of the free movement of goods, in *The Evolution of EU Law*, edited by P. Craig and G. De Búrca. Oxford: Oxford University Press, 349–376.

Weiler, J. 2001. Epilogue: The Judicial Après Nice, in *The European Court of Justice*, edited by G. De Búrca and J. Weiler. Oxford: Oxford University Press, 215–226.

Weiler, J. and Lockhart, N. 1995. 'Taking rights seriously' seriously: The European Court of Justice and its fundamental rights jurisprudence – Parts I & II. *Common Market Law Review*, (32) 1 and 2, 51–94 and 579–627.

Whorf, B. 1956. *Language, Thought, and Reality: Selected Writings of Benjamin Lee Whorf*, edited by J. Carrol. Cambridge, Mass.: MIT Press.

Wilhelmsson, T. 1986. Rättssäkerheten, rättsvetenskapen och de allmänna lärorna. *Retfaerd*, 9(2), 31–40.

Wilhelmsson, T. 1999. Jack-in-the-Box theory of European Community law, in *Dialectic of Law and Reality: Readings in Finnish Legal Theory*, edited by L. Eriksson and S. Hurri. Helsinki: Publications of the Faculty of Law, University of Helsinki, 437–454.

Wilhelmsson, T. 2004. Yleiset opit ja pienet kertomukset ennakoitavuuden ja yhdenvertaisuuden näkökulmasta. *Lakimies*, 102(2), 199–227.

Williams, A. 2010. *The Ethos of Europe. Values, Law and Justice in the EU.* Cambridge: Cambridge University Press.

Williams, B. 1985. *Ethics and the Limits of Philosophy*. London: Fontana.

Wróblewski, J. 1992. *The Judicial Application of Law*, edited by Z. Bankowski. Deventer: Kluwer Academic Publishers.

Zaccaria, G. 1990. Hermeneutics and narrative comprehension, in *Law, Interpretation and Reality. Essays in Epistemology, Hermeneutics and Jurisprudence*, edited by P. Nerhot. Dordrecht: Kluwer Academic Publishers, 251–274.

Index

For Product Safety Concerns and Information please contact our EU representative GPSR@taylorandfrancis.com
Taylor & Francis Verlag GmbH, Kaufingerstraße 24, 80331 München, Germany

www.ingramcontent.com/pod-product-compliance
Ingram Content Group UK Ltd.
Pitfield, Milton Keynes, MK11 3LW, UK
UKHW021302190926
475701UK00009B/585
* 9 7 8 0 3 6 7 6 0 1 2 1 8 *